FOLKLORE AND CULTURE
ON THE TEXAS-MEXICAN BORDER

FOLKLORE
AND
CULTURE
ON THE
TEXAS-MEXICAN
BORDER

AMÉRICO PAREDES

EDITED AND WITH AN INTRODUCTION BY RICHARD BAUMAN

CMAS BOOKS

CENTER FOR MEXICAN AMERICAN STUDIES

UNIVERSITY OF TEXAS AT AUSTIN 1993

A CMAS BOOK

Editor: Víctor Javier Guerra
Assistant Editor: Martha Vogel

The acquisition of this book was coordinated by Ricardo Romo, associate professor of history, University of Texas at Austin. The publication of the book was assisted by a grant from the university's College of Liberal Arts.

Library of Congress Cataloging-in-Publication Data
Paredes, Américo.
    Folklore and culture on the Texas-Mexican border / Américo Paredes; edited and with an introduction by Richard Bauman. — 1st ed.
        p.   cm.
    Includes bibliographical references.
    ISBN 0-292-72472-1
    1. Folklore—Texas. 2. Folklore—Mexico. 3. Folk literature, American—Texas—History and criticism. 4. Folk literature, Mexican—History and criticism. 5. Texas—Social life and customs. 6. Mexico—Social life and customs.   I. Bauman, Richard. II. Title.
GR110.T5P28 1993
398'.09764—dc20   91-43059

♾ The paper used in this book is acid free and conforms to the American National Standard of permanence for printed library materials, as approved by the American National Standards Institute.

Printed and bound in the United States of America.

First edition. First impression, May 1993.

Contents

Acknowledgments

Some years ago, when we were planning the festschrift for Américo Paredes that was published as *"And Other Neighborly Names": Social Process and Cultural Image in Texas Folklore* (1981), Roger Abrahams and I discussed the possibility of gathering together a collection of Don Américo's essays as well, and the discussions surrounding both projects helped shape this volume. More recently, Ricardo Romo helped materially to get this venture under way, and Ramón Saldívar provided welcome encouragement in its early stages. During the preparation of the volume, several people made valuable contributions: Beverly J. Stoeltje offered good advice on the selection of essays to be included, Frances J. Terry typed several parts of the manuscript and coordinated the correspondence between Bloomington and Austin, and Linda Kinsey Adams standardized the notes and references. I thank all of these colleagues for their help and good offices.

—R.B.

Introduction

Richard Bauman

Américo Paredes's richly textured collection of folksongs of the Lower Border, *A Texas-Mexican Cancionero* (1976), is dedicated

> To the memory of my mother
> who could sing a song or two;
> and to all the other singers
> of the Border,
> who left part of themselves
> in my keeping.

In this dedicatory poem and elsewhere in the introduction to the *Cancionero,* one feels a clear sense of the formative effect of this Border folk legacy on Paredes and of the moral and esthetic responsibility it engendered in him.

How to fulfill such a responsibility? One possibility is to sing the songs yourself, passing them on through performance as they were passed down to you. Another way is to answer the songs of the traditional singers with songs of your own; or to record and publish the songs as a means of preserving and presenting them; or to study the songs and the singers, to interpret them to others. Américo Paredes has done all of this and more. In his younger years, in the 1930s, he was a popular singer on the border and the author of evocative poetry that responded to the voice of Border tradition. Since then, as a scholar, he has carried out extensive field research and published a considerable body of Border folklore, and he has produced the most important and influential scholarship of our generation on the folklore of Greater Mexico in general and of the Lower Border in particular. His lifelong achievements have brought him many well-deserved honors, most recently the highly prestigious Charles Frankel Prize from the National Endowment for the Humanities and the Order of the Aztec Eagle from the Mexican government. They have also brought him other, less conventional validations of his work—of which he seems equally proud—as when a Texas Ranger threatened him with violence on the publication of *With His Pistol in His Hand* (1958). "Must be doing something right," he says.

A collection of Paredes's poetry has recently been published, as has his long-awaited novel,[1] and his scholarship in book form is widely known and relatively accessible. Less well known, however, and more difficult of access are his scholarly writings in article form. This collection, then, is presented in the interest of bringing some of Américo Paredes's most significant scholarly articles to a wider public. The selection process was difficult; a number of the editor's favorites could not be included, and those familiar with Paredes's work will doubtless miss still others. Nevertheless, the eleven articles included in this collection should give the reader a clear sense of the problems that have engaged Américo Paredes's intellect and of the rigor, elegance, and staying power of his scholarship. For those whose appetite is whetted by this selection and who wish to read further, a bibliography of the scholarly writings of Américo Paredes, compiled by Linda Kinsey Adams, is appended to this work.

Like the *tequileros, sediciosos,* and ordinary people of the border region from which he came and about which he writes, Paredes's scholarship cannot be contained by official boundaries. Life on a border can be tense, risky, dangerous, and filled with ambiguities, but it can also be energizing, with the potential to induce a depth of reflexivity and a breadth of perspective that the safety of the heartland seldom affords. This is as true of the intellectual borderlands between disciplines as it is of political borders. Paredes is claimed variously as a folklorist, an anthropologist, a literary scholar, and a social historian. One might say that he is all of these or, better, that his scholarship transcends such narrow categories. So integrative and transdisciplinary is his work, in fact, that an outline of its principal themes and perspectives may be useful as an orientation to the essays that follow.

From the beginning of his career, Américo Paredes's deepest interest has centered on the folklore and culture of the area he has termed the Lower Rio Grande Border, the region on both sides of the U.S.–Mexico border from the two Laredos downriver to the Gulf. This is his home territory, resonant with personal as well as scholarly meaning, from his youth in Brownsville and from a lifetime of visits and scholarly engagement.* It is important to emphasize that Paredes's intense focus on his native region never descends to a provincial narrowness of focus. One essential reason for this is that his work on the Lower Border is always— tacitly or explicitly—contextualized by a deep knowledge of Greater Mexico, a term that Paredes has coined to comprehend both "México de Adentro" and "México de Afuera," the former encompassed by the political borders of the Republic of Mexico, the latter taking in all those other parts of North America where people of Mexican descent have established a presence and have maintained their Mexicanness as a key part of their cultural identity. Parts of East Chicago and Detroit belong to Greater Mexico, together with Monterrey and Mexico City and migrant worker camps in Bakersfield. "The Folklore of Groups of Mexican Origin in the United States" (chap. 1) makes clear the productiveness of this broadly extended vision. With this breadth of perspective, extended still further by the folklorist's more global comparative frame of reference, Paredes is never drawn to parochial claims about *mexicano* folklore and culture of the kind made by Mexican folklorists who see the Lower Border as a fringe area of Mexico, or by North American scholars who see the Hispanic Southwest as a folk cultural region of the United States, or by the Hispanophile scholars of northern New Mexican folklore who construct their region as a preserve of old Peninsular culture. In significant part, it is Paredes's comparative and contextual perspective that makes his work on the Lower Border so persuasive and authoritative, despite the characteristic modesty with which he advances many of his findings. While the predominant focus of this collection is on the folklore and culture of the Lower Border, consistent with Paredes's life and career, the volume also includes several essays that reflect his interest in Greater Mexico more generally, and one, "The United States,

* For more biographical information, see José E. Limón, "Américo Paredes: A Man from the Border," *Revista Chicano-Riqueña* 8 (1980): 1–15.

Mexico, and *Machismo*" (chap. 9), that develops a comparison between Mexico and the United States.

While Paredes sees himself and is recognized and honored as part of the community of scholars dedicated to illuminating the folklore of Greater Mexico,* the richness and power of his scholarship, as noted, stems most strongly from his lifelong intellectual, artistic, and social engagement with the Lower Border. His work is an exemplary vindication of that premise on which the best of folklore and anthropology is built: that a deep, detailed, nuanced understanding of the local will illuminate and inspire a more global vision. What Américo Paredes tells us about the *corrido*, for example, can illuminate all of ballad scholarship, inspire a literary movement,[2] inform a political ideology,[3] and more.

A significant part of Paredes's contribution stems from his conceptualization of the Lower Border itself. As a cultural region, the Lower Border, as Paredes outlines its contours in his work, is a historical emergent, the product of a complex and turbulent development. Originally part of Nuevo Santander, a province of New Spain founded in 1749 to fill the gap between the established population centers of Tampico and Monterrey to the south and the Texas colony to the north, the area along the banks of the Rio Grande was from the beginning a place of in-between existence. After 1835, the people of the region found themselves under increasing pressure from the southward encroachment of Anglo expansionism. In the decade that followed, the Anglo-Mexican border region was relatively inchoate, but the Treaty of Guadalupe Hidalgo in 1848 had a decisive shaping effect on the region. By establishing the Rio Grande, formerly the focus of regional life, as the national border between Mexico and the United States, the treaty made the river "a symbol of separation" and left a Mexican population stranded in an alien country, though with firmly established ties on the opposite bank, only a shout or a short swim away. The responses of the border Mexicans to the marginal existence thus forced upon them have been the dominant focus of Paredes's career.

The Lower Border, then, as Paredes characterizes it in "The Problem of Identity in a Changing Culture" (chap. 2) and elsewhere in his writ-

---

* See, for example, Luis Leal, "Américo Paredes and Modern Mexican American Scholarship," *Ethnic Affairs* 1 (1987): 1–11; and Stanley Robe, "A Border *Cancionero* and a Regional View of Folksong," in *New Directions in Chicano Scholarship*, ed. Ricardo Romo and Raymund Paredes (La Jolla: Chicano Studies Program, University of California, San Diego, 1978), 257–268.

ings, is preeminently a contact zone, a region in which different cultures come face to face. It is thus fundamentally heterogeneous, defined by forces of social differentiation—ethnicity, class, language, power. Historically, the tenor of the contact, its dominant relational temper, has been one of conflict, engendered by the enforced domination of Anglos over a subject people. From the vantage point of the Texas-Mexicans, however, while survival has demanded some degree of accommodation, this accommodation has been tempered by currents of resistance to Anglo domination and by a struggle—psychological, expressive, social—to negotiate an identity in this environment of conflict. One constituent of this culture of conflict, and an instrument for the waging of the struggle itself, is a body of folklore: *corridos,* ethnic slurs, legends, jokes, proverbs. And while part of the overall folklore repertoire of Texas-Mexicans has been shared with other parts of Greater Mexico, what renders the folklore of the Lower Border distinctive is precisely the generative power of the struggle.

In his documentation and study of Border folklore, Américo Paredes has focused on both the widely shared and the locally rooted aspects of the repertoire. He has recorded the traditional *romances* sung on the border, for example, ballads descended from the old *romancero* that is part of the Hispanic legacy in New Spain, and he has given us some of our most illuminating studies of the *décima,* perhaps the most widely distributed form of folk poetry in the Western Hemisphere. Challenges abound in this work, as I will suggest a bit later, but it is in his writings on the Texas-Mexican folklore of resistance that the true boldness and power of his scholarship stand out most clearly. In order to comprehend why this should be so, it is necessary to understand how Paredes's conception of Border culture has challenged prevailing notions of folklore and what the ideological implications of his revisionist views have been.

In the two hundred years or so since the invention of the notion of folklore, the predominant conception of the folk, the social base of folklore, has been of a bounded, homogeneous, unsophisticated, tradition-oriented group sharing a common language and a collective body of vernacular knowledge, custom, oral tradition, and the like.* The weight of emphasis in such constructions has fallen upon group-internal, shared ways of life; group homogeneity has been taken as the touchstone of

* See Richard Bauman, "Folklore," in *Folklore, Cultural Performances, and Popular Entertainments,* ed. Richard Bauman (Oxford: Oxford University Press, 1992), 29–40.

folklore. Borders, as might be expected, have had a limited place in such models, perceived as barriers to diffusion, perhaps, or as zones in which heroic ballads or epics grew out of hostile face-offs on military frontiers, as between Greeks and Turks, Spaniards and Moors, English and Scots. Such border forms, however, have had little influence on the mainstream of folklore theory. Functionalist perspectives in anthropology, moreover, have reinforced the within-group frame of reference on which traditionalist folklore theory has rested, and emphasized the role of folklore in sustaining group equilibrium and the maintenance of the social system.

In the face of such deeply rooted foundational ideas concerning folklore and the folk, Américo Paredes's conception of Texas-Mexican Border society and folklore has offered a markedly revisionist view. In place of an understanding of folklore as founded on group homogeneity and operating within the boundaries of the group to maintain its social equilibrium, Paredes offers a far more subtle and complex picture. Certain elements of the Texas-Mexican repertoire, as noted, are part of the shared traditions of Greater Mexico, but this is only half the picture, for a significant portion of the repertoire, the most distinctive portion, is generated by the stark social oppositions of the border region, a response to differential—not shared—identity. Moreover, the generating force out of which such folklore emerges is conflict, struggle, and resistance, and the folklore operates as an instrument of this conflict, not in the service of systems maintenance. This is a bold challenge to traditionalist understandings, and to the extent that it has gained ground among folklorists in recent decades, Paredes's acknowledged influence as teacher, colleague, and author has been clear and significant.*

Nor has Paredes's contribution been limited in this respect to folklore theory, for traditionalist understandings of folklore have significant ideological and political implications as well. If one examines the history

---

* See, for example, Richard Bauman, "Differential Identity and the Social Base of Folklore," in *Toward New Perspectives in Folklore,* ed. Américo Paredes and Richard Bauman (Austin: University of Texas Press, 1972), 31–41; Richard Bauman and Roger D. Abrahams, eds., *"And Other Neighborly Names": Social Process and Cultural Image in Texas Folklore* (Austin: University of Texas Press, 1981); José E. Limón, "Agringado Joking in Texas Mexican Society: Folklore and Differential Identity," in *New Directions in Chicano Scholarship,* ed. Ricardo Romo and Raymund Paredes (La Jolla: Chicano Studies Program, University of California, San Diego, 1978), 33–50; and Manuel Peña, *The Texas-Mexican Conjunto: History of a Working-Class Music* (Austin: University of Texas Press, 1985).

of folkloristic and anthropological study of Mexican American folklore and culture, for example,* one discovers that conventional, consensus models have sustained and promulgated a particularly problematic image. In essence, traditionalist portrayals of Mexican American regional folk cultures have tended to give us constructions either of cultural relic areas that have preserved traces of Peninsular or classic Mexican folklore, or of regional enclaves of simple, fatalistically accepting and docile folk, quaintly backward in their customs and beliefs. There is no conflict to be found in this literature. The difficult truth is that for all the liberating potential of folklore study to illuminate the power of vernacular culture in resistance to oppression, the discipline has been all too susceptible to serving as an instrument of hegemonic containment by promulgating an image of the folk as romantically quaint, simple, anachronistic, and colorful at best, debased and backward at worst. Paredes's writings have offered an eloquent counterstatement, documenting and valorizing a culture and tradition of resistance, of standing up for one's rights in defiance of the forces of domination.† The *corridos* that Paredes's research has brought to full public view—celebrating the defiant and heroic exploits of Gregorio Cortez and Jacinto Treviño, the *sediciosos* of Aniceto Pizaña, and even the *tequilero* smugglers of the border— thus not only have provided a foundation for new theoretical perspectives, but more importantly they have constituted powerful symbolic and ideological resources for the Chicano political movement, a ground on which to reject the imputation of fatalistic accommodation. It is all too rare that academic scholars in the United States contribute significantly to movements for political liberation by the inspiration of their scholarship—or care to—and Américo Paredes is justly celebrated and revered for the inspiration he has provided.

One corollary of Américo Paredes's understanding of the Lower Border as a contact zone, a place shaped by the confluence—and conflict— of cultures and the struggle of identities, is a special sensitivity to the multiplicity of voices and ideologies striving for expression in Border folklore. Paredes's ear is open to them all, and this receptivity in turn has

* For a useful guide to this literature, see Olga Nájera Ramírez, "Greater Mexican Folklore in the United States: An Annotated Bibliography," *Ethnic Affairs* 1 (1987): 64–115.
† For an interesting parallel case dealing with the occupied West Bank of Palestine—not unlike the Nueces Strip of South Texas in many ways—see Ted Swedenburg, "Occupational Hazards: Palestine Ethnography," *Cultural Anthropology* 4 (1989): 265–272.

had a formative influence on his approach to the generic forms that constitute the repertoire of conflict—the slurs and insults, the proverbs, the songs, the stories. Paredes is always attuned to the dialogic resonances of Border genres, both insofar as they incorporate multiple voices within themselves and as they interact with each other in use and through time to constitute larger expressive systems.* These are not the self-contained and mutually exclusive genres of conventional genre theory in folklore, rooted in homogeneous folk communities, but the sorts of multivocalic, interpenetrating, and blended forms that one should expect from a heteroglossic culture of conflict.

Among the symbolic forms that give expression to border conflict, none has captured Paredes's attention more strongly than the *corrido,* and no scholar has done more toward illuminating the essence and capacity of this ballad form than he in his celebrated books *With His Pistol in His Hand* and *A Texas-Mexican Cancionero,* as well as in a series of essays, four of which are included in this volume (chaps. 6, 7, 8, 9). Part of the essence of the *corrido* of border conflict, as Paredes identifies it, is the dialogic face-off between the defiant hero and the cowardly agents of Anglo power—the *rinches* (Texas Rangers), sheriffs, and the like—rendered as direct discourse.†

Decía Gregorio Cortez	Then said Gregorio Cortez,
con su pistola en la mano:	with his pistol in his hand,
—No corran rinches cobardes	"Don't run, you cowardly rangers,
con un puro mexicano.	from a real Mexican."
. . . . .	. . . . .
Decían los americanos	Then the Americans said,
—Si lo hallamos ¿qué le haremos?	"If we find him, what shall we do?
Si le entramos por derecho	If we fight him man to man
muy poquitos volveremos.	very few of us will return."[4]

* The conception of dialogue that shapes this discussion of Paredes's work is drawn largely from Bakhtin (especially M. M. Bakhtin, *The Dialogic Imagination* [Austin: University of Texas Press, 1981]), though it accords well also with Marcus and Fischer's use of the term to identify a mode of ethnographic practice and representation: "the practical efforts to present multiple voices within a text, and to encourage readings from diverse perspectives" (George Marcus and Michael M. J. Fischer, *Anthropology as Cultural Critique: An Experimental Moment in the Human Sciences* [Chicago: University of Chicago Press, 1986], 68). See also José E. Limón, *The Return of the Mexican Ballad: Américo Paredes and His Anthropological Text as Persuasive Political Performance,* SCCR Working Paper no. 16 (Stanford: Stanford Center for Chicano Research, Stanford University, 1986).

† Compare John H. McDowell, "The *Corrido* of Greater Mexico as Discourse, Music, and Event," in

Here the forces of oppression are contained by the Texas-Mexican community; both voices are heard in the *corrido,* but the hierarchical tables are turned as the Americans are cowed by the "real Mexican."

As is characteristic of Paredes's work, one major frame of reference for his study of the *corrido* is historical, relating the external history of the border region to the origin and evolution of the genre. The historical study of the *corrido* as a form confronts the scholar with problematic continuities and discontinuities. Clearly the *corrido* has basic affinities with the classic Spanish *romance,* which was undeniably present in New Spain, including the border region (though never, apparently, very prominent in the Mexican folksong tradition on the border or elsewhere). What is one to make, then, of the apparent paucity of *corridos* before the 1860s as against the burgeoning of the genre from the 1880s onward? In Paredes's view, while the *corrido* as a form is descended largely from the *romance* (though with significant formal changes along the way), the emergence of a full-blown *corrido* tradition cannot be explained in terms of continuities with the *romance,* for the essence of the *corrido* lies in more than its form alone. For Paredes, the true *corrido* tradition centers around a spirit of heroic bravado, of defiant manly self-confidence, and this spirit is rooted in the emergent sense of Mexican nationalism "stirred into life by the war with the United States and the French invasion and developed slowly but steadily during the thirty years of Porfirio Díaz's rule, coming into flower with the Revolution."[5] In this light, and by appeal as well to the documentable record of *corrido* production very early in the Greater Mexican *corrido* period, Paredes argues that the border conflict of the 1850s might well have been the seedbed of the true *corrido* tradition: "The Lower Border produces its first *corrido* hero, Juan Nepomuceno Cortina, in the late 1850s" (page 140, this volume).

Origins, however, represent only part of Paredes's concern with the developmental trajectory of the *corrido;* the subsequent evolution of the genre and the tradition is fully as important. Paredes traces the *corrido* genre from its first coalescence in the mid-nineteenth century through a series of stages that culminated in the epic period of development from 1910 to 1930, followed by a subsequent period of decline from 1930 to the

"And Other Neighborly Names": Social Process and Cultural Image in Texas Folklore, ed. Richard Bauman and Roger D. Abrahams (Austin: University of Texas Press, 1981), 44–75.

present as the *corrido* was sentimentalized and otherwise transformed by the Mexican mass media. He notes, however, that vestiges of the older spirit show through from time to time even in our own day. This historical characterization applies to the *corrido* tradition as a whole, but Paredes's examination of the genre is not limited to the macroscopic tracing of the *corrido*'s evolutionary trajectory. On a more closely focused level, with regard to the life-course of individual *corridos*, Paredes has identified a developmental process with truly important implications for genre theory in general, namely, the interrelationship between the *corrido* and the *corrido* legend.

The *corrido* legend is a prose narrative that centers around the same figures and events as the ballad; in characteristic legend fashion, different legends may cluster around the same event complex, occasioned or prompted in the telling by different points of reference in the ongoing interaction: reference to a place, a person, a treasure, or the like. Paredes summarizes the relationship thus:

> Characteristically, the *corrido* of border conflict is realistic in tone. It exaggerates what it takes for fact, but it always gives us scenes taken from real life. The *corrido* legend, on the other hand, is more romantic, though it does not often make use of the marvelous. (page 194, this volume)

There is a complex dynamic in operation here, whereby different modes of folkloric discourse, different ways of giving expression to events, are interrelated in use and condition one another's development. If one makes even finer generic and stylistic distinctions—as between, say, the *corrido* of the outlaw type and the *corrido* of border conflict, or between the legend style and the style of the wonder tale, as they are variously used in giving voice to different personal and ideological perspectives on the "same" events—one may discover still more subtle dimensions of systemic interrelationship among genres. Paredes's "José Mosqueda and the Folklorization of Actual Events" (chap. 8) is a tour de force in this regard.

A process in some ways similar, in some ways different, operates on the *décima*. Like the *corrido*, the *décima* is an inherently dialogic genre, but while the *corrido* renders opposing voices as quoted speech, the *décima* is built on the exchange of verses by two parties, characteristically in a tone of challenge and competition. Paredes's essay "The Undying

Love of 'El Indio' Córdova" (chap. 11) presents an evocative account of such an exchange between the patriarch of a border family and the outsider suitor of his daughter—another manifestation of differential identity. Here again, as throughout Paredes's work, close attention to history adds nuance and texture to the explication of the folklore texts.

Like the *corrido*, the *décima* as a genre exists in close interrelationship with legend. As Paredes elucidates the process in "The *Décima* on the Texas-Mexican Border: Folksong as an Adjunct to Legend" (chap. 10), the *décima*—which flourished on the border before being largely displaced by the *corrido* by the end of the nineteenth century—retained a place in the repertoire by becoming embedded in a particular class of folk narratives.

> One must look for the legendary anecdote in order to find them. An incident is related, usually humorous, about some supposedly historical personage. Then some *décimas* are recited or sung, capping the narrative. The story is always that the main character in the anecdote composed the *décimas* as a result of the experiences just related. The *décima*, for so long a gloss to a quatrain, thus becomes a gloss or commentary in another sense. (pages 239–240, this volume)

But whereas it is the singing of the *corrido* that characteristically prompts the telling of a legend by way of further elaboration, when it comes to the *décima* it is the other way around: the reciting of the *décima* serves as a cap to an antecedent narrative.

Paredes carries the problem of generic interrelationships in still another direction in his "Folk Medicine and the Intercultural Jest" (chap. 3). In local terminology, the jests explicated in this essay are *tallas*, humorous anecdotes that are frequently personalized by being told as having happened to someone present or to one of their relatives and that are responded to in kind. The stories under examination, however, turn out to be parodies—dialogic forms par excellence—of another widespread narrative genre, the *caso*, a type of belief tale about a folk medical practitioner, or *curandero*, whose traditional healing practices succeed where modern (Anglo) scientific medicine cannot.[6] The *caso* parodies, told by successful Texas-Mexican professionals, mock the practice of the *curanderos* and the credulity of their patients, yet with a certain sympathy for their endurance, humor, and moral strength. Here is another instance in which the exploration of systemic interrelationships between genres is fundamental to a full understanding of their social meaning, in this instance as vehicles for the negotiation of identity. The generically ambiguous narratives test the fine line between rejection and acceptance of elements of what it means to be a Texas-Mexican on the border.

Paredes's subtle explication of the intercultural jests rests centrally on two critical dimensions of contextualization, namely, the social identity of the performers and the dynamics of the situational context in which the stories are told. The social meaning of these double-voiced narratives is understandable only as a function of their social use in context; they are told by middle-class professionals, deeply rooted in Border society and culture yet distanced in significant ways from those roots, and they emerge within a situational context that selects for humorous expressions of and responses to the social and psychological conflict of border life.

We find similar close attention to performers and contexts of use throughout Paredes's writings, especially in "The Concept of the Emotional Core Applied to the Mexican *Corrido* 'Benjamín Argumedo'" (chap. 7), "José Mosqueda and the Folklorization of Actual Events" (chap. 8), and the two related articles on the *décima* (chaps. 10, 11). This analytical focus on the social identity of performers and situational contexts of use, together with the understanding of genre as a flexible expressive resource, marks Paredes's work as part of the movement toward a performance-centered folkloristics that has burgeoned over the past fifteen or twenty years. In point of fact, Paredes's scholarship has been of foundational importance in this development. While his seminal contribution to performance-oriented analysis as coeditor of *Toward New Perspectives in Folklore* (1972) has been widely acknowledged, his influence goes back even further, at least to the 1964 article "Some Aspects of Folk Poetry" (chap. 5), a pioneering work linking form explicitly to performance, that had a strong influence on the subsequent scholarship of the University of Texas folklorists who have been closely identified with performance-oriented folkloristics.

In my view, however, Paredes's most eloquent and penetrating contribution to the study of performance and its wider applications is his essay "On Ethnographic Work among Minority Groups: A Folklorist's Perspective" (chap. 4). In this article, Paredes mobilizes all of the power of his knowledge of performance—social identity, situational context, expressive voice, communicative framing, and more—in a trenchantly reflexive critique of anthropological and folkloristic practice. The primary target of his critique is the literature on Greater Mexican—especially Texas-Mexican—society and culture, a literature riddled with interpretive inaccuracies that are deeply consequential not only in scholarly terms but in terms of the politics of culture. How is it, Paredes asks, that the work of apparently well-intentioned liberal scholars, generally fluent in Spanish, can go so astray, perpetuating damaging stereotypes that serve the interests of containment and domination? As I have suggested, this is an issue that Paredes has addressed from a number of vantage points throughout his career, but "On Ethnographic Work among Minority Groups" zeroes in on a new dimension of the problem, namely, the naively literalist referential bias of positivist ethnographic practice: asking people for facts and assuming that they will give you straight answers. What Paredes is able to show, by adducing example after example, is that the ethnographic encounter—yet another intercultural dialogue—is communicatively far more complex than has been acknowledged, and that the discourse of ethnographic subjects may well be shaped by other communicative motivations than acceding to the ethnographer's standards of truth value and expectations of straightforward responses. The ethnographic encounter invites the display of communicative skill, a touchstone of performance, just as the asymmetrical relationship between the "native informant" and the outsider ethnographer may invite joking, or leg-pulling, or circumspection, or playing to stereotypes—saying what the researcher expects to hear and then some. Taking such communication at face value will lead to just the kinds of ethnographic howlers that Paredes finds in the anthropological literature on Greater Mexico. This illumination of the expressive shaping of the ethnographic encounter is the essential contribution of "a folklorist's perspective," or, more specifically, of a performance-oriented folklorist's perspective, in which the getting and giving of information, the patterns and functions of speaking in society and culture, are themselves the focus of ethnographic investigation, to be discovered rather than assumed a priori.

Nor are the implications of Paredes's argument relevant to the ethnographic study of Greater Mexican culture alone; witness the recent critiques of Margaret Mead's classic *Coming of Age in Samoa* based on the recollection of one of her key informants that she and her fellows responded to Mead's probing questions about their sex lives by making up titillating answers they thought she would like, in the time-honored Samoan tradition of expressive leg-pulling.[7] Taken in its broadest terms, "On Ethnographic Work among Minority Groups" is about *all* ethnographic work: if you aren't attuned to the ways that people perform, joke, play, or otherwise frame and manipulate what they say, your ethnographic study of any subject—not just folklore—is susceptible to radical distortion.*

So central are the twin themes of multiple languages and multiple voices in Américo Paredes's studies of Texas-Mexican folklore that no commentary on his work would be complete without mention of the play of these same factors in his own writing, for the in-betweenness of his native Lower Border has marked his scholarly production no less than the folklore to which he has devoted his career.† First and most obviously, Paredes writes in both English and Spanish, for his scholarly constituency extends throughout the Western Hemisphere; the Rio Grande border, after all, links the United States not only with Mexico but with all of Latin America. For practical reasons, this collection of Paredes's writings is confined largely to articles published in English, the language of the academic milieu in which Paredes has spent his professional life. We have been able to include, however, one essay heretofore published only in Spanish, "The Concept of the Emotional Core in the Mexican *Corrido* 'Benjamín Argumedo'" (chap. 7). Paredes has also assumed at times the role of interpreter between United States and Latin American folklorists, publishing several articles that introduce the respective scholarly communities to each other (see the Paredes bibliography at the end of this volume).

Paredes writes not only in different languages but also in multiple voices. His scholarship is a richly textured expressive fabric, not at all confined to the standard expository prose and the we-they oppositions of conventional folkloric and anthropological scholarship. There is, to

* Compare Charles L. Briggs, *Learning How to Ask: A Sociolinguistic Appraisal of the Role of the Interview in Social Science Research* (Cambridge: Cambridge University Press, 1986).
† This point is developed by José E. Limón in *The Return of the Mexican Ballad: Américo Paredes and His Anthropological Text as Persuasive Political Performance*, SCCR Working Paper no. 16 (Stanford: Stanford Center for Chicano Research, Stanford University, 1986).

be sure, a fair share of expository prose in Paredes's writings, but it is a prose whose seriousness is constantly tempered by irony, Paredes's favorite critical trope, his own intercultural jest that simultaneously employs the discourse of mainstream scholarship and subverts it. Then, too, the expository prose alternates in Paredes's scholarly writings with dedicatory lyric poems, recollections of personal experiences, songs from his own repertoire, legends recast and retold from the tellings of others, and other styles and genres. As for we-they oppositions, there are certainly plenty in Paredes's work, including we the scholars and they the Texas-Mexicans, but often Paredes crosses the border, and it is we the Texas-Mexicans against the Anglo scholars.

Which is all to say, in the end, that there is a deep and resonant unity in Américo Paredes's life, his subject, and his writing, but it is a unity of diversity, a conjunction of the borders. And when you can balance the ambiguities, survive the conflict, and command the resources and repertoires of both sides of the border and the contact culture itself, as Américo Paredes has done, the result is inspired and inspiring writing. That is what you will find in the pages that follow.

FOLKLORE AND CULTURE
ON THE TEXAS-MEXICAN BORDER

Part One

The Social Base and
the Negotiation of Identity

– 1 –

The Folklore of Groups of Mexican Origin in the United States

In THE 1940S, around the time of the Second World War, a folk-inspired Mexican song was very popular. It went like this:

Como México no hay dos,   There are no two like Mexico,
no hay dos en el mundo entero   there aren't two in the whole world
ni sol que brille mejor. . .   nor a sun that shines brighter . . .
Como México no hay dos.   There are no two like Mexico.

And some Mexicans would observe with a characteristic irony, "¡Gracias a Dios!" (Thank God!)

Both the author of the song and those who commented on it were mistaken, since it is well known that there are in fact two Mexicos. Every Mexican knows that there are two Mexicos, just as he knows that there being two is not a purely metaphysical concept, although it has its transcendental implications. The concept of two Mexicos refers to facts to be understood in the world of things. One Mexico—the "real" one, in the Platonic as well as in the ordinary sense—is found within the boundaries of the Mexican republic. The second Mexico—the México de Afuera (Mexico abroad) as Mexicans call it—is composed of all the persons of Mexican origin in the United States. My present theme is the folk culture of this México de Afuera as manifested in folklore.

Mexican folklore and that of México de Afuera are commonly thought of as two related but distinct entities. There is no general agreement, however, about the differences which exist between the two. Scholars have distinguished Mexican from Mexican American folklore in at least three ways. I will call these (1) the Hispanophile, (2) the diffusionist, and (3) the regionalist views. To express the first view in its extreme form, we would have to stress the pronounced differences between Mexican Americans and Mexicans from Mexico. Mexican American folklore, we would say, is almost totally Spanish—Peninsular, in other words—in its origins, having come directly from Spain to the parts of the United States where it is found today. It has no more than a remote likeness to the folklore found south of the border between the United States and Mexico, since the latter is mixed with indigenous elements which have diluted its grace and elegance.

A less extreme Hispanophile view is based on chronology. While folklore of Spanish origin in the United States, we are told, has its sources in colonial Mexico, this folklore reached the southwestern United States long ago, when Mexico was New Spain, centuries before modern Mexico was formed. The Spanish folklore of the United States is thus superior to that of Mexico, not only because it is *criollo* (Spanish-American) with impeccable colonial credentials, but also because it represents survivals of ancient and valuable European forms. Adapting two terms well known in *romancero* (ballad) studies, the Spanish folklore of the United States is considered *antiguo* while the folklore of Mexico is simply *vulgar.*

The Hispanophile view does not appear in its extreme form in the work of any serious folklorist, though it is found in that of many amateur collectors, commentators, and novelists of the Far West. Interested persons can find all the necessary examples in the work of Cecil Robinson, *With the Ears of Strangers.*[1] This attitude is based on a racial snobbery of which no nation on earth is completely free, but which reached one of its high points in the United States in the late nineteenth and early twentieth centuries. The less extreme form of Hispanicism, which relies on chronology, has in fact influenced serious studies of Mexican American folklore. It is the tacit assumption on which the first studies of Mexican folklore were made in the United States, especially those in New Mexico. The renowned scholar Aurelio M. Espinosa, for instance, made admirable discoveries of remnants of Spanish folklore in the southwestern United States, but in general he was rarely concerned with the purely Mexican elements, which were decidedly in the majority—or if he did collect them, very seldom did he recognize them as Mexican.

Among his materials were Mexican *corridos* of very recent creation and of undoubted Mexican origin, like "De Ignacio Parra," yet he did not recognize them as Mexican because he was convinced of the purely Hispanic character of New Mexican folklore.* His prestige, in fact, made a sort of dogma of the supposed Peninsular origins of New Mexican folklore. For this reason, when in 1933 Arthur L. Campa affirmed its basically Mexican character, his observations seemed almost revolutionary, though they merely indicated what was evident to those who wished to see.[2]

The second way of interpreting Mexican American folklore—which we call diffusionist—sees it as a slight isolated ripple, moving far from its origin in the great waves of Mexican folk culture centered in Jalisco, land of the *machos.* There is no need to insist on the attractions of this view for any Mexican folklorist. The converse of the Hispanophile opinion, it regards Mexican American folklore as in no way different, original, or important, since it is merely a collection of decayed chips scattered from the trunk. We might perhaps find a few variants of texts well known in Mexico, variants which would serve as footnotes to Mexican folklore. That would be about all. Most native Mexican folklorists have viewed Mexican American folklore in this way, as the detritus of Mexican folklore, when they have taken it into account at all.

Mexican American and Mexican folklore can also be differentiated by considering the former a regional folklore and the latter a national folklore. A regional folklore tradition in the United States is defined as the offshoot of some distant trunk of national folklore, which has put down deep roots in North American soil and developed characteristics of its own. The members of a regional folk culture, according to Richard M. Dorson in *American Folklore,* "are wedded to the land and the land holds memories. The people themselves possess identity and ancestry through continuous occupation of the same soil."[3] In his survey of United States regional folklore in *Buying the Wind,* Dorson includes Mexican American folklore among regional folklores like those of the Pennsylvania Dutch and the Cajuns of Louisiana, thus giving Mexican American folklore an identity of its own.[4] This is the point of view, naturally enough,

* See, for example, Espinosa's "Romancero nuevomejicano" in *Revue Hispanique* 33 (1915): 446–560; 40 (1917): 215–227; and 41 (1917): 678–680.

of the modern North American folklorist who is interested in identifying the various threads making up the complex fabric of North American culture.

None of these three ways of seeing Mexican American folklore is completely wrong. If we are looking for survivals, we must admit that the Mexican folk culture of the United States is often more conservative than that of Mexico, and retains folkloristic data originally from Spain which seem to have disappeared in Mexico. The ballad "La bella dama y el pastor" is an example. Apparently Mexican folklorists have been unable to collect it in their country, although it is well known both in New Mexico and southern Texas.* No serious folklorist nowadays would doubt, however, that "La bella dama y el pastor" reached the southwestern United States from Mexico, in line with the most classic diffusionist principles, or that the groups of Spanish-speaking people in those areas are strictly Mexican in origin and culture.† Neither is it wrong to refer to the cultures of these groups as regional cultures. They are Mexican Americans who have been established for centuries in the regions where they live, and far from being immigrants themselves, can view the North American as the immigrant.

BUT THIS IS NOT the whole story. The attention of folklorists has been limited almost exclusively so far to regional groups, that is, to groups established for generations in certain parts of the Southwest. Only a minority of the Mexicans in the United States, however, live within these groups. If we consider Mexican American folklore as a totality, we find other kinds of groups besides regional ones. We also find evidence of a series of exchanges between endemic Mexican folklore and that of the México de Afuera, a continuous mutual influence moving in both directions which is not typical of other regional cultures in the United States. This is the result of a simple geographical fact: the Atlantic Ocean divides Pennsylvania from Germany, and Louisiana from France, but only an imaginary line divides México de Adentro (Mexico as a territorial unit) from México de Afuera. This line is easy to cross, legally or illegally.

* I should mention that I have collected versions of this ballad within the boundaries of Mexico, in the city of Matamoros, Tamaulipas. But Tamaulipas is the old province of Nuevo Santander, together with southern Texas.
† Of course I am not referring to recently immigrated groups like the Basques and the Sephardic Jews.

At least three kinds of folklore groups of Mexican origin can be found in the United States. First, there are the truly regional groups; second, the groups composed of rural or semirural immigrants; and third, the urban groups. The first, as we have said, are composed of descendants of the early settlers on the northern frontiers of New Spain. At present, they are found in only two areas. One, more or less equivalent to the former province of Nuevo México, includes the present state of New Mexico, West Texas, parts of Arizona and Colorado, and the Mexican state of Chihuahua. The second area, corresponding to the former province of Nuevo Santander, is comprised of southern Texas from the Nueces River to the Rio Grande, the Mexican state of Tamaulipas, and nearby areas of Coahuila and Nuevo León. Two similar regions existed in California and the former province of Texas, but it has been some time since they sustained Mexican American folk cultures of the regional type. After 1849, Mexican settlements in California were engulfed in the wave of North American immigration caused by the discovery of gold, so that only traces remain of *californio* traditions. The Mexicans who lived in the province of Texas—the region east and north of the Río Nueces—were almost all driven from their homes after Texas gained independence in 1836. Only in the areas which earlier formed part of the provinces of Nuevo México and Nuevo Santander have Mexican American folk groups of the regional type survived. In those areas, folklore materials from Spain and Mexico have been kept alive for many generations, and local adaptations have been made as well. These two regions are well known to folklorists. What is often not known is that their limits are not defined by the Customs and Immigration offices at the border. Parts of northern Mexico are included within the boundaries of each. These regional folk cultures thus include regions of two nations.

The folk groups composed of rural or semirural immigrants are formed to a large extent by *braceros* (migrant workers) from the interior of Mexico, who began to enter the United States in growing numbers at the turn of the century. In border areas they frequently displaced the day laborers born and brought up in those areas, who were forced to emigrate to the northern United States. In successive waves, *braceros* from southern Mexico established themselves among the regional groups, reoccupied formerly Mexican areas of California and Texas, and penetrated into parts of the United States to which Mexican culture had not extended before. Since they are almost all agricultural workers, they have congregated in farming communities, where they constitute a pool of badly paid labor. Their folklore has much in common with that of the regional groups, but it is enriched by material recently brought from the interior of Mexico. For example, the water spirit which haunted the shores of the Papaloapan in Veracruz now appears by the banks of the Rio Grande in Texas, or the Colorado in Arizona.

The third type of Mexican American folk group (the urban) is found in the Mexiquitos of North American cities like Los Angeles, Chicago, and San Antonio. Some members of these urban groups come from the regional groups, displaced by *braceros* migrating from Mexico. Others are enterprising ex-*braceros* who came to work in the fields and stayed on as employees in the factories of the big cities. Children and grandchildren of political refugees who left Mexico during the Revolution are also almost always found in cities. The folklore of these urban groups comes, for the most part, from the regional groups and from the immigrant farm workers, although it has been adapted to the needs of life in the city. A marked emphasis is given to such forms as the *caló* (dialect), the *albur* (wordplay), the *blason populaire,* and to the *chascarrillo* (joke) known to all the ethnic groups of the city.

Of the three groups, those least affected by the process of transculturation are the immigrant field workers; it would be difficult to decide which of the other two—the urban or the regional—has experienced a greater degree of transculturation, since both types are bilingual in varying degrees. The member of the urban group is more subject to external influences, and is thus also the object of greater hostility, caused by the pressures and complexities of urban life. As a result, he feels less at ease in his environment than the member of the regional group. The latter, in turn, while his regional consciousness may permit a more favorable synthesis, finds himself more isolated from North American cultural traditions. These three folk groups which make up México de Afuera are constantly influencing one another at the same time that they are the object of all sorts of influences from Mexico as well as from the United States. They also exercise a certain influence in both Mexico and the United States. Mexican folklore, that is, like the concept of a México de Afuera, knows no borders.

THE FIRST MEXICANS to become permanent residents of the United States—with the exception of a few political refugees—were the inhabitants of the Mexican territories ceded to the United States in 1848. This was the origin of the regional folk groups, and these were the first Mexican Americans—the majority of them very much against their will. They were at once involved in a long-drawn-out struggle with the North Americans and their culture. Cultural differences were aggravated by the opportunism of many North American adventurers, who in their desire for riches treated the new citizens from the start as a conquered people. Names like Juan Nepomuceno Cortina, Aniceto Pizaña, Gregorio Cortez, and Elfego Baca—all men who, as a *corrido* (narrative folksong) puts it, "defendieron su derecho" (defended their right)—were immortalized in songs and legends. This was the birth—ten years after the war between Mexico and the United States—of the first examples of Mexican American folklore. Some of these rebels against the government of the United States were killed or taken prisoner by the North American authorities, who naturally treated them as bandits and lawbreakers. Others escaped to Mexico, where they lived out their lives as symbols of Anglo-American injustice.

If we look at the history of Mexico from a general point of view, Mexican nationalist feeling does not define itself until the last third of the nineteenth century and owes a great deal to the French occupation during the reign of Maximilian of Austria. In the northern frontiers, however, and in the parts of the United States recently taken from Mexico, nationalism begins to be felt toward the end of the 1830s, if we may take the folklore of those regions as an indication. It is a blaze stirred up by the daily conflict between the quietism of the Mexican and the power, the aggressiveness, and the foreign culture of the Anglo American. On the one hand, this conflict was expressed almost immediately in folkloric data, in *corridos* and other songs, semihistorical legends, insulting labels for North Americans. On the other hand, these folk artifacts reinforced psychological attitudes toward the United States and helped to isolate the regional groups, making them more typically "folk" than ever.

The Mexican saw himself and all that he stood for as continually challenging a foreign people who treated him, for the most part, with disdain.

Being Mexican meant remaining inviolable in the face of overwhelming attacks on one's personality. Under those circumstances, for a Mexican to accept North American values was to desert under fire. Such a situation—creative of folk groups defined as minorities—is not historically unique. It has been repeated many times with other peoples whose identity has been menaced. Among people within their own borders—the Poles, let us say, the Finns, the Irish, or the Greeks—such a situation has created an intensified nationalism. In contrast, other peoples who have existed as minorities within a dominant group—the Jews in Europe, for example—have maintained their identity through very close cultural bonds. The border Mexican American, because of his special relationship to the United States, made use of both these solutions.

It is not until 1890 that the immigration of new Mexican elements to the United States really begins, as part of a reciprocal movement: at the same time that North American capital invades Mexico, the Mexican *bracero* invades the United States. The cause is the same: the expansion in industry and finance which occurred in the United States in the decades after the Civil War (1861–1865). By 1890 North American capital was strong enough to look for foreign investments, and the government of Porfirio Díaz welcomed it to Mexico. It was around this time that the Díaz government became oppressive. The exploitation of the nation's natural resources by foreign capital worsened the already miserable situation of the Mexican peasant.

Migrant work was nothing new to the field worker from the interior of Mexico, but now he began to extend his trips from the states neighboring his own to the northern part of the country, and finally across the border. In the United States everything was ready to welcome him. The Civil War had initiated a shift in population from rural areas to the city, at the same time that the nation's total population increased, causing a greater demand for agricultural products. European immigrants were arriving in great numbers, but they remained in the big cities as factory workers, or if they turned to agriculture it was in the northern part of the country. There were harvests to reap and railroad tracks to lay in the South and the Southeast. This demand was met by the *bracero*. *Braceros* immigrated to Texas at first, and to other border regions, but with time they moved farther and farther north—to the railroads of West Virginia and Pennsylvania, to the sugar beet fields in Michigan, and finally to the factories of the Great Lakes. According to the twelfth edition of the *Encyclopaedia Britannica*, in 1908 there were 71,000 Mexican immigrants in Texas alone; in 1920 there were a quarter million. In 1910, 2 percent of all the immigration to the United States was from Mexico; in 1920 it was 12 percent.

THE MEXICAN *BRACERO* in the United States became a more or less permanent source of labor—and a minority made up of immigrants in a situation little superior to that of the former slaves, with whom they competed for work. The great antagonism between blacks and Mexicans which resulted was often the cause of violence between the two groups. Also the Mexican *bracero* was identified with the black in the mind of the Anglo American. In this way racial prejudices were added to preju- dices based on linguistic differences and other cultural factors, resulting in exclusion from restaurants, beaches, and theaters, and segregation in special schools. As the number of Mexican immigrants in the United States grew, these discriminatory practices increased as well, including lynchings of Mexicans accused of raping North American women.

Treatment of the *bracero* has varied with the use which could be made of him, and the immigration laws have been applied at the convenience of the American farmers who hired him. In times when labor has been in short supply he has been well received. When the need for him was not so great, efforts were made to prevent his passage from Mexico to the United States, not only by legal means but also by intimidation and insults from customs and immigration agents. In times of economic de- pression, he has been suddenly deported and forced to abandon family ties formed during a stay of twenty or more years in the United States. In fairness, we must note that the Mexican immigrant's sense of continuing to "pass through" after twenty years or more of residence in the United States contributed to his problems, since he remained a perennial visitor in a foreign country, without exercising the rights and the duties of citi- zenship. And he brought up his children born in the United States in his own way of thinking. Here we see an extension of the concept of a México de Afuera already described in discussing the regional groups.

A brief mention of the urban groups remains to be made. Of course Mexicans have always lived in North American cities like San Antonio, where the Mexican element has been present since Texas was part of

Mexico. But we do not find really large groups or "colonies" of Mexicans in the cities of the United States until the Mexican Revolution, that is, from 1911 on. With the Revolution comes another type of Mexican immigrant: the refugee from fratricidal wars and the political exile, among whom were many of Mexico's intellectuals. These people naturally went to the cities—to suffer all the anxieties of exile in an environment hardly noted for its sympathy with the Mexican and his culture. These exiled intellectuals lost no time in becoming the leaders and models in the Mexican colonies of the big cities, so effectively that some cities like San Antonio and Los Angeles became Mexican cultural centers in exile for a time. But these colonies were not composed only of exiles; they also included many other Mexicans who had come to the United States not in flight from the Revolution, but in search of work. During the First World War large numbers of *braceros*—and Mexican Americans from the regional groups as well—abandoned rural areas and small farms for the cities, where they found work in the industries promoted by the war.

While others formed the majority in the *colonias mexicanas,* the refugees imposed the intellectual and emotional tone. To them, all the Mexicans in the United States were living in unhappy exile, outlawed from the homeland they longed for and eager to return at the first opportunity. Here once more the concept of México de Afuera appears, but with intellectual embellishments which were lacking in the viewpoints of the regional groups and the immigrants—all of this developing in *barrios* very similar to the ghettos of European Jews. As in the case of the Jews, segregation in the ghetto was in part imposed by external circumstances and in part was the result of cultural preference. This "exile"—that is, exile as a state of mind—lasted until the administration of Lázaro Cárdenas issued a general amnesty. Some few Mexicans abandoned El México de Afuera and returned to their homeland; the majority stayed in the Mexiquitos of North America's cities, without completely giving up the idea that they were living in exile. This is the older generation, of course. An entire generation of Mexicans has since been born and grown up in the big cities of the United States which does not understand the "exile" attitude adopted by its parents, yet through their behavior feels the differences which distinguish it from Anglo Americans. These young people have in self-defense adopted many ways of behaving different from those of their parents, exaggerating these traits as much as those they have inherited in the desire to create a new personality of their own. This is the origin of the *pocho,* the *pachuco*—the child born in the ghetto—although his mores have been extended in many cases to the regional groups and the rural immigrants.

AT THIS POINT, the reader may well ask the reason for so much attention to the relations between the United States and Mexico, and to the social and economic conditions of Mexicans within the United States, in a work whose theme is Mexican American folklore. The reason is that the shock of cultures and peoples in a continuing situation of cultural conflict has given Mexican American folklore the traits which distinguish it from other folklores, including that of Mexico. The rest is Mexican folklore, and by extension, Spanish-American, Spanish, or universal folklore. *Märchen* registered in the Aarne-Thompson index of types can be collected from Mexican Americans as from other folk groups, as Aurelio and José Manuel Espinosa demonstrated many years ago. The same may be said of the tales and *romances* (ballads) found especially in New Mexico. The links between Mexican American folklore and all of Spanish America were pointed out by Arthur Campa as far back as 1933, while already in 1891 Captain John G. Bourke was collecting in southern Texas folk material as typically Mexican as the *pastorelas* (Christmas plays).[5] This is all material of importance, worthy of the study it has received and continues to receive. But it does not mark Mexican American folk groups as the possessors of a distinctive folklore. A purely Mexican American folklore must be sought in the conflict of cultures. Its initial genre is the Mexican American or Border *corrido,* which appears as an anticipatory phase of the Mexican *corrido.* Vicente T. Mendoza tells us that the *corrido mexicano* "begins in the last quarter of the nineteenth century, with the singing of the deeds of various rebels against the government of Porfirio Díaz . . . [this was] the real beginning of the period in which the courage of the protagonists and their disregard for their lives was underlined and given emphasis."[6] But in southern Texas and nearby areas of northern Mexico, *corridos* of this type which sing the feats of the first Mexican American rebels against the North American government already exist at the end of the 1850s. The uprising led by Juan Nepomuceno Cortina in southern Texas in 1859 was celebrated in *corridos* of which we still have fragments. From the *corridos* of Cortina on, this Mexican American genre develops in a form similar to its Mexican counterpart, but with characteristics peculiarly its own. The hero is always a Mexican whose rights or self-respect are trampled upon by North American authority. Very often the conflict begins with the cruel and unjust death of the hero's brother at the hands of Anglo Americans. The hero takes vengeance and is attacked by large numbers of *rinches,* or Texas Rangers. He kills large numbers of the enemy but it is impossible for him to win a final victory because the odds are so unfair. One of these protagonists, Gregorio Cortez, describes such a situation: "¡Ah, cuánto rinche montado, para un solo mexicano!" (Ah, how many mounted Rangers, against one lone Mexican!) This is clearly an expression of the Mexican's general state of mind on seeing himself attacked on every level of his existence by a people more powerful and more numerous than his own.

Another type of Mexican American *corrido,* also older than the *corrido mexicano,* is that dealing with the adventures of a group of Mexicans whose work forces them to travel deep into the United States. Always narrated in the first person plural, these *corridos* recount the perils of the trip, the foreign cities and the strange things seen by the adventurers. An example is "El corrido de Kiansis," from the 1860s, which relates the journey of a group of *vaqueros* (cowboys) driving a herd of cattle from South Texas to the ends of the railroad lines in the south of Kansas:

Cuando salimos pa' Kiansis	When we left for Kansas
con una grande partida,	with a great herd of cattle,
¡Ah, qué camino tan largo!	Ah, what a long trail it was!
No contaba con mi vida.	I was not sure I would survive.

Sixty years later the type persists in "El corrido de la Pensilvania," which narrates the adventures of other Mexicans who go from Texas to Pennsylvania, not driving steers this time but to work on the railroad. The same narrative pattern is preserved, and the same tone and style of narration:

De la suidá de For West [Fort Worth]	From the city of Fort Worth,
a las seis de la mañana	at six o'clock in the morning
salimos en un enganche	we left on a labor contract
para el estado de Pensilvania.	for the state of Pennsylvania.

Other *corridos* about migrant workers are concerned not with adventures on the road but with the injustices and sufferings endured by the *bracero,* whether from his North American bosses, from racial discrimination, or from immigration agents. We find *corridos* with titles like "Los deportados" (The Deported Ones), "La discriminación," "Los enganchados" (The Work Gang), or "Tristes quejas de un bracero" (A *Bracero*'s Plaint). The expression of grievances—or more properly social protest—is evident in them:

Los gringos son muy maloras,	The *gringos* are very tricky;
se valen de la ocasión;	they take advantage of the opportunity,
y a todos los mexicanos	and treat us all
nos tratan sin compasión.	without compassion.

In the *canción* we find happier themes—comic compositions in bilingual form, and other satirical texts which ridicule North American customs. In some the Mexican American satirizes his situation, making use of his own propensity to mix Spanish with English:

En Texas es terrible	In Texas it is terrible
por la revoltura que hay;	how things are all mixed up;
no hay quien diga "Hasta mañana",	no one says "Hasta mañana,"
nomás puro "Good-bye".	it is nothing but "*Good-bye.*"

In another a newly arrived *bracero* criticizes the freedom of the North American woman:

Desde México he venido,	From Mexico have I come,
nomás por venir a ver	just to come and see
esa ley americana	this American law that says
que aquí manda la mujer.	the woman is the boss.

In prose narratives, the legend and the belief tale, as well as the comic anecdote, are used to develop themes of cultural conflict. "La muerte de Antonio Rodríguez" (The Death of Antonio Rodríguez), for example, is a story based on a historical event: the lynching of a young Mexican who was apparently burned alive in a small town in Texas in 1910. In a variant collected in 1962, the story retains its tone of outrage and indignation after half a century, but the additions of universal motifs like K2111, "Potiphar's wife," have converted the story into legend. Another example is the legend of José Mosqueda, which dates from the 1890s. Although Mosqueda was an ordinary train robber, his legend has been given traces of cultural conflict. In addition, some versions approach the *Märchen* in the variety of motifs which have been woven into the narrative—for example, G303.10.5, "Where the devil can't reach, he sends an old woman," and S241, "Child unwittingly promised: 'first thing you meet.'" At the end of the tale, the malevolent old woman sells José Mosqueda for a large sum in dollars but the North American she is working with betrays her and doesn't give her a single cent. If old women are worse than the devil, then according to this legend North Americans are worse than old women.

My INTENTION HAS BEEN not only to present a rapid overview of the genesis and development of Mexican American folklore but to demonstrate the importance of cultural conflict in its formation. I have also wished to point out the necessity of studying these factors, to which folklorists have given scant attention. Let us go back for a moment to the three points of view which most scholars have adopted toward Mexican American folklore. Naturally, nothing of what has interested us here can be hoped for from the Hispanophiles. A fragment of a ballad about El Cid inevitably has more interest for them than three dozen examples of folkloric data such as those I have given. True, Aurelio Espinosa was interested not only in Spanish survivals in New Mexico but in folkloric data which seemed to be genuine products of New Mexican folk groups. True, also, that his mistakenly identifying Mexican materials was less his fault than the result of the state of folklore studies at that time, which took little interest in its social context. Nevertheless, the contribution of the Hispanophiles to a modern understanding of these materials has been small.

The same may be said of "diffusionists" like Vicente T. Mendoza. As late as 1954, when *El corrido mexicano* appears, he is ignorant of an entire tradition of Mexican American Border *corridos*. It is true that he includes a variant of "El corrido de Kiansis" in *El corrido mexicano*, but he identifies it as proceeding from the mountains of Chihuahua. Not until 1964, in *Lírica narrativa de México*, does he recognize the existence of a type of *corrido* which deserves to be called *fronterizo* in a summary reference to "El corrido de Gregorio Cortez"—but he later identifies this same "Corrido de Gregorio Cortez" as from Coahuila![7] This is strange indeed, since I do not have the least doubt that by 1960 Mendoza was aware that "El corrido de Gregorio Cortez" comes from South Texas.

The "regionalists" are a separate case for two reasons: first, because they have been relatively numerous and active in the collection of Mexican American folklore; second, because the perspective they have taken toward that folklore sets it apart as something individual. They are interested in the Mexican American as such (in his role as Mexican American), and much might be hoped for from them in analysis of the folklore of El México de Afuera. But they disappoint us. The diffusionist may not be aware of the origin of Mexican American folklore or may ignore it; the Hispanicist may show a great preference for cultural survivals; yet authentic folklore texts can be expected from each. In contrast, many of the texts published by the regionalists have been vitiated by a limited knowledge of the language and by either a too romantic vision of the folk or an attitude of arrogant condescension. Their supposed informants talk like Castilian grandees or else stereotyped Mexicans in a third-rate film.

Most regionalists, moreover, have been romantics through and through. The romantic point of view deals not with living things but with idealizations of them, in a world where there are no contemporary problems. This romantic attitude very often follows the conquest of new territory. In the history of Spanish folklore, the vogue for everything *morisco* (Moorish) after the fall of Granada is well known. It is this tendency to sentimentalize a conquered people, with its elements of condescension, which directs the efforts of the majority of regionalists. They have focused their energies on the regional groups, that is to say, on the "Romantic Southwest." They look for local color, for the rare, the archaic, the bizarre, and as a result the sort of folklore with which we are concerned has small place in their collections.

Combine this with lack of personal communication between collector and informant, and you have the regionalists' most serious flaw. This is why J. Frank Dobie, for example, could spend his life among Mexican informants in Mexico as well as in the United States without ever really getting to know them; why John A. Lomax and others collected Mexican songs in South Texas without being aware of the existence of a whole tradition of Border *corridos* dealing with cultural conflict. They collected variants of the "Corrido de los sediciosos" (*Corrido* of the Seditionists) which relates the uprising in 1915 of a group of Texas-Mexicans commanded by Aniceto Pizaña, but they were variants which ridicule the *sediciosos* and give the role of hero to the Texas Rangers, hated so strongly by the regional folk groups!

A certain mistaken delicacy, or the desire not to offend, not to bring up painful matters which we all know have existed and which we all want to remedy, has convinced some folklorists that it would be in poor taste to expose the conflict between the Mexican and North American cultures. But this is to deny folklore study its place as a scholarly discipline. It belongs with the opinion that anyone who studies obscene folklore is an obscene person and that anyone who studies popular beliefs must be superstitious as well.

For one or several of the reasons given, the folklorists of the past paid little attention to the most characteristic aspects of Mexican American folklore. The task of making these known remained for investigators whose primary interest was not folklore—sociologists, economists, linguists, and anthropologists. The first published variant of the "Corrido de Gregorio Cortez"—the synthesis of the *corrido* of cultural conflict— appeared in 1930 and owes its appearance to Don Manuel Gamio.[8] The economist Paul S. Taylor published a variant of the "Corrido de la Pensilvania" in 1931, and both Gamio and Taylor have made various *corridos* of the *braceros* known through their writings.[9] Linguists have studied gestures, insulting names, and *caló* (dialect) in general, and there have also been studies of the social context by sociologists and anthropologists.[10]

Meanwhile, in the United States we have a new generation of folklorists with a different orientation and a better training in languages. They are responsible for a new and greater interest in Mexican American folk culture. In this way we are beginning to recognize throughout the United States that "como México sí hay dos."

~ 2 ~

The Problem of Identity in a Changing Culture: Popular Expressions of Culture Conflict along the Lower Rio Grande Border

CONFLICT—cultural, economic, and physical—has been a way of life along the border between Mexico and the United States, and it is in the so-called Nueces–Rio Grande strip where its patterns were first established. Problems of identity also are common to border dwellers, and these problems were first confronted by people of Mexican culture as a result of the Texas Revolution. For these reasons, the Lower Rio Grande area also can claim to be the source of the more typical elements of what we call the culture of the Border.

The *Handbook of Middle American Indians* divides northern Mexico into four culture areas: (1) Baja California; (2) the northwest area—Sonora and south along the Pacific coast to Nayarit; (3) the north central area—Chihuahua, Durango, and some parts of Coahuila; and (4) the northeast area—Tamaulipas, most of Nuevo León, and the lower-border areas of Coahuila, ending a few miles upriver from Ciudad Acuña and Del Rio.[1]

The culture of the Border is not only historically dynamic but has its regional variations as well. Because it is difficult to generalize on so vast an area, this essay focuses on one region, the northeast. It sometimes is referred to as the Lower Rio Grande Border or simply, the Lower Border.* In a strictly chronological sense, this region may claim priority over the other areas. If we view a border not simply as a line on a map but, more fundamentally, as a sensitized area where two cultures or

---

* See especially Américo Paredes, *"With His Pistol in His Hand": A Border Ballad and Its Hero* (Austin: University of Texas Press, 1958); and Américo Paredes, *A Texas-Mexican Cancionero: Folksongs of the Lower Border* (Urbana: University of Illinois Press, 1976).

two political systems come face to face, then the first border between English-speaking people from the United States and people of Mexican culture was in the eastern part of what is now the state of Texas. And this border developed even before such political entities as the Republic of Mexico and the Republic of Texas came into being. Its location shifted as the relentless drive south and west by Nolan, Magee, and their successors pushed a hotly contested borderline first to the Nueces and later to the Rio Grande.

Certain folkloric themes and patterns spread from the Nueces–Rio Grande area to other parts of the border as cultural conflict spread. That a distinctive Border culture spread from the Nueces–Rio Grande area to other border regions (as well as to other areas of the West) is a thesis explored by Professor Walter Prescott Webb in *The Great Plains*. In the chapter "The Cattle Kingdom," Webb sees his "kingdom" as developing a peculiar "civilization."[2] This "cattle culture" was the result of a union of northern Mexican *ranchero* culture, including techniques of raising cattle and horses, with new technological improvements brought in by Anglo Americans, especially such things as revolvers, barbed wire, and lawyers versed in the intricacies of land titles.

Much has been written about the blending of cultures in the southwestern United States, though less has been said about the impact of United States culture on northern Mexico. The number of books written about the influence of Mexican (or Spanish) architecture in the southwestern United States, if placed one beside another, would fill an extremely long bookshelf. Even more has been said and written about Mexican foods in the United States, an interest also manifest in the number of "Mexican" restaurants in almost any American town or city, patronized for the most part by WASP Americans. The ultimate in Mexican food in the Southwest and other areas are the quick-service chains that now sell tacos the way other chains sell hamburgers and hot dogs.

"Mexican food" is of course defined as tamales, tacos, enchiladas, chalupas, nachos, tostadas, frijoles refritos, and delicacies of that sort. What is rarely noted is that for the border Mexican of the past couple of centuries these foods have been almost as exotic as they are to the WASP American. One of the popular etymologies given for "greaser," an epithet applied by Anglo Americans to Mexicans, is that the term arose when the Anglos first encountered Mexicans in the Nueces–Rio Grande area and were struck by the greasiness of Mexican food. O. Henry has enshrined this stereotype in his poem "Tamales," according to which Don José Calderón Santos Espirition Vicente Camillo Quintana de Ríos de Rosa y Ribera takes revenge on the Texans for having killed his grandfather at San Jacinto by selling greasy tamales to Anglos:

> What boots it if we killed
> Only one greaser,
> Don José Calderón?
> This is your deep revenge,
> You have greased all of us,
> Greased a whole nation
> With your Tamales . . .[3]

The author of "The Little Adobe Casa," a parody of "The Little Sod Shanty on My Claim," has a much better idea of the border Mexican's fare, perhaps based on more direct experience than O. Henry's. The singer lives in Mexico, where "the Greaser roams about the place all day." Still, he keeps hoping that some "dark eyed mujer" will consent to be his wife. Meanwhile,

> My bill of fare is always just the same
> Frijoles and tortillas
> Stirred up in chili sauce
> In my little adobe casa on the plains.[4]

Frijoles, chiles, and tortillas were the standard fare along the border, as everywhere else in Mexico, except that the tortillas were more likely to be made of flour than of *nixtamal* (cooked maize), while the frijoles were never refried but boiled and mashed into a soupy stew—*caldudos*. Tamales were eaten once a year, at Christmas after the yearly hog was killed; and a taco was any snack made of a rolled tortilla with some kind of filling. For a more varied daily menu there might be rice with chicken or dried shrimp, beef either fresh or dried, as well as almost any other part of the steer. And for a real treat there was *cabrito* (goatmeat).

Bigfoot (El Patón) Wallace, who was captured by Mexican troops after the Mier Expedition, used his alleged sufferings in captivity as an excuse for the barbarities he committed against Mexican civilians when he was a member of Hays's Rangers during the Mexican War. One of the examples of his mistreatment at Mexican hands is mentioned in John Duval's romanticized biography of Wallace. Wallace complained that after being captured, and during the time he spent along the Rio Grande, all he ever was given to eat were beans, tortillas, and roast goatmeat.[5] Nowadays, many of Wallace's fellow countrymen journey all the way from Central Texas to "in" eating spots on the Rio Grande, to satisfy their craving for beans, tortillas, and roast goatmeat. But perhaps Bigfoot found border Mexican food too greaseless for his taste; he probably missed his sidemeat and the rich gravies he was accustomed to sopping his biscuits in.

A better case for the blending of Anglo-American culture with that of the northern Mexican *ranchero* may be made in respect to the more practical elements of the cattle culture. Cattle and horses, as well as land, were Mexican to begin with; and when the Anglo took them over he also adopted many of the techniques developed by the *ranchero* for the handling of stock. The vocabulary related to the occupation of the *vaquero* also became part of the blend. These things also have merited the attention of scholars and popular writers alike, especially those interested in the process whereby the rough Mexican *ranchero* was transformed into the highly romanticized American cowboy. All these subjects, from food and architecture to the birth of the cowboy, have attracted interest mainly from the viewpoint of their impact on the culture of the United States. My own interest in the cowboy has been a bit more intercultural, I believe, and it has focused on the manner in which an ideal pattern of male behavior has been developed interculturally along the border, subsequently to influence the male self-image first in the United States and later in Mexico. I refer to that familiar figure of popular fiction and popular song—the mounted man with his pistol in hand.[6] Take the Mexican *ranchero,* a man on horseback par excellence, add the six-chambered revolver, and you have the American cowboy of fiction and popular legend—the ideal figure of many an Anglo male. The cowboy as a *macho* image was carried by the Texan, along with other elements of the cattle culture, to other areas of the border, as well as to other parts of the West. The idea of the cowboy as the American *macho* becomes so pervasive that it can influence the private and public life of Theodore Roosevelt, as well as the scholarly writings of historians like Walter

Prescott Webb. Finally—aided in the last stages of the process by such books as Webb's *The Texas Rangers*—the cowboy has his apotheosis in Hollywood. The impact on a people of an idea or an ideal may be gauged by its influence on the folksongs of that people. Thus, it is worth noting that by 1910 the work of John A. Lomax, the great collector of North American folksongs, was beginning to make Americans see the cowboy as the national image and find the essence of the North American spirit in the cowboy, as expressed in the cowboy's songs. At that time the Mexican Revolution was just getting under way, and it would be almost a generation before romantic nationalists in Mexico would discover the essence of *mexicanismo* in the *corridos* of the Revolution.

The cowboy had influenced the border Mexican long before, and in a very direct way, because "cowboy" began as the name of the Anglo cattle thieves who raided the Nueces–Rio Grande area in the late 1830s, and who, revolver in hand, began the dispossession of the Mexican on the north bank of the Rio Grande. Understandably, the border Mexican developed a fascination for the revolver as a very direct symbol of power; he had learned the power of the pistol the hard way. Mexicans lent the image of the *vaquero* to their neighbors to the north, and the image returned to Mexico wearing a six-shooter and a Stetson hat. The cowboy *macho* image influenced the Revolution, in men such as Rodolfo Fierro; but it was after the Revolution that the cycle was completed, with the singing *charros* of the Mexican movies. And it was at about this same time that anthropologists and psychoanalysts discovered *machismo* in Mexico and labeled it as a peculiarly Mexican way of behavior.

BUT LIFE ALONG THE BORDER was not always a matter of conflicting cultures; there was often cooperation of a sort, between ordinary people of both cultures, since life had to be lived as an everyday affair. People most often cooperated in circumventing the excessive regulation of ordinary intercourse across the border. In other words, they regularly were engaged in smuggling. Smuggling, of course, has been a common activity wherever Mexicans and North Americans have come in contact; and this goes back to times long before Mexico's independence, when Yankee vessels used to make periodic smuggling visits to the more out-of-the-way Mexican ports. The famous Santa Fe Trail, begun about 1820 between Santa Fe and Independence, Missouri, may be considered one of the largest and most publicized smuggling operations in history. But even earlier, smuggling had been fairly general from the United States into Texas. The fact that the United States had consumer goods to sell and that Mexicans wanted to buy made smuggling inevitable, and many otherwise respected figures in the early history of the Southwest seem to have indulged in the practice. Smuggling could even be seen in those early days as a kind of libertarian practice, a protest against the harsh customs laws of the colonial times that throttled Mexico's economy. So, smuggling was not peculiar to the Nueces–Rio Grande area, while the romanticizing of the smuggler as a leader in social protest was not limited even to the border areas as a whole. One has only to remember Luis Inclán's *Astucia,* where tobacco smugglers in interior Mexico are idealized as social reformers of the gun and hangman's noose. (It is worth mentioning, however, that Inclán's hero sends to the United States for *pistolas giratorias* to accomplish his pre–Porfirio Díaz version of iron-fisted law and order.)

Borders, however, offer special conditions not only for smuggling but for the idealization of the smuggler. This sounds pretty obvious, since, after all, political boundaries are the obvious places where customs and immigration regulations are enforced. But we must consider not only the existence of such political boundaries but the circumstances of their creation. In this respect, the Lower Rio Grande Border was especially suited for smuggling operations.

To appreciate this fact, one has only to consider the history of the Lower Rio Grande. This area—presently Tamaulipas and the southern part of Texas—was originally the province of Nuevo Santander. Nuevo Santander differed from the other three northernmost provinces of New Spain—New Mexico, Texas, and California—in an important way. It was not the last to be founded, its settlement having preceded that of California by some twenty years. But it was the least isolated of the frontier provinces. Great expanses of territory separated the settlements in New Mexico and California from the concentrations of Mexican population to the south. The same was true of the colony of Texas until 1749. It was in that year that Escandón began the settlement of Nuevo Santander, and one of the aims of settlement was precisely to fill the gap between the Texas colony and such established population centers to the south as Tampico and Monterrey.

So from their very first days of settlement, the colonists of Nuevo Santander lived an in-between existence. This sense of being caught in the middle was greatly intensified after 1835. As citizens of Mexico, the former *neosantanderinos*—now *tamaulipecos*—faced an alien and hostile people to the north. As *federalistas,* they also had to contend with an equally hostile *centralista* government to the south. For the people of the Lower Rio Grande, the period from the mid-1830s to the mid-1840s was marked by cattle-stealing raids by Texas "cowboys" from north of the Nueces and incursions of Mexican armies from the south. It would be difficult to find parallels to this situation in the other frontier provinces; however, the bitter hatreds that developed in the Nueces–Rio Grande area during that bloody decade were soon diffused to other areas of the Southwest, along with other elements of the cattle culture.

The Treaty of Guadalupe Hidalgo settled the conflict over territory between Mexico and the United States, officially at least. It also created a Mexican American minority in the United States, as has often been noted. But it did not immediately create a border situation all along the international line. The *nuevomejicano* in Santa Fe, the *californio* in Los Angeles, and the *tejano* in San Antonio were swallowed whole into the North American political body. The new border—an imaginary and ill-defined line—was many miles to the south of them, in the uninhabited areas that already had separated them from the rest of Mexico before the war with the United States. The immediate change in customs demanded of *tejanos, californios,* and *nuevomejicanos* was from regional subcultures of Mexico to occupied territories within the United States.

Such was not the case with the people of the Lower Rio Grande. A very well defined geographic feature—the Rio Grande itself—became the international line. And it was a line that cut right through the middle of what had once been Nuevo Santander. The river, once a focus of regional life, became a symbol of separation. The kind of borderline that separates ethnically related peoples is common enough in some parts of Europe; but in the earliest stages of the border between Mexico and the United States, it was typical only of the Lower Rio Grande, with some exceptions such as the El Paso area. Here a pattern was set that would later become typical of the whole border between Mexico and the United States. Irredentist movements were shared with other occupied areas such as New Mexico, though the Cortina and Pizaña uprisings of

1859 and 1915 respectively were strongly influenced by the proximity of the international boundary. More to our point was the general flouting of customs and immigration laws, not so much as a form of social or ethnic protest but as part of the way of life.

When the Rio Grande became a border, friends and relatives who had been near neighbors—within shouting distance across a few hundred feet of water—now were legally in different countries. If they wanted to visit each other, the law required that they travel many miles up or down stream, to the nearest official crossing place, instead of swimming or boating directly across as they used to do before. It goes without saying that they paid little attention to the requirements of the law. When they went visiting, they crossed at the most convenient spot on the river; and, as is ancient custom when one goes visiting loved ones, they took gifts with them: farm products from Mexico to Texas, textiles and other manufactured goods from Texas to Mexico. Legally, of course, this was smuggling, differing from contraband for profit in volume only. Such a pattern is familiar to anyone who knows the border, for it still operates, not only along the Lower Rio Grande now but all along the boundary line between Mexico and the United States.

Unofficial crossings also disregarded immigration laws. Children born on one side of the river would be baptized on the other side, and thus appear on church registers as citizens of the other country. This bothered no one since people on both sides of the river thought of themselves as *mexicanos,* but United States officials were concerned about it. People would come across to visit relatives and stay long periods of time, and perhaps move inland in search of work. After 1890, the movement in search of work was preponderantly from Mexico deep into Texas and beyond. The ease with which the river could be crossed and the hospitality of relatives and friends on either side also was a boon to men who got in trouble with the law. It was not necessary to flee over trackless wastes, with the law hot on one's trail. All it took was a few moments in the water, and one was out of reach of his pursuers and in the hands of friends. If illegal crossings in search of work were mainly in a northerly direction, crossings to escape the law were for the most part from north to south. By far, not all the Mexicans fleeing American law were criminals in an ordinary sense. Many were victims of cultural conflict, men who had reacted violently to assaults on their human dignity or their economic rights.

Resulting from the partition of the Lower Rio Grande communities was a set of folk attitudes that would in time become general along the United States–Mexican border. There was a generally favorable disposition toward the individual who disregarded customs and immigration laws, especially the laws of the United States. The professional smuggler was not a figure of reproach, whether he was engaged in smuggling American woven goods into Mexico or Mexican tequila into Texas. In folklore there was a tendency to idealize the smuggler, especially the *tequilero,* as a variant of the hero of cultural conflict. The smuggler, the illegal alien looking for work, and the border-conflict hero became identified with each other in the popular mind. They came into conflict with the same American laws and sometimes with the same individual officers of the law, who were all looked upon as *rinches*—a border-Spanish rendering of "ranger." Men who were Texas Rangers, for example, during the revenge killings of Mexicans after the Pizaña uprising of 1915* later were border patrolmen who engaged in gunbattles with *tequileros.* So stereotyped did the figure of the *rinche* become that Lower Rio Grande Border versions of "La persecución de Villa" identify Pershing's soldiers as *rinches.*

A *corrido* tradition of intercultural conflict developed along the Rio Grande, in which the hero defends his rights and those of other Mexicans against the *rinches.* The first hero of these *corridos* is Juan Nepomuceno Cortina, who is celebrated in an 1859 *corrido* precisely because he helps a fellow Mexican.

Ese general Cortina	That general Cortina
es libre y muy soberano,	is quite sovereign and free;
han subido sus honores	the honor due him is greater,
porque salvó a un mexicano.	for he saved a Mexican's life.

Other major *corrido* heroes are Gregorio Cortez (1901), who kills two Texas sheriffs after one of them shoots his brother; Jacinto Treviño

* The uprising occurred on the Lower Rio Grande Border and involved a group of Texas-Mexican *rancheros* attempting to create a Spanish-speaking republic in South Texas. Pizaña endeavored to appeal to other United States minority groups. [Original Editor's Note]

(1911), who kills several Americans to avenge his brother's death; Rito García (1885), who shoots several officers who invade his home without a warrant; and Aniceto Pizaña and his *sediciosos* (1915). Some *corrido* heroes escape across the border into Mexico; others, like Gregorio Cortez and Rito García, are betrayed and captured. They go to prison but they have stood up for what is right. As the "Corrido de Rito García" says,

. . . me voy a la penitencia	. . . I am going to the penitentiary
por defender mi derecho.	because I defended my rights.

The men who smuggled tequila into the United States during the twenties and early thirties were no apostles of civil rights, nor did the border people think of them as such. But in his activities, the *tequilero* risked his life against the old enemy, the *rinche*. And, as has been noted, smuggling had long been part of the border way of life. Still sung today is "El corrido de Mariano Reséndez," about a prominent smuggler of textiles into Mexico, circa 1900. So highly respected were Reséndez and his activities that he was known as "El Contrabandista." Reséndez, of course, violated Mexican laws; and his battles were with Mexican customs officers. The *tequilero* and his activities, however, took on an intercultural dimension; and they became a kind of coda to the *corridos* of border conflict.

The heavy-handed and often brutal manner that Anglo lawmen have used in their dealings with border Mexicans helped make almost any man outside the law a sympathetic figure, with the *rinche,* or Texas Ranger, as the symbol of police brutality. That these symbols still are alive may be seen in the recent Fred Carrasco affair. The border Mexican's tolerance of smuggling does not seem to extend to traffic in drugs. The few *corridos* that have been current on the subject, such as "Carga blanca," take a negative view of the dope peddler. Yet Carrasco's death in 1976 at the Huntsville (Texas) prison, along with two women hostages, inspired close to a dozen *corridos* with echoes of the old style. The sensational character of Carrasco's death cannot be discounted, but note should also be taken of the unproved though widely circulated charges that Carrasco was "executed" by a Texas Ranger, who allegedly shot him through the head at close range where Carrasco lay wounded. This is a scenario familiar to many a piece of folk literature about cultural conflict—*corridos* and prose narratives—the *rinche* finishing off the wounded Mexican with a bullet through the head. It is interesting to compare the following stanzas, the first from one of the Carrasco *corridos* and the other two from a *tequilero* ballad of the thirties.

El capitán de los rinches	The captain of the Rangers
fue el primero que cayó	was the first one to fall,
pero el chaleco de malla	but the armored vest he was wearing
las balas no traspasó.	did not let the bullets through.

* * *   * * *

En fin de tanto invitarle	They kept asking him to go,
Leandro los acompañó;	until Leandro went with them;
en las lomas de Almiramba	in the hills of Almiramba
fue el primero que cayó.	he was the first one to fall.
El capitán de los rinches	The captain of the Rangers
a Silvano se acercó	came up close to Silvano,
y en unos cuantos segundos	and in a few seconds
Silvano García murió.	Silvano García was dead.

Similar attitudes are expressed on the Sonora-Arizona border, for example, when the hard-case hero of "El corrido de Cananea" is made to say,

Me agarraron los cherifes	The sheriffs caught me
al estilo americano,	in the American style,
como al hombre de delito,	as they would a wanted man,
todos con pistola en mano.	all of them pistol in hand.

The partition of Nuevo Santander was also to have political effects, arising from the strong feeling among the lower Rio Grande people that the land on both sides of the river was equally theirs. This involved feelings on a very local and personal level, rather than the rhetoric of national politics, and is an attitude occasionally exhibited by some old Rio Grande people to this day. Driving north along one of today's highways toward San Antonio, Austin, or Houston, they are likely to say as the highway crosses the Nueces, "We are now entering Texas." Said in jest, of course, but the jest has its point. Unlike Mexicans in California, New Mexico, and the old colony of Texas, the Rio Grande people experienced the dismemberment of Mexico in a very immediate way. So the attitude developed, early and naturally, that a border Mexican was *en su tierra* in

Texas even if he had been born in Tamaulipas. Such feelings, of course, were the basis for the revolts of Cortina and Pizaña. They reinforced the borderer's disregard of political and social boundaries. And they lead in a direct line to the Chicano movement and its mythic concept of Aztlán. For the Chicano does not base his claim to the Southwest on royal land grants or on a lineage that goes back to the Spanish *conquistadores.* On the contrary, he is more likely to be the child or grandchild of immigrants. He bases his claim to Aztlán on his Mexican culture and his *mestizo* heritage.

Conversely, the Texas-born Mexican continued to think of Mexico as "our land" also. That this at times led to problems of identity is seen in the folksongs of the Border. In 1885, for example, Rito García protests illegal police entry into his home by shooting a few officers of Cameron County, Texas. He makes it across the river and feels safe, unaware that Porfirio Díaz has an extradition agreement with the United States. Arrested and returned to Texas, according to the *corrido,* he expresses amazement:

Yo nunca hubiera creído	I never would have thought
que mi país tirano fuera,	that my country would be so unjust,
que Mainero me entregara	that Mainero would hand me over
a la nación extranjera.	to a foreign nation.

And he adds bitterly:

Mexicanos, no hay que fiar	Mexicans, we can put no trust
en nuestra propia nación,	in our own nation;
nunca vayan a buscar	never go to Mexico
a México protección.	asking for protection.

But the *mexicanos* to whom he gives this advice are Texas-Mexicans.

An even more interesting case dates back to 1867, the year Maximilian surrendered at Querétaro. A few days before this event, on May 5, Mexicans celebrated another event just as historic, the fifth anniversary of the defeat of the French at Puebla by Mexican troops under Ignacio Zaragoza. The little town of San Ignacio, on the Texas side of the river, celebrated the Cinco de Mayo with a big festival at which a local *guitarrero* sang two of his songs, especially composed for the occasion. One was "A Zaragoza," in praise of the victor over the French at Puebla; the other was "A Grant," in praise of Ulysses S. Grant, the victor over the Confederacy. The same set of symbols—flag, honor, country—are used in both songs.*

THE SIMPLEST FORMS of verbal folk expression are names; they are also the first level of expression of stereotypes developed as a result of intergroup relations. When we name things, we give them a life of their own; we isolate them from the rest of our experience. By naming ourselves, we affirm our own identity; we define it by separating ourselves from others, to whom we give names different from our own. By naming others we also identify them, and thus make them easier to cope with. It has been a widely held belief throughout human history that one can acquire power over others—mortals and immortals alike—by knowing their names.

The names Mexicans and Americans have called each other along the border are a rich source of information about the history of their attitudes. We invent names—usually derogatory—for other ethnic groups by reference to the stereotypic image we have of the particular outgroup. Some names make reference to physical appearance, language, diet, or customs—the most obvious ingredients in the development of ethnic stereotypes. Others may be the names of occupations or social classes identified with the outgroup. Still others are personal names that evoke for the ingroup a fully realized image of the stereotype they attribute to the outgroup. Finally, some derogatory ethnic labels may be corruptions of the accepted, nonderogatory name for the group in question. And occasionally we have a situation in which a name coined for one outgroup is transferred to another group that demands more of the ingroup's attention.

American English has always been rich in derogatory labels for various ethnic groups. In *The American Thesaurus of Slang,* Berrey and Van den Bark list as many as 150 derogatory terms for the American Negro alone.[7] We would expect border English to be generously endowed with names for the Mexican, and we are not disappointed. The most

* For a fuller treatment of these two songs, see Américo Paredes, "Folklore e historia: Dos cantares de la frontera del norte," in *25 estudios de folklore,* ed. Fernando Anaya Monroy, Estudios de Folklore, no. 4 (Mexico City: Instituto de Investigaciones Estéticas, Universidad Nacional Autónoma de México, 1971), 209–222.

common has been "greaser," which focuses on an aspect of physical appearance, the color and appearance of the skin—and perhaps of the hair. Along with its derivatives—"greaseball," "goo-goo," and "gook"—it once had a much wider ethnic range in American English.[8] In recent times, however, "gook" has been restricted to Orientals, while "greaser" long ago became the identifying epithet for the Mexican, to whom the term has been applied at least since 1836.* The Mexican's trouble with the long and short versions of the English *i* qualify him as a spic. "Spic," however, and its derivatives—"spig" and "spigotty"—are not used exclusively for the Mexican but may be applied to any speaker of Spanish, Portuguese, or Italian. The Mexican diet has been a much richer source of derogatory names, among them "pepper belly," "taco choker," "frijole guzzler," "chili picker," and (of a woman) "hot tamale." Aside from diet, no other aspect of Mexican culture seems to have caught the fancy of the Anglo coiner of derogatory terms for Mexicans.

More fruitful sources have been names used by Mexicans to denote class or occupational distinctions among themselves, such designations being turned into derogatory terms for all Mexicans, or at least all those Mexicans the Anglo speaker disapproves of. Chief of these are *peón, pelado, mojado* or its English equivalent "wetback," *bracero,* and most recently *pachuco.* Various corruptions of "Mexican" also have been used as derogatory terms. Aside from the clipped form "Mex," the most common are "Meskin" (originally a nonderogatory, dialectal form of "Mexican") and its derivatives, "skin," "skindiver," and "diver." A special twist in the insulting use of national or ethnic names—one that seems peculiarly North American—is the application of the outgroup's ethnic designation to another member of one's ingroup. Southern whites, it is well known, have long insulted other southern whites by calling them "niggers." Similarly, border Anglos have insulted each other by use of the epithet "Mexican." On occasion, one Anglo might insult another simply by calling him *señor,* the implication being that the person so addressed was a Mexican. Not surprisingly, the Anglo came to consider "Mexican" an insulting term when applied to Mexicans as well. The use of "Spanish" as a euphemism for "Mexican" is old on the border. As Bigfoot Wallace said of the surgeon who treated him kindly while he was a pris-

---

* In *Letters from the Frontiers* (Philadelphia: J. B. Lippincott, 1868), G. A. McCall refers to northern Mexico as "Greaserdom."

oner in Perote in the early 1840s, "He was a Castilian, or Spaniard, by birth, and not a Mexican, which may account satisfactorily in a great measure for the fact that he was not a bigoted tyrant in disposition. At any rate I hope he may live a thousand years."[9]

"Latin" is another current euphemism for the Mexican, but it seems to be fairly recent, having gained currency only in the 1920s, with the founding of the League of United Latin American Citizens. I am not aware of any names that were originally used by Anglos specifically for some other ethnic group and that were later transferred in toto to the Mexican. Mexicans occasionally have been called "niggers," but this seems to be merely an extension of the custom of using "nigger" as a form of insult.[10] The names mentioned reveal a stereotypic view of the Mexican that may be encapsulated in a proper name. Two names are especially favored in this respect. "Pedro"—usually pronounced with a long *a* as "Paydro"—evokes the fat, stupid but basically harmless peon. "Pancho" suggests the bandit stereotype, the Mexican with the long mustaches and the cartridge belts crossed over his chest.

There is still another form of ethnic insult of long standing in American English, though it has not been especially notable in Border culture—what Ed Cray has called the derisive ethnic adjective.[11] Some of these are very old, such as "Dutch widow" for a prostitute and "Dutch courage" for drunken belligerence. Collecting in Los Angeles, Cray lists a number of phrases using "Mexican" as a derisive adjective: Mexican car wash (leaving your car out in the rain), Mexican credit card (a piece of hose to siphon gasoline out of other people's cars), Mexican overdrive (driving downhill in neutral), Mexican promotion (an increase in rank without a raise in pay), and Mexican two-step (dysentery). These phrases, however, are wandering and adaptable forms that, like some jokes, may be fitted to many situations. One also hears of Jewish overdrive, Jewish car wash, Oklahoma credit card (in Texas, of course), and Irish promotion. Not even "Mexican two-step" (better known by its victims as the *turista* or Montezuma's revenge) can claim the honor of original coinage. In some parts of the South, dysentery has been known as the Kentucky or the Tennessee two-step. However, the tendency to use "Mexican" as an adjective to denote a makeshift job or product is an old one on the Rio Grande border. Cray also reports it among Anglos in Los Angeles.[12]

In *The American Language* H. L. Mencken observes that as far as terms of opprobrium go "the American language boasts a large stock, chiefly directed at aliens."[13] Mencken's observation is entirely correct, but he goes on to remark that in the exchange of insults the United States gets off very lightly, "for only the Spanish-speaking nations appear to have any opprobrious names for Americans, and these are few in number." He cites but two, *yanqui blofero* and *gringo*.[14] Mencken is too quick to claim superiority in the art of the insult, for Spanish-speaking people have done much better than he suggests. Along the border I would estimate that there are between forty and fifty names used by Mexicans for the Anglo, about the same number that Anglos have used for the Mexican. Names for the Anglo, however, show a different distribution in the categories cited above. In devising names based on the Anglo's physical appearance, the Mexican has noted not only the Anglo's skin color but also the color of his hair and eyes, as well as the size of his feet, which are seen not only as huge but also as having a very bad smell. A few examples are *blancanieves, canoso, colorado, cara 'e pan crudo, cucaracho, cristalino, ojos de gato, güero,* and *patón*. Etymologically, *gringo* belongs to the names originating from the outgroup's difficulties with an ingroup's language, since *gringo* has a long history among Spanish-speaking peoples as a derogatory term for the non-Spanish-speaking foreigner. Few border Mexicans, though, are aware of the origins of *gringo,* and there are many who believe the U.S.-originated legend that the word was coined by Mexicans during the American occupation of Mexico City in 1846. But *gademe* certainly is a local invention, going back to the 1840s, and based on the Anglo's alleged custom of uttering a "goddam" with every sentence he spoke. *Sanavabiche* is often used in a similar manner, though at times it is difficult to determine whether the speaker is merely using the American expletive "son of a bitch." But much is made about *San Avabiche* as an American saint, leading to the phrase *Hijo de un santo de los americanos.* Names referring to the Anglo's diet are few indeed. The most common one has been *repollero,* deriding the Anglo's taste for boiled cabbage, though at times I have heard *repollero* as a term for the Anglo truck farmer. The American taste for ham plays a big part in Border folklore, and now and then one hears the term *gringo jamonero.* It is more common, however, for Americans to be derided as ham-eaters in prose narratives or in ballads such as "El corrido de Jacinto Treviño," in which the hero derides a bunch of *rinches* who are besieging him in a Brownsville saloon:

Éntrenle, rinches cobardes,	Come on, you cowardly Rangers,
validos de la ocasión,	who like to take unfair advantage;
no van a comer pan blanco	this is not like eating white bread
con tajadas de jamón.	with slices of ham.

In Border versions of "La persecución de Villa," Pershing's troops are derided in much the same way:

Cuando llegaron a México estos gringos	When these *gringos* arrived in Mexico, they were looking for bread and for
buscaban pan y galletas con jamón,	crackers and ham;
y la raza, que estaba muy enojada,	but the people, who were very angry,
lo que les dieron fueron balas de cañón.	gave them nothing but cannonballs.

Still another Anglo habit, tobacco chewing, has resulted in *mascatabaco*. No names that I know of have been coined on the border in reference to Anglo class or occupation designations, though some have borrowed from other areas. Poor whites in Central Texas were known among other Anglos as cedar choppers, a term the Texas-Mexican renders as *postero* (fence-post maker) and which may be applied to any Anglo American. Border Mexicans also use *turista* for any Anglo they do not like, in ironic reference to the stereotyped American tourist of interior Mexico. The Mexican has no derogatory names at all based on official designations for the English-speaking citizen of the United States. They do use *míster* as the Anglo uses *señor,* to suggest ethnic origins in a contemptuous sort of way, as in the phrase *el míster ese. Los primos* might also fit in this category. Aside from the connotations of stupidity in the term, *primos* is explained as meaning *hijos del Tío Sam*. Neither *americano* and *anglosajón* nor the clipped forms *anglo* and *sajón* carry the derogatory connotations that "Mexican" and "Mex" carry for the Anglo. *Anglo* is the most neutral of the two clipped forms. If a border Mexican is comparing Mexicans and North Americans to the detriment of the latter, he is more likely to use *sajón*. The border Mexican uses no English proper names to evoke the stereotype of the Anglo, as the Anglo does with "Pedro" and "Pancho." Nor does he use any of the names for the Anglo as derogatory adjectives.

The border Mexican is unique perhaps in the number of derogatory ethnic names he has transferred to the North American from other referent groups. Leaving *gringo* aside, which underwent a restriction of meaning, as did "greaser" in English, we have *birote, bolillo, gabacho, godo, güero,* and possibly *patón. Gabacho* is an old derogatory term for the Frenchman that began to be used for the Anglo during the 1930s among the urban Mexican Americans of Los Angeles, El Paso, Laredo, and San Antonio. As late as 1959, none of my colleagues in Mexico City had recorded the term in this sense. But in the early 1960s, *gabacho* was reported among the students at UNAM as a term for the North American. According to some informants from East Chicago, Indiana, *gabacho* (meaning American) had been taken to the Bajío area in the 1950s by returning migrant workers. *Güero* is a very common term for American on the border, though its use as an ethnic label is not recorded in the dictionaries I have seen. In his *Diccionario de mejicanismos,* however, Santamaría gives us this stanza from a song dating from the French occupation. It is found under "Mariachi."

Dicen que por el Naguanchi	They say that around Naguanchi
no puede pasar ni un güero	not a single *güero* can pass,
porque le arrancan el cuero	because they will take his hide
pa' la caja del mariachi.[15]	for the drum in the mariachi.

The reference is, of course, to the French invaders. *Bolillo* and its variant *birote,* both used for the Anglo on the border, are difficult to explain except in relation to the French troops of the same period. Anglos are associated in the border Mexican's mind with ham, not with French bread. I have to date found no written evidence of the direct use of *bolillo* for Frenchman, but there is evidence that the *juaristas* taunted the French and their allies with mocking references to French bread. In an article about folklore from northeastern Mexico during the French occupation, Manuel Neira Barragán says that the *norteños* sang a version of "Las torres de Puebla" in which the victorious Mexican soldiers taunt the retreating French at the close of the battle of the Cinco de Mayo:

¿Qu'es de las piezas de pan?	Where are the loaves of bread?
Aguárdenlas que ahí les van. ¡Pam![16]	Get ready, for here they go. Bang!

Another song, quoted by Vicente Mendoza, shows the Mexican women who associated with the French in a desolate state after the fall of Querétaro and the capture of Maximilian:

¡Pobrecitas afrancesadas	Poor Frenchified girls,
que piden piezas de pan!	who keep asking for loaves of bread!
Apárenlas, que allá van.[17]	Get ready, for here they go.

Godo, another Border term for the Anglo, is widely known in Spanish America as a derogatory term for the Spaniard, though it seems to be rare in modern Mexico, since Santamaría does not list it in his *Diccionario de mejicanismos. Patón,* according to Santamaría's *Diccionario general de americanismos,* is applied to the Spaniard in Cuba. Again, Santamaría fails to list the term in *Mejicanismos,* though it has been used for the North American on the border since the early 1840s. In sum, we have at least four and perhaps six derogatory terms, once applied to Frenchmen and Spaniards, that have been transferred to the North or Anglo American.

In recent years anthropologists, sociologists, and even cultural geographers have been interested in the Mexican American's self-image as it is expressed in the names he uses in reference to himself. The results of such studies have been less than satisfactory, mainly because two important variables have either been ignored or not given their due weight. One of these variables is the Mexican American's bilingual-bicultural makeup, which allows (or forces) him to occupy somewhat different viewpoints at different times, depending on the language he happens to be using as an instrument to calibrate his experience. The other is the influence exerted on the Mexican American's (and even the Mexican's) self-awareness by the derogatory ethnic labels discussed above. In Spanish, border Mexicans use terms like *mexicano, raza,* and *chicano* in reference to themselves, these being ingroup terms for the most part, to be used only among other *mexicanos.* In his more jocular moments the border Mexican is likely to refer to himself by such labels as *chicaspatas* or *ganado cebú,* the mirror opposites of *patón* and *ganado Hereford.*

When speaking in English, he may refer to himself as Latin, Spanish, or perhaps Mexican American. Only rarely will he call himself a Mexican, in English, especially if he is talking to an Anglo.

As has been noted, the border Mexican uses no derogatory adjectives based on names for the Anglo. He does, however, use "Mexican" as an adjective in some contexts resembling Anglo derisive adjectives such as "Mexican car wash." In most cases, though, "Mexican" is used to suggest a kind of simplicity and ingenuity that more than makes up for lack of complex technology. A *molcajete* (kitchen mortar used to grind spices) becomes a "Mexican blender," and a tortilla a "Mexican fork"; chile peppers are "Mexican vitamins," tacos are "Mexican hamburgers," and mezcal is "Mexican penicillin," a play on the old saying "Para todo mal, mezcal." These are employed equally well in English and Spanish, though usually only among other Mexicans. *A la mexicana,* always in Spanish, means doing something with wit and ingenuity rather than with much equipment and expense. All these denote a kind of ironic pride in identifying oneself as a Mexican. But when a border Mexican rolls down his car windows so he can enjoy his "Mexican air conditioning," he has moved very close to the Anglo's point of view. Again, a border Mexican foreman may correct another Mexican working for him, telling him "¡No seas . . . mexicano!" instead of saying "No seas pendejo." This is most common on the Texas side of the border, it is true, but it is not unheard of on the opposite side of the river. It is worth remembering that the saying that "p.m." in Mexico means not "post meridian" but *puntualidad mexicana* is common in the northern Mexican states and much farther south as well.

There is no doubt that the border Mexican is ambivalent about the terms "Mexican" and *mexicano,* and there is little doubt also that the Anglo's use of "Mexican" as an insulting term has much to do with the Mexican's ambivalence. It is little wonder, then, that when English-speaking anthropologists ask unsuspecting *mexicanos* what they call themselves, the informants will answer "Spanish," "Latin," *raza,* "Chicano," or what have you—anything but "Mexican."

If we compare the derogatory names that Anglos and Mexicans have given each other in close to a century and a half of border existence, we will agree that both have been equally inventive in insulting each other. But if we look at the names discussed above in relation to all other ethnic groups known by each culture, we will note significant differences. Berrey and Van den Bark list the following numbers of derogatory ethnic names for different groups in the United States: Negro, 150; Jew, 50; Irishman, 43; Frenchman, 25; German, 24; Italian, 13. These figures are far from complete, when we note that for the Mexican, Berrey and Van den Bark list only fourteen names. The Mexican, on the other hand, does not seem to have extended his inventiveness to other ethnic groups besides the American. He has a couple of names each for the Spaniard and the Chinese and half a dozen or so for the Negro (mostly taken from English), and that is all. Furthermore, some of the insulting names the Mexican formerly used for the Frenchmen and Spaniards have been transferred to the American. This seems to be the result of a factor we might call ethnic visibility—the physical, cultural, economic, or political qualities of a group that draw the attention of others, either in a positive way or as an irritant. From Berrey and Van den Bark's list, it is obvious that the Negro is the most visible minority in the United States. In the Southwest the Mexican may claim honors for high visibility, but he is just one of many minorities that affect the WASP majority with feelings of tension and unease. For the Mexican, however, the Anglo fills the horizon, almost to the total exclusion of other ethnic groups—capable of excruciating visibility and high irritant power.

There are several other things worth noting about the names we have used in neighborly interchange along the border. One involves the matter of culture flow. It is the usual consensus that culture moves like water, from the high places to the low. This is not always true, and no better examples of an opposite view can be found than in the history of Spanish literature, where folk forms and themes were a major source for the literature of the Golden Age. In Mexico, also, scholars have usually believed that the folklore of the frontier regions is made up of local versions of items imported from interior Mexico. In other works I have attempted to show that this may not be entirely true of the *corrido*.[18] A similar case, I believe, may be made about Mexican folklore concerning the United States, especially in regard to names. It is a thesis that cannot be developed at length in this essay, but perhaps some short examples may gain it a hearing. During 1847 and 1848, American troops occupied Mexico City and other areas of interior Mexico. There was, of course, a great deal of popular feeling against the invaders, which was expressed in songs, *pasquines,* and *décimas.* I have delved into the records of the period to the best of my ability, and nowhere have I been able to find any other name used for the Americans but *yanqui.* On the Rio Grande, however, names like *gringo, patón,* and *gademe* were being used for the Anglo by 1842. Almost a century later, in the 1930s, *gabacho* gains currency along the border as a derogatory name for the American; but it is not until the 1960s that it is reported in Mexico City. Perhaps some Mexicanist with more resources than mine will come up with contrary evidence to overturn this thesis; but on the basis of available data it seems that the derogatory names for the American gained currency on the border before they moved south into interior Mexico.

In "The Esoteric-Exoteric Factor in Folklore," William Hugh Jansen makes the point that our awareness of other groups besides our own is intimately related to our consciousness of ourselves as a group.[19] It would appear, then, that it is on the border that a Mexican national consciousness first manifests itself on the popular level. Intrusion by a foreign, greatly different people minimized differences among border Mexican subgroups. The necessity to identify and label the outsiders inevitably led to a need to establish one's identity, to ask the question of emerging national consciousness: "Who are we?"

But the appearance of an awakening sense of identity was coupled with a challenge to that same identity. Another thing we may note about the study of Border ethnic names is the impact that the Anglo's insulting terms for the Mexican has had on the Mexican's ego, so strong an impact that it has affected the Mexican's terms of self-reference. The Mexican American is proud to call himself a *mexicano,* but he is often ashamed to be known as a Mexican. *A la mexicana* may have connotations of ethnic pride, but "¡No seas mexicano!" may be used as a half-insult even by some people on the Mexican side of the border.

It is questionable whether an identity crisis occurs with the border Anglo; at least the folklore does not seem to show it. One may observe identity problems among some individuals but rarely among groups. This obviously is due to the aggressive role of the Anglo culture in the border situation. The Anglo has taken liberally from the Mexican in creating his own version of a Border culture, but such borrowings have not always been acknowledged. Even when borrowings are recognized, they are not seen as threats to the culture of the United States. They are cheerfully stirred into the great mix that is North American culture, whether one sees that culture as a pot of stew or as a bowl of tossed salad. The Mexican, on the other hand, has always been on the defensive in the border situation, afraid of being swallowed whole. He does not have to be sophisticated or an intellectual to realize the risk to his way of life that culture contact entails. The folklore shows his preoccupation about remaining Mexican even when he is becoming most American-ized. Still, the Anglo does show clear signs of tension and unease in his relationship with the Mexican.

Each group seems to have a double-faceted view of the other; we might say that one aspect expresses active hostility while the other one expresses animadversion of a latent sort. The Anglo's actively hostile ste-reotype of the Mexican is well known: he is dirty and greasy; he is treacherous, cruel, and cowardly; thievery is his second nature; further-more, the Mexican American has always recognized the Anglo Texan as his superior. The Mexican American's actively hostile stereotype of the Anglo is not so very different: the Anglo is cruel and treacherous if he can get you in his power, but he is easy to outwit because he is so big and stupid; his victories over the Mexican are made possible by superior numbers and superior weapons; man for man, however, the Anglo is too fat and soft, too used to easy living, to measure up to the Mexican. The less actively hostile stereotype of the Anglo shows him as good-hearted but boorish; he is very rich, having made his money by cheating other people—for example, cheating the Mexicans out of Texas; he is cagey and clannish, but he is so greedy and gullible that he can be tricked out of his money or even out of his wife by appealing to his cupidity; in gen-eral, he is not really a bad fellow, even though he speaks funny Spanish and allows himself to be ruled by his women. The corresponding stereo-type of the Mexican shows him as a colorful but impractical character who speaks funny English; if old, he is a kind of Uncle Remus, full of an-tiquated and useless wisdom; if young, he loves flowers, music, and a good time, but it is hard to get a good day's work out of him.

There is an interesting difference in the Mexican and Anglo stereo-types of each other as they appear in Border folklore and in related popular literature. The Anglo in border Mexican folklore is usually face-less and nameless, an idea or a feeling rather than a man. When he is singled out in a ballad or prose narrative, he represents a broad type: the major sheriff or the chief of the Rangers in the *corridos,* the gullible tourist, or merely the stupid American who is tricked out of his money or his wife by the Mexican in the jokes. The Mexican, on the other hand, is rarely mentioned in the English-language folksongs of the border country. He plays a bigger role in the Anglo-American legendary anecdote, especially in tales of buried treasure and in miscellaneous stories with a border-country setting. In tales such as these, the Mexican is never the major character but the companion, servant, or guide of an Anglo American. Nonetheless, the Mexican of the Anglo-American legendary anecdote seems to be much more of an individual than is the Anglo American of border Mexican folklore. He is Juan, the goatherd with a sense of humor and a flair for telling a good story; Jesús, the drunken but faithful servant; Alberto, the wise old *vaquero*—still stereotypes, apparently, but with more personality than the generic *cherife mayor* of the *corridos* or the *gringo pendejo* of the Mexican jokes.

Even in the most recent types of folklore, this difference in stereotyping appears. Young Anglos have combined the contemporary mock riddle with the well-known American institution of Colonel Sanders' Kentucky Fried Chicken and the "Mexican greaser" stereotype, to produce the following:

Q. What is brown, greasy, and sells fried chicken?
A. Colonel Sánchez.

Young border Mexican Americans, on the other hand, have taken two proverbs that go back to the Mexican colonial period: "Indio con puro, ateo seguro" and "No tiene la culpa el indio sino quien lo hizo compadre." (An Indian smoking a cigar is certain to be an atheist *and* The Indian is not at fault but rather he who trusts him.) To these they have added two real but nameless types in their experience: the Anglo politician who is very friendly and speaks Spanish to them only when he is running for office, and the cigar-smoking Texas-Mexican political boss who sells out to the Anglo. The result is a proverb in the traditional style:

No te fíes del mexicano que fuma puro,
ni del gringo que te dice "compadre".

Never trust a Mexican who smokes a cigar,
or a *gringo* who calls you *compadre.*

We noted the American habit of using proper names as derogatory ethnic labels, not only Pedro and Pancho for the Mexican or Mexican
American but Fritz for the German, Pat for the Irishman, Pierre for the
Frenchman, Ivan for the Russian, Giuseppe for the Italian. There is a
slightly literary air involved in this kind of ethnic naming, if seen from
this broader perspective. And perhaps the difference is there—that the
Mexican stereotype of the Anglo appears in songs and narratives belonging to a truly folk tradition (artistic but unreflecting expressions of a
whole people), while the Anglo anecdotes about the Mexican most often
betray the reflective eye of the conscious artist, or would-be artist. They
are on the edge of that literature of the Southwest that J. Frank Dobie la-
bored to bring into being, mostly by means of folklike sketches dealing
with "colorful" Mexican characters. On the other hand, except for
names and ethnic jokes of a fairly general kind, Anglo folkore almost ignores the Mexican. One might say that he has been observed by the
Anglo, while the Anglo has been experienced by the Mexican.

So far we have dealt with generalizations about males made by other
males. The stereotypes of Anglo and Mexican women also show some
similarities. In both cases, the woman belonging to the opposing ethnic
group is seen as both desirable and easy of access, but not worth marrying; however, the details fleshing out the pattern are different. In a way,
the Anglo stereotype idealizes the Mexican woman. She is exotic, romantic, desirable; full of vivacity and sexual know-how. But, alas, she is
Mexican, and marriage to her involves falling into the sin of miscegena-
tion. As an old cowboy ditty put it:

But she was Mex and I was white,
and so it could not be.

On the other hand, the Mexican stereotype of the Anglo woman por-
trays her as visually striking, all pink flesh and yellow hair, but not particularly satisfying in a sexual way; furthermore, she is shameless and
dominates her husband.

It should be emphasized that these stereotypes, though often expressed in the performance of folk literature, do not necessarily jibe with

observed behavior, either now or in the past. For example, Anglos did marry border Mexican women from the very earliest days, though when such marriages are mentioned in Anglo anecdote and song the women are called Spanish rather than Mexican. At the present time, moreover, one may hear from border Mexican informants about the shamelessness of Anglo girls, who date and wear revealing clothes, but the observer may also note that the informant's teenage daughters are wearing skimpy clothing, going out on dates, and acting very much like Anglos.

In the latter case we seem to have an example of culture lag, while in the former it is a matter of prejudice toward people with darker skins. At all events, the Anglo view of the Mexican woman seems to be less unfavorable than the Mexican view of the Anglo woman. In the Anglo stereotype, the Mexican woman has definite personal qualities as a woman, at least, though not necessarily as an individual. Such things as vivacity, a quick temper, faithfulness, jealousy, compassion, bravery, or even the ability to play the guitar add something to the stereotype. It is only the question of race that makes the Mexican woman an undesirable mate for the Anglo. The Mexican stereotype of the Anglo female, however, is based on a few very physical qualities; they are fair of skin and buxom of figure: "gordas y bien coloradas" as "El corrido de los ambiciosos patones" says. But the Mexican claims to have no real sexual interest in these red-faced, well-fed women, who, he avers, are insipid lovers. Their conquest is merely a way of injuring the Anglo man, like tricking him out of his money or using him homosexually. One must keep in mind that in reality unions of Mexican men to Anglo women were extremely rare on the border until recent years, while instances of Anglo men marrying Mexican women go back to the very first years of contact between the two peoples.

The border Mexican rarely gets to put his prejudices into action, if one discounts the rumors that circulated after La Raza Unida gained political control of Crystal City. Jokesters were passing the word around that Anglos were no longer being served at Crystal City's better restaurants and bars. But even these jokes make the point that the Mexican folklore about the Anglo is mainly compensatory, while the Anglo can on occasion put his own prejudices into action. In 1942 and 1943, young Mexican Americans of Los Angeles were subjected to beatings and other persecutions by police and military personnel during the so-called *pachuco* riots. The police justified their treatment of young Mexicans on biological grounds. Captain E. Duran Ayres of the Los Angeles police, in an official report, claimed that the Mexican will not use his fists, or even his feet, in a fight with a Caucasian, since the Mexican

> considers all that to be a sign of weakness, and all he knows and feels is a desire to use a knife or some lethal weapon. In other words, his desire is to kill, or at least let blood. That is why it is difficult for the Anglo-Saxon to understand the psychology of the Indian or even the Latin. . . . When there is added to this inborn characteristic that has come down through the ages, the use of liquor, then we certainly have crimes of violence.[20]

Carey McWilliams, who quotes Ayres in *North from Mexico*, emphasizes Ayres's view that the Mexican has an inborn blood-lust, the result of his ancestry, which leads him naturally to crime. McWilliams mockingly refers to Ayres as an anthropologist.

Captain Ayres, however, is not the only amateur anthropologist who has had harsh words for the young Chicanos of Los Angeles. Having visited Los Angeles about the time of the "*pachuco* riots," Octavio Paz has some interesting things to say in *The Labyrinth of Solitude*. For Paz, the *pachuco* is "an impassive and sinister clown whose purpose is to cause terror instead of laughter." He is at once a sadist and a masochist. He seeks to become a criminal so he may bask in notoriety; he provokes Anglo society into taking action against him until retribution finally bursts over his head in a saloon fight, a raid, or a riot, from which all that the *pachuco* derives is "painful self-satisfaction."[21] If we are capable of imagining Captain Ayres reading *The Labyrinth of Solitude*, we may be able to picture his enthusiasm.

Ayres would have been even more enthusiastic about Paz had he been present in Batts Hall at the University of Texas, Austin, one night in 1969, when Octavio Paz delivered the Hackett Memorial Lecture of that year, "Mexico: The Last Decade." The bloody events of Tlatelolco the year before were still fresh in everyone's mind, and Paz's indignation was more than justified. That much would have troubled our hypothetical visitor, Captain Ayres, who might not have seen much difference between the beating and shooting of young Mexicans in Los Angeles and the same thing in Mexico City. But Ayres would have felt at home when the speaker assigned the blame for the massacre. It was not a case of overreaction by a group of armed men who took a brutally literal interpretation of their mission to preserve law and order. Mexican biology was to blame. Paz found the massacre to have "correspondences with the Mexican past, especially with the Aztec world, [which was] fascinating, overpowering, and repelling."[22] Behind the masked figure of the *tapado** was the masked figure of the Aztec priest, holding a bloody obsidian knife on high.

Captain Ayres was not in the audience, but hundreds of young Anglo students were; they formed the major part of the audience, in fact. I remember trying to study their faces for a clue to their thoughts. Many of them were products of the Border culture of conflict we have been discussing. Their grandparents, and perhaps their parents, had grown up convinced that Mexicans were cruel and bloodthirsty because of their history and their "blood." Caught in the liberalism of the sixties, these students had come to label the attitudes of their ancestors as racism. And here they were now, listening while a prominent Mexican intellectual confirmed their discarded prejudices.

If I have given some space to Paz and his fondness for masked figures, it has not been out of mere captiousness but in the hope of making a point. It is worth noting that even intellectuals may indulge in self-derogatory stereotypes, all for the sake of art, of course. But the anonymous Mexican American who creates still another self-derogatory joke is an artist, too. I doubt that any one of us would want to charge Paz with racism. He does get carried away now and then by his fascination with the bloodier aspects of the pre-Columbian cultures. A kind of inverted *indigenismo,* one might call it—the reverse of some contemporary revisionists, who would have us believe that the Aztecs never indulged in human sacrifice at all.

Paz's insensitivity to the problems and the potentialities of the young Los Angeles Mexicans is rooted in other causes. He speaks to us not with the voice of the future but with that of the past. His view of the *pachuco* is the same jaundiced view taken of the *pocho* by the Mexican intellectuals of the Revolutionary period. Paz's real complaint is that the *pachuco* does not act the way Paz thinks Mexicans should act.

* The unrevealed presidential candidate. [Original Editor's Note]

Pocholandia, as we all know, is supposed to begin in the northern Mexican states, extending northward into the southwestern United States. It is synonymous with the Border culture that occupies our attention here. And it has not been viewed any more sympathetically from the south than it has from the north. The *pocho-pachuco,* with apologies to Octavio Paz, is not so much a creature hiding behind a mask as a poor soul wedged between the pyramid and the skyscraper.

But perhaps things are changing. Reading Mexican periodicals and listening to Mexican radio and television, one gets the impression that in a cultural sense the border has shifted south a bit, to a point somewhere below Mexico City, let us say. And that may be why the younger Mexican intellectuals are more sympathetic toward the *pocho-chicano* than their elders were; they are much more aware of our problems. Because in this, Octavio Paz did not miss the mark. He was wrong in assuming that the Mexican American had lost all his heritage. But he was right in noting that the *pocho,* living between two cultures, existed in a state of permanent crisis; and that the *pocho*'s search for identity was a state shared by all Mexicans, and perhaps by all the world. If there was truth to such a view in the 1950s, it may be truer today, when the character of life has made borders less meaningful than they once were.

- 3 -

Folk Medicine and the Intercultural Jest

THIS PAPER IS A DISCUSSION of six jests collected in Spanish at the lower end of the Texas-Mexican border and presented here in English translation. They were part of several hundred texts recorded in 1962 and 1963, during a series of field trips in search of jests and legendary anecdotes that might reveal attitudes of Mexicans and Mexican Americans toward the United States. I will attempt to relate them to Texas-Mexican attitudes toward culture change. They are not peculiar to the group from which they were recorded. Some of them have been collected from other Mexican groups, and their basic motifs are universal. The six were recorded from two informants, one narrator telling five, but I heard the same stories from other people during my collecting. It is the circumstances in which the texts were collected that I believe important, and for this reason I will describe them in some detail.

All six texts were collected on tape during two recording sessions at Brownsville, Texas, a bilingual and bicultural community. Jests of this sort are called *tallas* in the regional idiom, and they are told during regular *talla* sessions. Francisco J. Santamaría, the Mexican lexicographer, lists *talla* as a "Texas-Mexican barbarism" for any narrative, anecdote, or jest, saying it is derived from the English "tale."[1] This certainly would emphasize the intercultural character of the *talla*, were it not for the fact that Santamaría is wrong. Whatever the origins of *talla*, they certainly are not in "tale," to which it has merely a visual resemblance. Santamaría seems to have known, furthermore, that *talla* is found as far away from Texas as Costa Rica. The term may derive from the verb *tallar*, to rub or to chafe and by extension to tease. The *talla* as it is practiced in

49

South Texas often does have a relationship to the Mexican wordplay known as the *albur*. Under these circumstances, the jests are told as having happened to one of those present, or to one of their close relatives. The victims answer in kind, of course. *Talla* sessions are common occurrences along the border among males of all ages and at occasions varying from wakes to beer-drinking parties. Women are rarely present.

In collecting, my first consideration was to re-create as closely as possible the circumstances of a *talla* session in its natural context. In Brownsville the sessions were held at a house just outside of town, which happened to be vacant at the time. A group of men would be invited, enough so that a total of ten to fifteen people were present at one time, including the collector. Sessions began around nine or ten at night and were held outside on the darkened patio or the lawn, with the participants sitting in a circle. Outside the circle was a washtub full of beer and ice. Also outside the circle was the tape recorder, but in a direction opposite to that of the tub with beer and just behind where the collector sat. An empty beer case was placed in the middle of the circle, on which the microphone rested on top of a cushion. The machine was a four-track Revere set at a speed of 3¾ inches per second, recording one hour per track on a 7-inch tape. This made it possible to record four hours on one tape without having to bother with the machine more than three times during the night. Four hours was the usual length of a session, from about ten until two in the morning.

The disadvantages to this method of collecting are the relatively poor quality of the recordings and the extreme tediousness of transcription. A four-hour session might well result in a dozen usable texts. But it is the best method I know for capturing the free, unself-conscious idiom in which the jests are told. The informants knew they were being recorded, of course, but a fairly natural atmosphere could be achieved after the first few minutes. The beer was partly responsible, as was the fact that the microphone was barely visible in the dark, so that the group forgot about it once beer and talk flowed freely. Most important, though, was the presence at each session of one or two assistants planted among the group, whose business it was to make the *talla* session as natural as possible and to elicit the kind of materials I was seeking without having to ask the informants for them. Their first job was to get everybody in the right mood by passing out the beer and making the usual small talk. The main purpose of my collecting, however, was to tape-record jokes and other lore about Anglo Americans. So the "plant" went on to tell some familiar joke on the subject, usually one of the large cycle of jests I have tentatively labeled the "Stupid American" joke. Since those invited were chosen because of their abilities as narrators, they responded with jests of their own, one story suggesting another. The plant had one other important function. The party sometimes wandered off in other directions, into small talk or verbal dueling, for example, or into reminiscing and sentimental songs. The plant tried to bring things back into line by telling another of his stories, usually texts I had already collected. He could do this as long as he stayed sober himself, something that did not always happen.

The main purpose of my field trip, as has been said, was to collect folklore making covert or direct expression of attitudes toward Anglo Americans and their culture. Materials were recorded in between a series of digressions that the plants attempted to control and redirect toward our agreed-on objective. On first examining the transcribable texts I brought back with me, I set aside the six discussed here as belonging with the digressions rather than with the material I was looking for. Americans scarcely appear in them. In text 6 we do have a character of the "Stupid American" stereotype, but it is the Mexican villagers who appear in a ridiculous light rather than he.

All six of the stories do have in common a general situation: there is a sick person, and a group of people seek a cure for him. It is not the patient himself but his family or the community as a whole that seeks help. A doctor or healer is found, who recommends a cure with varying results. Texts 1–5 all are concerned in one way or another with Mexican folk-curing practices. Only in text 6 is *curanderismo* absent, but the story is a variant of other *curandero* jests known to the collector in which it is the folk healer who recommends the wrong purgative to the patient, or the right purgative to the wrong person. That is to say, all six jests are parodies of a folktale type known to Latin American folklorists as the *caso* and sometimes called the belief tale in the United States—a relatively short narrative about miraculous or extraordinary events supposed to have happened to the narrator or to someone he knows. The particular type of *caso* parodied here is based on a formula well known to students of *curanderismo,* a simple pattern pitting the *curandero* against medical science, with science driven from the field in utter confusion.

Somebody falls ill and is taken to a doctor, but the doctor can do nothing for him. The patient gets worse and worse. There may be a consultation attended by several doctors—"a meeting of the doctors," as the *casos* put it—but the men of science cannot find the cause of the disease or recommend a cure. Or perhaps they say the patient is beyond hope of recovery. Again, they may recommend a painful and costly operation requiring a long stay at the hospital. Then someone suggests going to Don Pedrito or Don Juanito or some other *curandero*. The patient's relatives are skeptical at first but they finally agree. The whole group journeys to the *curandero*, who receives them kindly but chides the doubters about their skepticism, which he has learned about by miraculous means even before they arrived. Then he asks a standard question, seemingly unnecessary for his diagnosis but very important to the structured arrangement of the narrative: "And what do the doctors say?"

He is told what the doctors say, and he smiles indulgently at their childish ignorance. Then he prescribes some deceptively simple remedy: an herb perhaps, drinking three swallows of water under special circumstances three times a day, washing at a certain well or spring, or the like. The patient recovers completely. There may be a sequel in which the former patient goes and confronts the doctors. They are surprised, incredulous. They visit the old *curandero*, seeking to find out the secret of the cure. The old man tells them nothing, or he will answer in words such as "God cured him, not I." The doctors leave, chastened and still mystified.

A number of these *casos* have been current in South Texas and northern Tamaulipas for generations, most often in association with the saintly figure of Don Pedrito Jaramillo, the famed healer of Los Olmos, Texas. Ruth Dodson published a number of stories related to Don Pedrito, first in Spanish and later in English translation.[2] More recently, Octavio Romano has studied Don Pedrito as a charismatic figure.[3] Not all *curandero* belief tales follow the strict pattern of this formula, though it is perhaps the most widely retold. Another important narrative pattern deals with the scoffer who comes to the *curandero* pretending to be ill, merely to ridicule or expose him. The *curandero* punishes him by causing him to have a debilitating and embarrassing case of diarrhea.

The function of the *curandero* belief tale among Mexican folk groups is clear enough. It helps bolster belief in folk medicine; it encourages acceptance by the younger generation of the old traditions, especially when the group must live among an increasingly skeptical majority. This may be equally true whether the Mexican folk group is living in the United States or across the border in Mexico, since Mexican physicians are at times even more intolerant of folk medicine than their Anglo-American counterparts. But this type of *caso* plays an important role among rural and semirural Mexican groups in the United States, who see their folk culture assailed not only by modern science and technology but by the belief patterns of rural Anglo-American neighbors, who may have their own folk beliefs but tend to be contemptuous of those held by foreigners.

It is this type of belief tale that is parodied in jests such as the six we are considering. They quite consciously mock the defenses set up by the *curandero* belief tales, and they express an equally conscious rejection of the folk culture holding such beliefs. On the surface they represent as violent a rejection of Mexican values as that of William Madsen's Mexican American from Hidalgo County, Paul, who wishes he could get the Mexican blood out of his veins and change it for something else.[4]

Pertinent is the fact that parodies of *curandero* belief tales are widespread among Mexican Americans, certainly one of the reasons why these six intruded into a session of "Stupid American" jokes. The earliest printed example I know of appeared in the *Journal of American Folklore* in 1914 in one of Aurelio M. Espinosa's collections of New Mexican folklore. It is a variant of our text 6, except that it is a *curandero* rather than a veterinarian who gives the purgative to the wrong person. It works, though, so the *curandero* justifies his action saying, "Haciendo la cosa efecto, no importa que sieso sea" (As long as the thing works, who cares whose ass it was).[5] In the late 1920s, when the celebrated Niño Fidencio was curing the sick, the halt, and the blind in Nuevo León, Mexico, similar stories were circulated along the border about some of his cures. In one he cured a hunchback by breaking his spine. The hunchback screamed, "I'm dying!"

"But you'll die straight," Fidencio replied.

These are, of course, adaptations of other stories ranging much farther in space and time. All six contain universal motifs found in Stith

Thompson's *Motif Index of Folk-Literature,* either under J2450, "Literal fools," or J2412, "Foolish imitation of healing."[6] Texts 5 and 6 resemble Spanish folktales about the numskull who is told to bathe his grandmother in hot water and boils her to death instead. Or he is told to clean a child, so he cuts its belly open and takes out the intestines. Texts 2 and 3—especially text 2—are based on motifs listed by Thompson under B700, "Fanciful traits of animals." There are several methods by which animals that have introduced themselves into people's stomachs are disposed of. For example, in B784.2.1, reported from Ireland, Italy, and the United States, "The patient is fed salt or heavily salted food and allowed no water for several days. He then stands with mouth open before a supply of fresh water, often a running brook. The thirsty animal emerges to get fresh water." Thompson does not tell us if the animal is then beaten to death. Then there is motif B784.2.1.2, reported from India, about which Thompson tells us, "A husband ties a cock near his wife's feet so that a snake-parasite in her stomach will come out to catch the cock. The snake is then killed by the husband." Thompson does not tell us how the snake comes out of the woman's body, an important omission especially for the psychoanalytically oriented investigator. It might also be worth mentioning that we could find parallels to these jests somewhat nearer at hand; text 6 is very much like North American sick jokes.

The prevalence of feces and other anal motifs as a source of humor in our jests certainly would interest the psychoanalyst. This characteristic may reflect influence from one type of *curandero* belief tale discussed above, seriously told and believed but causing mirth instead of wonder, when the listener thinks of the discomfiture suffered by the skeptic inflicted with diarrhea. At least, this points to a favorite source of humor among groups telling the same tales. But it is the other *caso* formula—in which the *curandero* vanquishes medical science—that is alluded to in texts 1–5, all beginning very much in the serious belief-tale style but becoming *tallas* when the ending takes a ludicrous twist, by means of which the *curandero* and his methods are satirized.

Text 1 reproduces the sequel following many of the *casos,* when the doctors come to the *curandero* and humbly seek to know the secret of his powers—truly a triumph of folk healing over medical science. But our *curandero* is not reticent about explaining his methods, nor does he attribute his success to divine power. His answer, in fact, has a logic all its own, based on a folkish kind of empiricism one might say. The hit-or-miss character of many folk remedies, their farfetched sense of causality, and the actual use of dung in *curanderismo* all come in for ridicule.

Texts 2 and 3 are variants of the same tale, based on an old and widely traveled motif, B784.2, "Means of ridding person of animal in stomach." It is significant that they were told by the same informant in the order given, text 2 before text 3, so that text 3 is an emphatic restatement of text 2. This jest includes a good part of the belief-tale formula: A man falls gravely ill. He is taken to the hospital, where nothing is done for him. Hospital personnel recommend an operation, something the unsophisticated Mexican American dreads. Madsen, for example, reports that for his Hidalgo County informants the hospital is the most dreaded place next to prison and that hospitalization "can become a nightmarish experience when surgery is involved."[7] Frightened by the prospect of an operation, the relatives take the patient to the *curandero,* who asks the formal question "And what did they say at the hospital?" The hospital wants to operate, but the *curandero* is reassuring. No operation is necessary; he will cure the patient without much trouble. Up to this point the joke and the belief tale follow more or less identical lines, and it is at this point that the ridiculous is introduced.

There are some other features about texts 2 and 3 that should be noted before passing on to the other jests, even though they do not pertain to our belief-tale formula. The action is set in Hidalgo County though the story was recorded in the county of Cameron. The narrator first calls the *curandero* Don Pedrito, evidently in reference to the celebrated Don Pedrito Jaramillo, though he forgets later and calls him Don Juanito. Still later, in text 3, the *curandero* becomes Don Fulanito (Mr. John Doe or Mr. Such-and-Such), making him just any folk healer. More interesting still is the matter of the hospital. According to the belief-tale formula, the patient's family refuses to put him in the hospital because of their horror of operations, or the American doctors do get him into the hospital but are unable to find a cure. It is different with our *bracero's* friends, who do want him treated there. Nor do they question at this point the ability of the American doctors to make the patient well. The hospital attendants refuse to admit the patient, and it is because of this that he is taken to the *curandero.* If we keep this in mind, the emphatic character of the second variant, text 3, becomes significant. The same is stated, but in stronger terms. The demand for money on the ~~~~ of the hospital staff is emphasized by putting it into English: "Who's gonna pay?" pronounced in a drawling, decidedly unpleasant tone. The "All right. Get out!" of text 2 becomes "All right. Get out, *cabrones!*"* Even the gentle old *curandero* suffers a change with his "There'll be no fuckin' operation!" The narrator has warmed up to his theme, whatever his theme may be. At least we can be sure that he intends to be more than merely funny.

Text 4 makes an interesting contrast with texts 2 and 3. Again the setting is in Hidalgo County and again the *curandero*'s name is Don Pedrito. But in this story the American doctor is sympathetic; he offers to take the sick girl to the hospital. It is the girl's family who decide to take her to Don Pedrito because he "never goes around recommending operations." Up to this point the jest closely follows not only the usual pattern of the *curandero* belief tale but also certain supposedly factual cases reported by nonbelievers in *curanderismo,* in which Mexican Americans are said to have died of such things as appendicitis rather than go to a hospital. Satire begins when Don Pedrito is shown in anything but a humble or saintly mood; he calls the American doctors a bunch of *cabrones.* His diagnosis of what the doctor has called appendicitis is a parody of such folk diseases as *mollera caída* and *susto pasado* (fallen fontanelle and an advanced case of fright sickness).† Also satirized is the belief, often encountered by collectors, that only Mexicans can get "Mexican" diseases like *ojo* and *susto,* though it should be mentioned that one encounters just as often belief tales about Anglo Americans who are healed by *curanderos.* Almost 20 percent of Don Pedrito Jaramillo's cures as related by Ruth Dodson are said to have been done to Anglo Americans.[8]

At first glance text 5 seems to be different from the preceding four jests, but it really is based on one small part of the belief-tale formula we have been considering: the actual treatment of the patient by the *curandero.* The rubbing down with alcohol is prescribed by *curanderos* and by old-fashioned M.D.s alike for any number of ailments. In the original

---

* *Cabrón, cabrones* (singular and plural). Literally "he-goat"; in formal Spanish usage it is the word for cuckold; in current usage, as in the jests, the term is roughly equivalent to the English "bastard."
† In text 4 the *curandero*'s diagnosis is *carne juida, sangre molida o pedo detenido.*

Spanish the doctor prescribes that an egg (*huevo*) be put on the patient's forehead, *huevo* being such a common synonym for "testicle" that many prudish people avoid the word altogether, substituting it with *blanquillo*. The use of an egg and of ashes, however, will be recognized by those familiar with Mexican folk medicine as part of the treatment for diseases like *susto* and *ojo*. Even the doctor's reassurance to the patient's family at the beginning, that "It's not as bad as all that," is part of the *curandero* belief-tale formula. Medical science has made a great deal of fuss over the patient's illness, but it will be an easy thing for the *curandero* to make the patient well. It is obvious that the M.D. in this story really is a *curandero* in disguise. The sense of the ridiculous is heightened by having an M.D. playing the part of the *curandero,* or vice-versa, but we must also keep in mind that the doctor to whom the joke is attributed is a Mexican American. The jest is not identified with any particular doctor, by the way. Even the same narrator will use different names in retelling the story, but the name of a real Mexican American doctor always is used, most often one that the narrator's hearers know well. I can attest to having heard this same informant tell the same jest downtown, away from a tape recorder, using the name of a different Mexican American doctor.

Text 6 does not seem to go with the others at all; as it stands there is no *curanderismo* involved. But a comparison with text 5 reveals an identical plot structure: a naive group of Mexicans misinterpret instructions for the treatment of a patient, with fatal results for the patient, the ending in both cases being very much like that of the cruel or sick joke common in North American urban lore. The characters giving medical instructions in the two stories also bear comparison. The American veterinarian is portrayed as a likable simpleton, along the lines of the "Stupid American" stereotype. But he is working for the Aftosa commission, engaged in slaughtering the Mexican peasant's cattle to control the hoof-and-mouth disease, and thus a much resented figure. The Mexican American doctor, on the other hand, acts like a *curandero* and thus is comically seen as "one of our boys," but he is also a representative of American medical science and American culture and therefore must share some of the resentments generated by intercultural conflicts.

It is this double nature of our texts that makes them especially interesting. In the satirizing of folk medicine and *curandero* belief tales they express a mocking rejection of Mexican folk culture; in their expression of resentment toward American culture they show a strong sense of identification with the Mexican folk.

The texts, as has been said, were recorded during two sessions in Brownsville, Cameron County, Texas, a bilingual and bicultural community with an influential Mexican American middle class including doctors, lawyers, teachers, well-to-do merchants, and individuals in elective and appointive public office. These are for the most part descendants of the old Mexican settlers of the region, people with their roots in a past when Brownsville was a "Mexican" town, rather than immigrants and children of immigrants from Mexico. By usual North American standards they would belong to the middle class; according to Madsen's class divisions for Mexican Americans in Hidalgo County, they would be upper class.[9] The participants in the *talla* recording sessions were bilingual males between the ages of twenty-five and fifty-five. They speak good English and have received advanced education in American colleges and universities. They play important roles in community life, not in the life of a "Mexican colony" but in that of the city and the county as a whole. In other words, they would seem to be completely acculturated, having adapted to American culture and functioning in it in a very successful way. At the same time, when they are away from the courtroom, the school, the office, or the clinic and congregated in a group of their own, they think of themselves as *mexicanos.* Not only will they speak Spanish among themselves, but it is quite obvious that they place a high value on many aspects of Mexican culture and are proud of the duality of their background. They do in a sense live double lives, functioning as Americans in the affairs of the community at large and as Mexicans within their own closed circle.

In each of the two sessions, groups of about a dozen individuals of the type described told jests of the "Stupid American" type, in which tension and hostility toward the majority culture were expressed in joking situations. The *curandero* parodies were introduced into this context by two of the informants, one at each session. Text 5 was told by a lawyer, a friend of the doctor to whom the story was attributed in this particular variant. The doctor was not present at the session. Had he been present the joke might have been interpreted in another way, as part of a verbal duel, with the doctor replying by telling a joke about lawyers in which his friend would have been the main character. This is one way the *talla* is performed, as was said in discussing the probable origins of the word. In this case, however, the doctor's name was used because he is well known and representative. The narrator practices criminal law; his work brings him into contact with many Mexican Americans of the poorer class, much less acculturated than himself, who are usually in trouble when they come to him. His knowledge of Spanish gains him their confidence, and his Mexican background leads him to identify with them in many ways, but his profession demands that he comport himself in the role of an American lawyer functioning in an American court rather than assuming a "Mexican" role as he does when he is with a group of intimates. Many things repressed in the courtroom find an outlet in the *talla* sessions. The lawyer always has amusing anecdotes to tell within his own group, some of them revealing the comic naiveté of his clients, others showing their folk wit and hardheaded common sense.

Texts 1–4 and 6 were told by the same person, one of the best narrators I know. Only a sound recording can show his sense of intonation and mimicry, and even then his gestures are lost. He told all five stories in the same session, but not consecutively since he was alternating with other narrators present. It is quite clear, however, that one tale brought another to his mind. These are not his stories any more than text 5 belongs to the lawyer alone. They are common property, but this informant is recognized as telling them better than most other people do. He works for a school system somewhere in Cameron County, and his job brings him into contact—at times into conflict—with Mexican American parents of the laboring classes. He also has his anecdotes about his job: the naiveté of some of the parents he deals with, their lack of understanding of American values, their reluctance to keep their children in school. Often he parodies these people when he is among his own group. Just as often he will become exasperated with his job, complaining that his work shows no results, that he is butting his head against a stone wall. He seems sincerely committed in his efforts to raise the educational level of Mexican Americans in the county and is emotionally involved in the situation.

The two informants are typical of their group. They are socially conscious members of the middle class, impatient about the slow acculturation of the average Mexican American and his low economic and social status. At the same time, they reveal a strong feeling of identification with the unacculturated Mexican. They are highly acculturated Mexican Americans who value their ancestral culture in spite of such aspects as *curanderismo,* which they would include among the things the Mexican American must reject in order to compete successfully in an English-speaking world. But their attitude toward the *curandero* is not a hostile one. They will admit that some of these old men are pretty good psychologists in their own way, and they also point out with evident pride that many Mexican herbs have been put to use by modern medical science. Furthermore, the belief in *curanderismo* is something in their own recent past. Such celebrated *curanderos* as Don Pedrito Jaramillo were patronized a half-century ago not only by the poor and illiterate but by many of the land-owning families of the area. Some of those present during the *talla* session I recorded had been treated by *curanderos* in their early childhood. So there is identification on the part of the group not only with the unacculturated Mexican but with *curanderismo* itself. This is most clearly seen in text 5, in which the *curandero*'s role is given to a highly acculturated Mexican American physician, an absent member of the group in which the tale was told.

Curanderismo for this group is a subject viewed with a good deal of ambivalence, but the ambivalent attitude is anything but rare in jokes. The best dirty jokes about priests and nuns are told by Catholics; to be truly effective, the contemporary cruel or sick joke has to be told among people who are highly sensitive to human suffering. The *curandero* jests release a complicated set of conflicting emotions ranging from exasperation to affection in respect to the unacculturated Mexican American, coupled with a half-conscious resentment toward the Anglo-American culture. Also involved is a definite element of masochism, often expressed in the proverbial phrase "¡Ah, que mexicano!" (Ah, what a Mexican!), used to express jesting disapproval of some bumbling or foolish act. We must keep in mind that members of this group are quite explicit in identifying themselves as *mexicanos,* and that the above phrase is used only in Spanish, never in English.

So these jests are not after all intrusions into a session of stories expressing intercultural conflict; they also are expressions of the same kind of conflict. Only in text 4 does the doctor, representative of American culture, appear in a favorable light. In texts 2 and 3 the matter is quite explicit. The poor *bracero* must go to the folk healer because he is re-fused treatment at the American hospital. The *curandero* asks for so little—a small fee or a gift, something the poorest laborer can pay. One does not have to be a rich man to visit Don Fulanito. Many such inci-dents are seriously told by Mexican Americans of the poorer classes. We find the same subject matter here in jokes, told by people who can afford to be treated at hospitals, but the stories are not quite in the comic vein. There is a good deal of emotional involvement, which members of the group would readily acknowledge among themselves, and that gives an edge to the humor. They may tell you, with a kind of self-directed exas-peration, about Mexican laborers who died of appendicitis because they refused to go to a hospital. But they will also tell you other stories of Mexican laborers who died for lack of attention, and it is obvious that these stories arouse their resentment.

Why the events in texts 2, 3, and 4 are placed in Hidalgo rather than in Cameron County I am not prepared to say. It may be that Mexican Americans in Cameron County feel that their people in Hidalgo live un-der worse conditions than they do. It may be a narrative device, placing the action at some distance from narrator and audience. If such is the case, it is worth noting that the device is not a comic one. The comedian uses the opposite approach, relating his story to familiar events and to people close at hand. The introduction of people in the narrator's audi-ence as characters in his jests has been mentioned as typical of one of the aspects of the *talla* session, when it becomes a verbal contest. Narrators tend to place events some distance away for reasons other than comedy. If characters and events are very far away, in a distant time and a distant land, the effect is one of wonder and romance. But to achieve a feeling of verisimilitude, required in the legendary anecdote, events are placed not too far off—in the next town, the next hollow, or the next county. This again is evidence that these jests are not intended to be as funny as they appear on the surface.

This is not, then, a relatively simple case of second-generation Ameri-cans ridiculing the culture of their ancestors and thereby rejecting it. As parodies of the *curandero* type of belief tale the jests do express the Mexican American's rejection of his traditional culture. But combined with parody is a good deal of resentment against Anglo-American culture, expressed in a stereotypic view of American physicians and hospital attendants as caring little about Mexican patients of the poorer, less educated class. Since the informants are not poor and badly educated themselves but belong to the middle class, the ambivalence of their attitudes is quite marked. Members of the group telling the jests have not lost the feeling that beneath their Americanized exterior they still are *mexicanos*. There is an underlying conflict between their Spanish-Mexican heritage and an Anglo-American culture they have embraced intellectually without completely accepting it emotionally, in great part because Anglo-American culture rejects part of themselves. The jests help resolve these conflicts brought about by acculturation, involving not only a change from rural to urban values but from a basically Mexican culture to the generalized, English-speaking culture of the majority.

Text 1

They tell about an old man who was a *curandero,* that they brought him a patient who was sick in the stomach. And he said, "Give him goat turds."

Said, "But what do you mean, give him goat turds!"

"Yes," he said, "boiled."

Well, so they did it, and the man got well. And then there was a meeting of physicians. Said, "Listen, man," he said, "we never could find out what was wrong with him. And he got well with goat turds."

So they called the old *curandero.* Said, "Well, why did you give goat turds to this man?"

He said, "It's very simple. Because I knew the ailment he had," he said, "could be cured with some sort of herb. But I didn't know which one," he said. "And since goats eat all kinds of weeds and herbs, I knew the plant that was needed would be there in the shit."

Cuentan de un viejito curandero, que le trajeron un enfermo que estaba mal del estómago. Y dijo:

—Delen la cagarruta de cabra.

Dijo:

—¡Pero cómo le van a dar la cagarruta de cabra!

—Sí —dijo—, hervida.

Bueno, pues lo hicieron y se alivió aquel hombre. Y entonces hubo junta de médicos y dijo:

—Pos hombre —dijo—, nosotros no le hallábamos la enfermedad. Y se alivió con la cagarruta de cabra.

Y ya le hablaron al viejito curandero y dijo:

—Bueno, ¿por qué le dio usted la cagarruta de cabra a este hombre? Dijo:

—Es muy sencillo. Porque yo sabía que la enfermedad que tenía él —dijo— se curaba con una yerba. Pero no sabía qué yerba era —dijo—. Pero como las cabras comen de todas yerbas, allí en la cagada tenía que ir la yerba que necesitaba.

—Informant no. 24
Brownsville, Texas
October 20, 1962

Text 2

They went to see Don Pedrito about a poor *bracero* who was around there in Hidalgo County, and this poor man got up one night to get a drink of water and he swallowed a spider. Well, he got sicker and sicker, so they took him to the hospital at Edinburg.

And they said, "Who's going to pay?"

"Well, there's no money, I guess."

"All right. Get out!"

"So what can we do?" they said. "Nobody can pay. Let's take him over to Don Pedrito."

Well, so the little old man came and looked him over. "And what happened to him?" he said.

"Well, it's like this." Said, "This boy swallowed a spider."

He said, "And what did they say at the hospital?"

Said, "Oh, no! At the hospital they want money to operate on him."

"No," he said, "don't talk to me about operations. I'll take care of him right now. Let's see, turn him over for me with his ass sticking up, with his butt in the air."

They turned him over.

"Now, pull his pants down." They pulled his pants down.

He said, "But bring him out here in the yard." They laid him down in the yard.

He said, "Do you have some Karo corn syrup?"

"Well, yes. Here's some."

Gave his asshole a good smearing with it. "All right, now," he said, "everybody stand back." And he picked up a stick.

Said, "But what are you doing, Don Juanito?"

He said, "I'm waiting for the flies to gather," he said. "When the flies start buzzing the spider will come out, and I'll kill it with this little stick."

☆

Le llevaron a don Pedrito a un pobre bracero que andaba por allí en Hidalgo y este pobre se levantó en la noche a tomar agua y se tragó una araña. Pos que malísimo y malísimo y lo llevaron al hospital de Edinburgo.

Y dijeron:

—¿Quién va a pagar?

—Pos que no hay dinero.

—Bueno ¡pa' fuera!

—Pos no hay más —dijeron—, pos no hay quién pague, pos tráiganlo con don Pedrito.

Y ya vino el viejito y lo vio.

—¿Y qué le pasó? —dijo.

—Pos no —dijo—, pos este muchacho se tragó una araña.

Dijo:

—Y ¿qué dicen en el hospital?

Dijo:

—No. Pos en el hospital quieren dinero para hacerle operación.

—No —dijo—, qué operación ni qué nada. Orita lo arreglo. A ver, voltéenmelo con las nalgas pa' arriba, con la rais pa' arriba.

Lo voltearon.

—Pos túmbenle los pantalones.

Le tumbaron los pantalones.

Dijo:

—Pero pónganmelo acá en el patio.

Lo acostaron en el patio.

Dijo:

—¿No tienen melaza Karo?

—Pos que sí. Aquí hay.

Le dio una embarrada en el ojete.

—Ora sí —dijo—, retírense todos.

Y agarró una varita.

Dijo:

—¿Pos qué está haciendo, don Juanito?

Dijo:

—Estoy esperando que se junten moscas —dijo—. Al ruido de las moscas sale la araña y la mato con esta varita.

—*Informant no. 24*

Text 3

And then there was this other guy who drank the kerosene, this other poor man living in a tent around there who picked up a glass. And they had a lot of milk bottles there, made of glass, and they had water and kerosene in them. And this poor man picked one of them up and downed half a liter of kerosene. And he was choking, so there they go to the hospital at Edinburg.

And they took him there. "Who's gonna pay?" [Underscored part said in English.]

"Well, there's no money, I guess."

"All right. Get out, *cabrones!*"

Well, there was no money, so out! So they took him back, and the poor man was choking. He had downed half a liter of kerosene. Said, "Call Don Fulanito."

So the old man came. "What's the matter?" he said.

"He drank half a liter of kerosene."

"All right. So what did they say at the hospital?"

Said, "Well, at the hospital they want money. For the operation."

"Ah, no. There'll be no fuckin' operation," he said. "Let's see. Bring him out here for me. Just put him out here and leave him to me." He said, "Don't you have a lantern there?"

"Well, yes."

"Let's see, then. Take the wick out of the lantern." They took out the wick. "Does anybody have a pencil around there?"

"Well, yes. Here's the pencil."

"Now get out of the way," he said. "Pull his pants down." He stuffed the wick in his asshole with the pencil and said, "Let's have a match." He lighted the wick. He said, "All right, now. Everybody stand back. When the fire is gone," he said, "when the wick goes out, then all the kerosene will be out of him."

★

Y luego el otro que se tomó el petróleo, el otro pobre que en una carpa por allí agarró un vaso. Y tenían una bola de botes de leche allí, de cristal, y allí tenían agua y petróleo. Y este pobre agarró y se metió medio litro de petróleo. Pos que se estaba ahogando, pos que al Edinburg Hospital.

Y lo llevaron allá.

—*Who's gonna pay?*

—Pos que no hay dinero.

—Bueno, ¡pa' fuera, cabrones!

Pos no hay dinero, pos ¡pa' fuera! pos que lo llevaron pa' allá y aquel hombre ahogándose; se había metido medio litro de petróleo. Y dijo:

—Traigan a don Fulanito.

Y ya vino el viejito.

—¿Qué pasó? —dijo.

—Pos que se tomó medio litro de petróleo.

—Bueno, ¿pues qué dijeron en el hospital?

—Pos en el hospital quieren dinero —dijo— por la operación.

—No, hombre, qué operación ni qué una chingada —dijo—. A ver. Sáquenmelo pa' acá. Nomás pónganmelo aquí y déjenmelo solo.

Dijo:

—¿No tienen un farol por ahi?

—Pos que sí.

—Pos a ver. Sáquenle la mecha al farol.

Le sacaron la mecha.

—¿No tienen un lápiz por ahi?

—Pos sí. Tenga el lápiz.

—Pues quítense de aquí —dijo—. Túmbenle los pantalones.

Le metió la mecha de la lámpara en el ojete con el lápiz y dijo:

—A ver un cerillo.

Prendió la mecha. Dijo:

—Ora sí. Retírense todos. Cuando se acabe la lumbre —dijo—, que se apague la mecha, es que ya se le salió el petróleo.

—Informant no. 24

Text 4

This is something they say happened in Mission or McAllen or somewhere over there, in Hidalgo County, you see? A girl began to feel very sick in the stomach, and they took her to the doctor. And the doctor said, "This girl has appendicitis." He said, "We'll have to take out her appendix, no other way. If she isn't feeling better by tomorrow at ten," he said, "I'll come for her."

So then a woman said, "Look," she said, "Don Pedrito is in town. He's a *curandero*," she said, "and he's a very wise old man."

Said, "What for?"

"He never goes around recommending operations," she said, "and he never makes a mistake."

Well, so they called him. He said, "Let's see, let's see," he said. "What does the doctor say?"

"Oh, the doctor says it's her appendix."

He said, "Oh, no. Those doctors are a bunch of *cabrones;* all they know is about diseases in English. But this little girl is sick in the Mexican way; she has a Mexican disease," he said. "And it can be only one of three things: fled flesh, bruised blood, or a blocked fart."

Éste es un caso que dicen que pasó en Mission o McAllen o por acá, aquí en Hidalgo, ¿ves? Una muchacha que comenzó a estar muy mala del estómago y la llevaron con el doctor y el doctor dijo:

—Esta muchacha tiene apendicitis. —Dijo— Hay que sacarle el apéndice, no hay más. Si para mañana a las diez de la mañana no se le corta —dijo—, yo vengo por ella.

Y ya entonces dijo una señora:

—Mire —dijo—, aquí está don Pedrito. Es un curandero —dijo— y ese viejito es muy acertado.

—¿Para qué? —dijo.

—Ése nunca anda recomendando operaciones —dijo— y es muy acertado.

Pues ya lo trajieron. Dijo:

—A ver, a ver —dijo—, ¿qué dice el doctor?

—Pues el doctor dice que es el apéndice.

Dijo:

—No, hombre. Estos doctores cabrones nomás saben ellos las enfermedades en inglés. Pero esta muchachita tiene una enfermedad en el mexicano. Ésta es enfermedad mexicana —dijo— y debe de ser, de tres cosas una: carne juida, sangre molida o pedo detenido.

—Informant no. 24

Text 5

Z—— P—— [narrator names a Mexican American M.D.] went to call on a patient. He examined him and said, "It's not as bad as all that. I'm going to write you a prescription. But I want you to do exactly what I tell you, and I'll come back tomorrow morning. He'll get well, I assure you. But listen very carefully," he says, "because I want you to do it exactly as I am going to tell you."

"Very well, doctor."

He says, "I want you to give him a sponge bath, all right? Soak the sponge in alcohol and give him a good rubbing all over his body. And before the alcohol can evaporate, cover him with a sheet all the way up here to the neck. Then you take a little bit of ashes and sprinkle them around the bed. Pray one Paternoster and three Hail Marys. Then take a ball and balance it very carefully on his forehead," he says. "I'll come back around six or seven in the morning, and I assure you he'll be perfectly all right by then."

Well, so they did as they were told. Next morning the doctor came. But no, the poor man was already dead. "How's the patient?" he says.

"But he already—he's dead."

"But how could he be dead! It wasn't all—it wasn't a fatal disease. You must have failed to do exactly what I told you."

"Oh, no . . . We did, *señor* doctor."

"Well, did you give him the sponge bath with alcohol?"

"Yes, of course. As soon as you left. And we covered him with the sheet so the effect would not be lost."

"And the ashes?"

"Well, see for yourself; there they are. Look there, on the bed; you can still see the ashes there."

"And the ball on his forehead?" he says.

"Well, now there, you see doctor. There's where we had a bit of trouble. We had to call three of the neighbors," he says. "And we tried to do it between us four," he says. "But we couldn't pull it up any farther than his navel."

★

Fue Z—— P—— a ver a un enfermo. Y lo examinó y dijo:

—No es para tanto la enfermedad. Le voy a dar una receta. Nomás que quiero que la sigan al pie de la letra, y yo vuelvo en la mañana. Y yo les aseguro que va a sanar. Pero pongan mucho cuidado —dice— porque quiero que lo hagan exactamente como se los voy a dar.

—Muy bien, doctor.

Dice:

—Quiero que le den un baño de esponja, verdad. Pongan alcohol en la esponja y luego lo tallan bien-bien todo el cuerpo. Y antes de que se vaya a evaporar el alcohol le ponen una sábana hasta aquí al cuello. Luego le ponen una cenicita alrededor de la cama. Récenle un Padrenuestro y tres Avemarías y le ponen un huevo en la frente —dice— y yo vuelvo aquí como a las seis, siete de la mañana y les aseguro que para entonces está perfectamente bien.

Pues así lo hicieron. Otro día en la mañana vino el doctor. No, pues ya estaba muerto el pobre hombre.

—Pero ¿cómo sigue el enfermo? —dice.

—Pos, si ya—ya murió.

—Pero ¡cómo murió! Si no era para—no era de muerte la enfermedad. Es que no han de haber llevado a cabo la receta como yo se las dije.

—No. . . Sí, señor doctor.

—Bueno, ¿le dieron el baño de esponja con alcohol?

—Sí, cómo no. Tan pronto como se fue usted. Y le pusimos la sábana para que no se fuera a ir el efecto.

—¿Y la ceniza?

—Pues vea usted; ahi está. Vea usted, en la cama, todavía se ve la ceniza allí.

—¿Y el huevo en la frente? —dice.

—Bueno, pos allí. . . ve, doctor. . . es donde tuvimos una poca de dificultad. Tuvimos que llamar a tres de los vecinos —dice— y entre los cuatro tratamos de hacerlo —dice— pero nomás se lo pudimos estirar hasta el ombligo.

> —*Informant no. 10*
> Brownsville, Texas
> September 7, 1962

Text 6

There was a veterinary out there with the Aftosa, a *bolillo* from around here.* And then this little old man was very sick; he had indigestion or I don't know what. So they went. "Here's a doctor from the other side of the border. What more do you want!" So they went to see him.

He said, "Oh, no! Me doctor by the cow. But not by the man. No gotta permit." [Vet's dialogue is in heavily accented Spanish, except underscored part, which is in English.]

Said, "No matter, doctor. What do you give the cows when they are sick in the stomach?"

"Well, *hombre*," he says, "me give a little Epsom salts."

Said, "How much Epsom salts do you give the cow?"

He says, "Oh, by one big cow me give her a pound of salts in one gallon of water."

So then they said, "Now we can figure the dose ourselves." They went home and measured half a gallon of water and half a pound of Epsom salts. And they made the old man drink it.

---

* *Bolillo*. One of the many derogatory names for the Anglo American. It seems to have been used originally for the French (*bolillo* is a small loaf of French bread), but later it was transferred to the North American.

Well, so next morning they came. Said, "Oh, doctor, we came to see you."

"How is sick man doing? Is he better?"

"Oh, no, he's dead."

He said, "But how could he be dead!"

"Yes, we came to invite you to the funeral, this afternoon. But don't feel guilty about it, doctor." Said, "It isn't your fault."

He said, "Why you say not my fault?"

Says, "We gave him the salts and the salts worked. He must have died of something else, because even after he was dead he still moved his bowels three times."

Andaba un veterinario allá con la fiebre aftosa, un bolillo de aquí. Y entonces el viejito este estaba muy malo, tenía una indigestión o no sé qué. Y ya fueron.

—Aquí está un doctor del otro lado, ¿qué mejor quieres?

Pos ya fueron con él.

Dijo:

—¡Oh, no! Mí ser doctor por la vaca. Poro no por el hombre. *No gotta permit.*

Dijo:

—No li' hace, doctor. ¿Qué le da usted a las vacas cuando están malas del estómago?

—Pues hombre —dice—, mí dar un poco de sal d'higuera. [Heavily accented, especially on *r*'s.]

Dijo:

—¿Cuánta sal de higuera le da usted a la vaca?

Dice:

—Oh, por una vaca grande mí darle una libra de sal en un galón de agua.

Y entonces dijeron aquellos:

—Pos acá le medimos nosotros.

Se fueron a la casa y midieron medio galón de agua y media libra de sal de higuera. Se lo metieron al viejito.

Pos otro día en la mañana vinieron. Dijo:

—Oh, doctor, veníamos a verlo a usted.

—¿Cómo seguir el enfermo? ¿Se alivió?

—Oh no, ya se murió.

Dijo:

—Pero cómo murió.

—Sí. Lo vinemos a convidar a usted que vaya al funeral, ora en la tarde. Pero no se sienta usted culpable, doctor —dijo—, no es culpa suya.

Dijo:

—¿Por qué usted decir no culpa mía?

Dice:

—Nosotros le dimos la purga y la purga hizo su deber. Él se murió de otra cosa porque todavía después de muerto le ha hecho tres veces.

—Informant no. 24

~ 4 ~

On Ethnographic Work among Minority Groups: A Folklorist's Perspective

W<small>E ARE WELL AWARE</small> of the current quarrel in this country between minority groups and the social sciences. Nowhere has this quarrel reached greater proportions than between Chicanos and anthropology, with Chicanos bitterly attacking ethnographies made of their people by Anglo anthropologists. Octavio Romano, who himself received his doctorate in anthropology and did his fieldwork in a Chicano community, is perhaps the best known and most persuasive of the Chicano critics of anthropology. The main target of Chicano wrath has been anthropologist William Madsen, Romano's erstwhile colleague, who has become a sort of *bête blanche* of the *movimiento*. Madsen's little book *Mexican-Americans of South Texas* is Exhibit A, to which all Chicanos point with disgust.[1] Ethnic studies instructors risk censure by their students if they use *Mexican-Americans of South Texas* as a text or even assign it for outside reading.

It seems unfair to single Madsen out for something that—rightly or wrongly—can be said of other anthropologists who have written about Chicanos or Mexicans. In fact, Chicanos sometimes praise other ethnographers who make the same generalizations Madsen does. But it has been Madsen's misfortune to become a symbol of what Chicano activists feel is wrong with the whole field of anthropology in the United States. It is a field of inquiry, they would say, that is racist to the core.

Anthropologists are likely to respond with a countercharge and an invitation. Finding yourself an object of study, they argue, is not always a pleasant experience, especially for hypersensitive people. "We are giving you a substantially true picture of yourselves," they will say, "if only you would look at things objectively. Of course, we do have a need for a more subjective view to complement our own, a view from within. So why don't you join us. Let us make anthropologists out of you so we can get your point of view."

But that is exactly what Chicanos are not doing. They do not want to be brainwashed, they say. So they are avoiding the field of anthropology, to the detriment of both sides in the dispute.

Are such criticisms justified, or is it all a matter of Chicano hypersensitivity? I cannot say that my own reactions may be completely objective, since I am a Chicano myself, and that should color my judgment. But attempting to be as objective as possible—and that is as much as one may expect either of anthropologists or the subjects of anthropologists—I must say that I find the Mexicans and the Chicanos pictured in the usual ethnographies somewhat unreal. Of course, each ethnography is an individual case and should not be used as the basis for generalization, as ethnographers are careful to point out just as they begin to generalize. And, in all fairness, some of our criticism has been a bit shrill so that its very tone betrays a lack of objectivity. But there are too many voices joined in criticism. I am thinking especially of the reaction to studies such as those by Madsen, Arthur Rubel, and others on the part of the average Chicano student, especially those students coming from the communities studied by the Hogg Foundation Hidalgo County Project in 1957–1962. It is not so much a sense of outrage, that would betray wounded egos, as a feeling of puzzlement, that *this* is given as a picture of the communities they have grown up in. Many of them are more likely to laugh at it all than feel indignant.

This essay, then, takes the position that Chicano criticisms are not unjustified, that it is possible for anthropologists to give us distorted views of Chicano groups, and perhaps of Mexican peasant groups as well. But I will reject the charge of racism, which has been made by some Chicanos, if by racism is meant active ill will or contempt for the people being studied. The individuals responsible for the studies under criticism are for the most part liberal in their racial and political views, with a real respect for the cultures they study. Most Chicanos would answer, however, that they do not accuse anthropologists of overt racism. They do charge unconscious bias, the fitting of data to preconceived notions and stereotypes. This is a much more plausible assertion, which seems to be borne out by careful consideration of the materials.

We know that the anthropologist is conditioned to make allowances for his own biases; his training is supposed to discipline him in viewing potential data with the highest degree of objectivity possible. But perhaps the methodological safeguards to compensate for a normal degree of bias are not working very well. Anthropologists may need to reexamine the argument that they can give us substantially true pictures of a culture by following time-honored methods. And when the group under study is part of one of our own minorities, the situation takes on a good deal of urgency. It was one thing to publish ethnographies about Trobrianders or Kwakiutls half a century ago; it is another to study people who read what you write and are more than willing to talk back. The present-day anthropologist writing about minority groups in the United States faces fieldwork problems undreamed of by Malinowski or Boas. The question, then, is what may be done to improve ethnographic methods for working with minority groups. The advantages or disadvantages of using "ethnics" as ethnographers is not an immediate issue here, if the ethnics are to receive the same kind of training that has been received by their mentors in the past.

The use of better sampling techniques could help us avoid some major pitfalls. Such is Thomas Weaver's thesis in "Sampling and Generalization in Anthropological Research on Spanish-Speaking Groups."[2] There is no doubt that poor sampling can result in badly skewed data, though the best sampling techniques will not take us very far if they lead us to think of all individuals in a category as interchangeable units rather than as people with emotions and goals of their own. Even so, sampling techniques used for Chicano groups have often been modeled on those used for "simple" societies, without regard to the fact that Chicanos, as Americans, are part of the varied fabric of modern life. Age, sex, and economic status have been the main criteria, without regard to other factors such as factionalism and differences in political philosophy. This perhaps is the reason why members of the Hidalgo County Project could work so close to the Hidalgo communities without perceiving the political ferment that would produce the Raza Unida movement shortly thereafter.

Closer to the heart of the problem is the matter of language, a truly thorough knowledge of the language, both standard and dialectal. A common criticism advanced by Chicanos is that anthropologists do not really know the Chicano's language. The anthropologist is likely to respond that he is fluent in Spanish, for most ethnographers seem to be satisfied if they have what is called fluency. It is hard to convince some of our colleagues that fluency in a language can be a dangerous thing. There is a guidebook flavor to the whole idea of fluency. It is the sort of thing that quickie language courses promise you as you embark on a visit to foreign lands. You will be able to order a meal or ask where the railroad station is without stumbling over your phrases or retreating to your dictionary. Fluency is equivalent to readiness or smoothness of speech. It is the ability to speak complete sentences without having to stop and grope for a word. As a matter of fact, some of us less-gifted verbalists are not particularly fluent speakers even in our native tongue. We may console ourselves, however, with the thought that parrots and very small children are terrifically fluent without knowing much of what they say.

Fluency does allow you to communicate; and the ability to communicate was enough of a goal for the ethnographer who wanted to elicit kinship terms or to work out taxonomies of plants, animals, or statuses. It is a different matter when you attempt to interpret people's feelings and attitudes in actual speech situations. One should seriously question the competence of a "fluent" ethnographer who cannot even keep his tenses and genders straight, if he comes before us as an interpreter of a people's ethos or worldview on the basis of their linguistic behavior. Unwarranted generalizations may be reached on the basis of a misinterpretation of words, especially if a dialect expression is taken in its standard dictionary meaning or a metaphorical expression is taken literally.

An interesting example occurs in Rubel's *Across the Tracks*. The author is observing Chicano political behavior in New Lots during a political campaign; he drops by the Chicano candidate's campaign headquarters, where the "workers," he notes, "were not working; they were conversing." Listening to their conversation, he is able to record the following:

> Sometimes the conversation of the campaigners focused on strategy. At such times there was much talk of *hacienda* [sic] *movida, hay mucha movida*, and "moving the people." Such phrases implied that the Mexican-American electorate—the *chicanazgo* [sic]—was a dormant mass, which had to be stirred into activity.[3]

Let us ignore such slips as *hacienda* for *haciendo* and *chicanazgo* for *chicanada*. The most interesting thing here is the author's interpretation of *movida*. *Mover*, of course, means "to move." Most Spanish dictionaries do not recognize *movida* except as the feminine of *movido*, an adjective meaning "agitated." But Chicanos long ago substituted *movida* (apparently a direct translation of the English noun "move") for *jugada*, in the sense of a maneuver or move in a game of strategy. The term usually has negative connotations: *movida chueca* (crooked maneuver), *hay mucha movida* (there's dirty work going on), *hacer movida* (to look out for number one). Not knowing the significance of *movida*, Rubel misinterprets the conversation, drawing unwarranted, stereotyped conclusions about Chicano behavior from what he thought he heard, seeing Chicanos as passive, apolitical, and incapable of organizing much of anything.

Madsen seems to fall into a similar trap by attributing literal meanings to figurative expressions, when he tells us about Mexican American naiveté in regard to the germ theory of disease.

> Much of the opposition to modern medicine stems from the rejection of the germ theory of disease. Mexican-Americans of the lower class are aware of the germ concept but many of them refuse to recognize the actual existence of microbes. Germs are thought of as mythical little animals called *animalitos*. Because these creatures cannot be seen by the naked eye, they are often dismissed as an invention dreamed up by Anglo doctors to dupe the people. The majority of uneducated Mexican-Americans have never looked through a microscope. Their view of microscopic life comes from cartoons shown in TV advertisements and public health clinics. They do not find this evidence very convincing.
>
> "When they show me a live, moving germ that I can see and touch, then I'll believe," said old Joaquín. "These stupid TV pictures of little animals that look like fly specks or Mickey Mice mean nothing."[4]

Apparently, it did not occur to Madsen that old Joaquín could have been pulling his leg, but the references to television pictures and Mickey Mouse might have told him something. Anglos, educated or otherwise, whether they have looked through microscopes or not, are also influenced in their "ideas" about germs by television commercials and cartoons. Many an Anglo explains his absence from shop or office by saying, "The flu bug bit me." No one jumps to the conclusion that he literally thinks of the flu virus as an insect. He is speaking figuratively, and without a doubt he is influenced in his imagery by television commercials and cartoons. It just happens that border Mexicans use *animalito* as equivalent to the English "bug" in the sense of small insects or vermin. About all the use of *animalito* tells us is that Madsen's Mexican Americans have undergone a good degree of acculturation through mass media, so that they are expressing their misconceptions about disease in general American rather than traditional Mexican terms.

Madsen follows this with another passage, illustrating stubborn "incredulity" about germ theories.

> A public health nurse who makes regular home visits scolded Rosa for allowing her new baby to drink from a bottle after flies had touched the nipple. "You must see that the nipple is crawling with germs," the Anglo nurse said. After the nurse departed, Rosa carefully examined the nipple and gave the bottle back to her baby. "There is nothing on it at all," she commented to her mother who was visiting at the time. "That nurse must have spots on her glasses."[5]

Here it is the trained Anglo nurse who is indulging in "Mickey Mice" language, as if the germs were bedbugs or cockroaches, crawling about for Rosa to see. Apparently (Madsen leaves so much detail out of these vignettes) the nurse does nothing about the offending nipple except to scold Rosa. Anyone with some idea of the arrogance public health nurses can display toward the poor and the nonwhite can appreciate Rosa's reaction. Her words convey not incredulity about germs but hostility toward the nurse.

Some of Madsen's Chicanos, however, have been converted to germ theory.

> . . . experimentation with patent medicines has led them to believe in the possible existence of germs. When such medicines bring relief, some Mexican-Americans accept advertising claims that the efficiency of the medication is due to its power to kill germs. "When I have a sore throat, I buy this gargle and it always makes my throat feel better," Valentin explained. "Maybe it really is like it says on the label that the hurt comes from germs biting me."[6]

Madsen's Chicanos are not only literal-minded, they never crack a joke.

Madsen and Rubel, however, are not alone in the cavalier use of linguistic data to illustrate ethnocentric preconceptions, nor are all available examples from the literature on the Chicano. The same sort of thing has been going on in the anthropological study of the Mexican peasant. Michael Kearney, for example, writing about the Zapotecs of Ixtepeji, feels that their "dominant present time orientation" and fear of the future are expressed in their grammatical usage.

> These observations which indicate a dominant present time orientation are supported by the Spanish grammatical usage, common in Ixtepeji, of indicating probability, doubt, and conjecture in the present by use of the future tense. Since the future is seen as uncertain, unpredictable, and undependable, it is logically consistent to indicate doubt and conjecture in the present by use of the future tense and all that thought of the future implies. Furthermore, this usage most often has an element of anxiety associated with it as well. For example, the phrase *¿Quién será ese hombre que viene?* translates as "Who will this man be who is coming now (in the present)?" and expresses a certain uneasiness about an approaching stranger.[7]

The phrase, of course, does not translate as Kearney would have it, but as "Who can that man be who is coming?" Not only in Ixtepeji but elsewhere in the Spanish-speaking world, a form borrowed from the future tense of "to be" is used to express a variety of moods: doubt, wonder, probability, potentiality, condition, emphasis. It should be unnecessary to point out that the presence of *será* does not make them statements about the future. Consider these usages of the verb:

¡Que cosa *será* la muerte	I wonder what death is like;
que viene tan despacio!	it comes so very gently.
¡Que cara *estará* la harina	Just think how dear flour must be;
que hacen el pan tan chiquito!	they bake it into such little loaves!
(*Argentina*)	
Si *serán* buenos los mozos,	The boys of La Herrera
los de la Herrera,	are really something;
que cogen los tomates	they use ladders
con escalera. (*Spain*)	to harvest tomatoes.

Kearney's attempts to use Spanish grammar in psychoanalyzing the people of Ixtepeji may prompt the Spanish-speaking reader to say, "¡Cómo serás, hombre!" (You're just too much, man!)

Somewhere there must be a Spanish-speaking anthropologist with preconceived notions about North Americans as grasping, greedy individuals obsessed with the idea of possessions, of having things. He should be able to support his generalizations with an appeal to English grammar, noting that Americans cannot express a great many tenses and moods without recourse to the verb "to have": I have been; he would have come; he may have done it, and so on.

Kearney, after all, was a beginner when he wrote his *Winds of Ixtepeji*. But one of the most flagrant examples of an anthropologist letting his preconceptions decide his interpretation of the Spanish language comes from a much more experienced source, Munro Edmonson. Writing about the narrative folklore of the Middle American Indians, Edmonson discourses on Middle America's tradition of human sacrifice and "the fatalistic philosophy which underlies it [and] that is the central feature of the Guatemalan and Mexican Indian in his literary as in his religious life." It is not only the Indian who has been infected by fatalism; "there is continuity and generality to the fatalistic tradition" that reaches into the psyche of the *mestizo* and the *criollo*. As evidence, Edmonson gives us a bit of translated song:

> When one searches even the modern tin-pan-alley songs of Mexico or Guatemala for gaiety, he is almost invariably disappointed. Even in a near-nonsense song:
>
> > Guadalajara on a plain;
> > Mexico on a lake.
> > I have to eat this *tuna*
> > even if it pricks me.[8]

This is no doubt a vivid picture of the fatalistic Mexican accepting his lot. He is destined to be wounded by the prickly pear, poor man. The Spaniard fights against his fate, but the Mexican bows to it. Let us, however, go back to the Spanish-language original that Edmonson has translated for us, and we may get a very different picture:

Guadalajara en un llano,
México en una laguna;
me he de comer esa tuna
aunque me espine la mano.

The stanza, by the way, is no product of Mexico's Tin Pan Alley but has a respectable place in oral tradition. It is in the classic Spanish *copla* form, and like many other *coplas* its first two lines have no direct relation to the message of the second two. They are not nonsense, however; they are a conventional device that prepares the listener for what the last two lines will say. In these last two lines the first thing worth noting is the presence of *he,* a form of the helper verb *haber.* Bilingual dictionaries usually translate *haber de* as "ought to" or "must." But any Spanish speaker knows that *he de* denotes a strong determination to do something. What the singer is saying is, "No matter what, I *will* eat that prickly pear, even if I get my hand full of thorns." And the pear in question is not an actual fruit, of course, but a woman's favors.*

Shakespeare's Hotspur expresses a similar sentiment in referring to a lord who refuses to join him in a plot against the king because it is too dangerous: ". . . but I tell you, my lord fool, out of this nettle, danger, we pluck this flower, safety" (I Henry IV, act II, scene iii, lines 8–10).[9] Similarly, our *copla* says, "Out of this thorny cactus, danger, I will pluck this *tuna,* beauty." Fatalism, indeed!

Mexicans, and Chicanos as well, are capable of subtle uses of verbal art, and it is strange that so little attention has been given to these aspects of folklore in the ethnographic literature. A striking aspect of such ethnographic works is the presence of passages that resemble jokes, legends, or other folkloric performances in content, style, or structure but are presented in print as examples of factual communication. Since the authors give us no information as to the specific situations in which the words were uttered, we cannot be sure that we are dealing with folklore, but there is a strong doubt that what have been recorded are straightforward data. In some cases, however, the similarity to contemporary jokes is too close to ignore. Ethnographers may find it worthwhile to keep in

---

* Compare the following from a slightly bawdy *son veracruzano:*

| Me picaron las abejas | The bees stung me |
| pero me comí el panal. | but I ate the comb. |

mind that Chicanos and Mexicans do have a sense of humor, and that they love to put strangers on. In another essay, Munro Edmonson has said, "Even a highly competent ethnographer is usually lost when his informants begin to joke among themselves."[10] But when his informants begin to joke with or about the ethnographer, he is more than lost, especially if he is not aware that joking is going on.

In the past, the ethnographer was on much surer ground, when his main interests were such "classic" ethnographic chores as taking censuses, mapping out kinship systems, or recording overt behavior; but distortion is extremely likely when he attempts to interpret feelings and attitudes on the basis of artistic expression, especially if the ethnographer is not sufficiently aware of the kind of behavior taking place and assumes that his informants are simply giving him information. In such cases, it is quite likely that he will end up as the butt of the joke, like the greenhorn in the old frontier anecdotes.

When is an ethnographer's informant giving him information, and when is the informant doing something else? Ethnographers working with Chicanos sometimes fail to make this distinction between factual report and the possibility of joking or some other types of performance. Part of the trouble—as has been noted—arises from a lack of real familiarity with the language. At times, perhaps, a more rigorous application of methods well known to anthropologists might have helped. But most important is the tendency to proceed as if language had only one level of meaning, or as if informants were incapable of any kind of language use but that of minimum communication. There is a lack of recognition of the artistic possibilities of language, and perhaps an underestimation of the informant, who is seen as somewhat naive, eager to give the fieldworker all the facts he knows once the latter has established that magic condition known as rapport. The informant is seldom seen as a competent artist in language use, who may in fact be taking the anthropologist's measure.

Anthropological training is supposed to teach one a certain degree of objectivity, but anthropologists are well aware how fragile are the defenses we build against subjectivity and unconscious bias. The history of modern anthropology, in a sense, has been a continuous effort to make corrections for that bias. The majority of such efforts, unfortunately, have led toward a greater and greater tendency to make of anthropology a computerized science, to think of raw anthropological data in terms of mathematical formulas. "Unfortunately," because anthropology at the same time has become particularly interested in human emotions, tendencies, and attitudes. And the type of data that can be worked into graphs or fed into computers usually ignores the nuances of human interaction. This is the crux of the matter. Too much of the ethnographic work conducted among Mexican Americans has been aimed at compiling data by the most direct means possible—that of asking people for facts. Every utterance seems to have been received as communicating the information asked for and is duly noted as such, without taking too much into account either the rhetorical and figurative uses of language or the structure of any given speech event, which may demand one response rather than another.

Even when the ethnographer does recognize artistic expression, he is likely to ignore most of its behavioral aspects. Kearney's *Winds of Ixtepeji* is a case in point. Kearney can give the reader a beautifully complete description of ritual drinking behavior, but he gives us no details on how the legend of "La Llorona" is performed. Even more, he does not give us a single text of the legend as it is told in Ixtepeji, where presumably he heard it many times. He works with a summary (a tale type if you will) published elsewhere by other authors.[11] Yet, he bases some sweeping generalizations about Ixtepejano family and interpersonal relations on this folk narrative. Kearney's readers may be pardoned if they are skeptical about his conclusions.

A greater awareness, on the part of the ethnographer, of the informant as a performer of folklore certainly would not be amiss. And it is here that contemporary methods in folkloristics could be of some help to ethnographers working among minority groups such as the Chicano. Especially useful to the ethnographer should be the work of those folklorists who take a performance-oriented approach to verbal art, or who see the informant as an artist engaged in a creative act. Drawing concepts from sociolinguistics, literary criticism, and sociology, folklorists like Roger Abrahams, Richard Bauman, Dan Ben-Amos, Dell Hymes, and others have made us very much aware of such things as performance frames and the keys or signals that identify them.* Earlier,

---

* For a recent survey of the folklore-as-performance approach, see Richard Bauman, "Verbal Art as Performance," *American Anthropologist* 77 (1975): 290–311.

Abrahams had pointed out the rhetorical nature of folkloric performance and the use of performance as a device for self-assertion or attention getting,[12] while Daniel J. Crowley emphasized the dramatic element in the performance of folk narrative in a study of Bahamian folklore.[13] Even earlier, William Bascom drew attention to the artistic qualities of verbal folklore,[14] while William Jansen was a pioneer among folklorists not only in seeing the folkloric act as a performance but in noting the part played by role playing and role shifting in expressive behavior.[15]

The fact that they deal with materials immediately recognizable as involving some measure of art has made folklorists very conscious of two points of importance to the subject at hand. One is the recognition of the informant as a potential performer, whatever the circumstances. The other is a preoccupation with the varied results of the face-to-face interaction that occurs between informant and fieldworker. Thus, the folklorist tends to view the informant not only as a more-or-less representative member of a group but as a potential artist, and an individual person as well, with interests and goals of his own.

These considerations can be of great importance in dealing with Mexican or Chicano informants. Insinuation and veiled language, for example, occupy a prominent place in Greater Mexican verbal art. The use of indirect language has been refined in the wordplay of the *albur* to double or triple levels of meaning. Euphemism, circumlocution, and allusive language are employed, not to soften the force of an insult but rather to heighten its effect. Ethnographers have been aware of this in a general sort of way. Madsen, for example, reports the existence of verbal dueling in Hidalgo County.

> Words and phrases with double meanings are used to insult the masculinity of one's drinking companions. Such verbal dueling may be developed into a fine art. The champions are those who can disguise their attacks with words of flattery so that the victim feels complimented rather than insulted.[16]

Madsen seems to be reporting at second hand rather than from direct observation. Verbal dueling occurs not only during drinking bouts but in many other contexts as well; and the object is not to fool the victim into thinking he is being flattered but to exhibit the virtuosity necessary to make an insult sound like a compliment or courteous speech. Chicano victims are seldom fooled. Many of these apparent compliments are stereotyped and easily recognized by any member of the group. Mexicans and Chicanos alike are familiar with the story about the two *compadres* from Alvarado, Veracruz, who say to each other on parting:

—No se olvide, compadrito. (Don't forget, my dear *compadre*.)
—Ni usted tampoco, compadrito. (You neither, my dear *compadre*.)

A touching example of the respect and affection that goes with *compadrazgo,* but what the two ritual brothers are saying to each other is: "Don't forget to go fuck your mother, *compadre*." "Don't you forget to do the same."

Anglo social scientists—and even some Mexican intellectuals—have remarked on the Mexican's alleged sensitivity to any reference about his womenfolk. A simple remark concerning a man's mother or sister may be taken as an insult, a tendency that has often been seen as a pathological condition in the Mexican. After all, why should a youth take it amiss if a friend asks in the politest of voices, "How is your sister this morning?" For quite good reasons, we would agree, if we know that in the verbal art of both young men the phrase is a stereotyped euphemism for "What is your sister's condition this morning after the rough riding I gave her last night?" What is remarkable here is not the Mexican's degree of sensitivity to insult but his virtuosity in its practice.

In the situation just mentioned, whether the concern about the health of someone's sister is real or whether a fight or a verbal duel is about to begin depends on a great many factors not always apparent in the words of any text. Where we have only a recorded text to go on, and none of the circumstances that prompted it, we may not be able to judge whether the utterance occurred in a literal or an artistic frame. A good example is the text attributed by Madsen to Joaquín, who did not believe in stupid television pictures of *animalitos* that looked like Mickey Mice and demanded to see a living, moving germ he could see and touch. Not knowing the circumstances, we cannot really say that Joaquín was performing for the ethnographer, playing the role of the seeing-is-believing, doubting-Thomas rustic just for laughs. Perhaps he really was convinced that what he could not see did not exist.

But it may be interesting to compare him with an old *ranchero* I knew in Brownsville before Pearl Harbor. He used to come into town every Saturday afternoon and sit in his favorite barbershop, regaling audiences with his tongue-in-cheek commentaries about war, politics, the economy, or just life in general. Some of his best performances had the weather as their subject. One extremely hot, still afternoon he told us that it was quite clear the weather was getting hotter, year by year, and that he knew why. The growing number of automobiles was to blame. He pointed out that when a breeze was blowing from the Gulf, it was much cooler. But now we had fewer and fewer of these *airecitos* because all the air was being used to inflate automobile tires. Our old *ranchero* used to tell his stories with the gravest of faces, acknowledging the laughter that followed with a pleased expression but rarely with a broad smile. Everyone understood and appreciated him as a virtuoso in deadpan humor. As far as I know, he never met up with an ethnographer. Otherwise we might have a study or two in the literature about Chicano concepts concerning the weather.

The *ranchero*'s performance is a good example of the kind of situation in which the performer assumes the role of the dumb hick for the amusement of people very much like himself. His performance, in fact, involves double role-casting: himself as the hick and his auditors as the type of people (outsiders) who would consider the *ranchero* stupid. This type of double imitation is based on what Jansen called the esoteric-exoteric factor in folklore, specifically the ingroup's perception of what the outgroup thinks of it. The "I'm just a poor, dumb Mexican peon" persona is a favorite with the border Mexican jokester, who can use it for plain fun among his own group—as in the example just given—or work it on outsiders with a barbed intent.

In joking, as we well know, the persona assumed by the performer may be a stereotype created by the outgroup but used in apotropaic fashion by the ingroup to which the performer belongs. The crude-backwoodsman persona in American frontier humor is a familiar example. Bluestein has written about this particular strategy in American humor in his essay on "The Arkansas Traveler."[17] His only mistake is to think that the "strategy of humor 'The Arkansas Traveler' employs is uniquely American."[18] Consider Bluestein's description of this type of humor: "The squatter knows that the traveler considers him a backwoods barbarian. The strategy of the humor, consequently, is based on the squatter's willingness to act the role of an ignorant rustic, thus taking advantage of the traveler's gullibility as well as his prejudices . . . the backwoodsman adopts a pose of innocence and naiveté that reverses the roles, making the city slicker the butt of the joke."[19] Substitute "Mexican" for "backwoodsman" and "American tourist" for "city slicker" and you have the basic situation of dozens of "Stupid American" jokes told by Mexicans and Chicanos alike. But folk art too is imitated by life. There is reason to believe that the "Stupid Mexican" persona in Chicano humor—equivalent to the Arkansas squatter—has sometimes been taken seriously by Anglo ethnographers. The ethnographer is quite likely to recognize masks of this type in his own culture, for he has more or less unconsciously learned how to identify them as part of the process of socialization. He is not likely to spot the same kind of play in a Chicano context, unless he is oriented toward an awareness of artistic verbal expression. Failing that, the "Stupid Chicano" persona strikes a responsive chord in his latent biases, and he interprets a joking situation as a straight communicative event.

A clear example of mistaken joking behavior is furnished by Rubel. Telésforo, a young man, is asked to describe how his mother knew when any of her children were ill. Telésforo's answer covers the better part of a page in small print. The first thing the mother does when a child complains is to give him aspirin, then more aspirin, "and if you were still sick she would start on the herbs. She would go through all the teas that she knew, and then she would ask the neighbors. If none of these things worked, and you had tried all the teas and medicines that people knew of, then they figured that you suffered from *ojo*." So they would cure the child of *ojo*. "Then if this didn't help the sickness, and if you're not dead yet, they would turn you over and start curing you for *empacho*." And finally, after all these treatments the narrator would recover, only to be given "a purge to clear the stomach of all the herbs."[20]

If this is not intended as comedy, there is no such thing as humor among Chicanos. In fact, the text belongs to a class of jokes parodying the methods of the *curandero* and showing him as a bumbling old fool who works on a hit-or-miss basis and does the patient more harm than good. One variant of this same joke has the *curandero* taking a shortcut. Instead of trying one herb after the other, he feeds the patient goat turds, since goats eat all kinds of herbs and the herb the patient needs will be in the dung.[21] What Rubel's informant seems to have done is to cast himself as the protagonist in a well-known joke, a common practice among border humorists. Rubel, however, takes his informant's words at face value, remarking that "every specific pathogenic condition is associated with a cluster of symptoms, but no single symptom (with the probable exception of dramatic mania) is the exclusive property of any one illness. Because of overlapping symptoms Chicanos have difficulty in arriving at definitive diagnoses and precipitating causes for any one condition."[22]

The attribution of the main roles in a humorous narrative to oneself or to others is greatly favored by performers of Border jokes. In such case, it is not the assumption of a stereotyped role in order to turn around the stereotype and use it against the outsider; rather, it is the playful addition of real-life actors to a well-known plot, to make it more vivid or more ridiculous. Often, the narrator will attribute a comic role not to himself but to some other person, who may or may not be present at the joking session. If the victim is present, he will answer in kind; and the situation develops into a dueling session, which may include jokes, rhymes, songs, and other less structured verbal forms. If the victim is not present, he may be chosen for role attribution because he fits the bill: the protagonist in the joke is a lawyer, a politician, a newly married man, or nearsighted, or very short, for example, and the absent victim happens to have the required attribute central to the plot. Undeniably, the element of aggression—conscious or unconscious—is involved, as it is in most jokes. If aggression or resentment against the absent victim is quite on the surface, the joke may fall into the category of gossiplike banter. But even in such cases, the audience understands the whole thing as artistic license rather than as a statement of alleged fact, as gossip would be.

On most occasions, however, role attribution is meant as a rhetorical device, an added artistic dimension in the performance of a joke. A deputy sheriff, for example, embellished a rather mild joke based on the motif of misunderstanding words in a foreign language by telling it as follows:

> I had been to Austin to deliver a prisoner, and I had this guy along with me [*gestures toward the man sitting next to him*]. And on the way back I was very tired and I was afraid I would run a stop sign in one of those little towns. So I told this guy, "Keep an eye out for any signs that say 'Stop.'"

But this *cabrón* can't read much, especially English, so I tell him, "It will be a sign with four letters on it." Pretty soon he yells, "Stop! Stop!" And I stop but there's no stop sign, only a *cantina* with a neon sign that says, "Beer." And he says, "There it is; it has four letters." So we stop and have a beer.

In this joke the narrator not only attributed a role to himself but also one to his friend. Austin was worked into the story because I was down on a visit from Austin, so in a sense even I became part of the joke.

This type of performance poses no problems when everyone understands the rules and knows what is going on. When such is not the case, an unwary outsider may accept as fact what is intended as parody or humorous fiction. And if an accomplished jokester smells a pigeon, he can lead his dupe on with mock memorates—possibly the most dangerous form of verbal art to the ethnographer, especially if he is an outsider without a complete command of the language. Americans, of course, are familiar with the mock memorate as a stock-in-trade of early frontier humor, in the form of the outrageous lies told by old-timers to tenderfeet. Ethnographers working among Chicanos would do well to keep the mock memorate in mind in evaluating confidences given them by informants, especially when recording among a group with the remotest resemblance to a joking or kidding session.

Even without the element of role attribution in any of its variations, the ethnographer may mistake a joke for literal communication. This seems to have happened to Madsen. In a discussion of illegal immigrants from Mexico and their problems, Madsen tells us how they "must constantly be on guard against apprehension and deportation by the authorities." When caught the wetback attempts to brazen it out and at times is successful. But not always.

> Such play acting sometimes fails because of ignorance about the United States. One wetback stopped for questioning was asked where he was born. Standing proud and straight, he looked into the eye of the border patrol officer and replied, "Chicago, California."[23]

This is one of several "wetback" jokes that were being told along the border in the late 1950s and early 1960s, when the *bracero* situation was reaching something of a crisis, and when the Hidalgo Project was under way. The most popular was the "¿Dónde nació?" joke (interpreted by the wetback being questioned as "¿Dónde está Ignacio?"), but the "Chicago, California" joke also was widespread. In Brownsville it produced a special variant used to satirize a Chicano policeman who was supposed to be excessively stupid. The policeman stops a tourist and asks him where the tourist is from. The tourist answers, "Chicago." "Don't give me any of that bullshit," says the cop. "Do you think I'm stupid or something? Your license plates say 'Illinois!'"

"Wetback" jokes do tell us a great deal about the attitudes of native Texas-Mexicans toward the newly arrived *bracero*, and this was a subject that interested Madsen. But he missed its potentialities because he thought he was recording factual verbal reports instead of humor.

The Brownsville variant of the *bracero* joke, with the stupid cop as protagonist, involves a somewhat different kind of role attribution from that exemplified by the deputy sheriff's joke about the sign with four letters on it. The policeman was never present when the joke was told; in fact, he was not considered a regular member of the groups gathered in joking sessions when the joke was performed. No one took the story about the cop's encounter with the tourist from Chicago as anything but humorous fiction, yet most of those present did believe the policeman to be stupid. Here the main function of role attribution is not as a device to achieve interest or immediacy of performance but as a vehicle expressing a conscious attitude shared by the group. In a way, it is a form of insinuation; what on the surface appears to be a joke really is a kind of insult.

This particular use of role attribution is also found in the type of frame set up during verbal dueling and other kinds of wordplay (the *albur* or *choteo*), where the object is artistic insult, and which usually includes other verbal forms. On the surface the banter may sound like gossip, especially if the victim is not present. The difference is that in gossip the events are alleged to have happened, while in this type of verbal dueling no such assumption is made.

The young Chicanos who were among Rubel's primary informants seem to have indulged in a good deal of wordplay when he was present during meetings of what Rubel calls his *palomilla*. Throughout *Across the Tracks* there are instances of what appears to be wordplay or gossiplike banter, which Rubel records as literal communication. This leads to some astonishing statements, such as:

> A young man whose attachment to his household interferes with the more manly activities with his palomilla causes serious concern to his family and to the others of his palomilla. When such a situation is feared to exist, members of the society exert pressures to pry the man from his home to the more appropriate palomilla. In one instance a young man of about thirty-two years was believed to be too closely attached to his wife and children. His mother complained, accusing his wife (her daughter-in-law) of refusing him permission to leave the house during the night.[24]

That Chicano mothers can be possessive about their sons and jealous of their daughters-in-law is undeniable, though the same may be said about mothers of other culture groups in the United States. But that Chicano families and society in general should put pressure on a young husband to keep him attached to his youthful gang rather than encouraging him to become a responsible family head, is more than one can swallow. However, this image of the *palomilla,* as such a vital institution that all Chicano society combines to preserve its integrity, is one that would appeal to and be fostered by active gang members, who naturally feel threatened every time one of their numbers leaves the group.

Rubel's acceptance as fact of the self-aggrandizing chatter of "his" *palomilla* leads him to one of the most amusing boo-boos of the book, the story of "The Mabel Caper."[25] Jaime, "previously notable for his successes with women," marries and changes his way of life. He breaks with the *palomilla* and refuses to run around anymore. But after a few months of marriage, his wife goes to Houston to see her mother; and Jaime is thrown into the waiting arms of his former gang, who punish him by making him a victim of "The Mabel Caper," apparently a well-established custom of the group. A fake tryst is arranged for Jaime with "Mabel," supposedly a young Anglo farmwife married to a husband much older than herself and working on the night shift. Jaime is led by Homero, one of the conspirators, to an abandoned farmhouse where others of the *palomilla* are waiting. Homero knocks and calls Mabel's name. The door is thrown open, a powerful light is shined on their faces, and the angry voice of the "husband" is heard: "I'll teach you to fool with my wife!" There are several shots, and Homero falls to the ground feigning agony. The dupe Jaime takes off into the brush; and it is several hours before searching parties find him, "scratched, weary, fearful, and soaking wet."

Rubel is so impressed with "The Mabel Caper" as an institutionalized mechanism for maintaining discipline in the *palomilla* that he mentions it later as a part of the traditional culture of the Chicano. In summing up the influence of the "institution" of the *palomilla* on the institution of marriage, Rubel says: "An unduly warm relationship between a young man and his wife and children is frowned upon. Gossip, the Mabel caper, and more direct reprimand function as adequate sanctions to prevent such an attachment."[26]

But there is one fishy little detail in the story of Jaime and Mabel that should have been apparent to anyone looking at the story with the critical eye of the social scientist. "The Mabel Caper," we are told, is a well-established custom with Jaime's *palomilla;* the trick has been played on "others of Mexiquito" before Jaime becomes the victim.[27] Yet, Jaime is no innocent; less than a year before, he had been an active member of the group and a noted womanizer. It is strange that he should not know about the Mabel trick, and that—assuming his ignorance—he should act like a young teenager eager to have his first sexual experience.

Any folklorist will have recognized the familiar "Visiting the Widow" anecdote. In *American Folklore* Richard M. Dorson includes it in his section on "The Folklore of College Students" as a variation on the "Fatal Fraternity Initiation" legend. In most examples of this legend, the hapless freshman undergoing hazing dies from the experience, while in the "Visiting the Widow" variation he is merely scared half to death.[28] By the time Dorson's book appeared, the story had filtered down from the college campuses to the high schools. During the early 1960s, the "Visiting the Widow" anecdote was submitted in every one of my beginning folklore classes at the University of Texas, usually by two or more students. None of the students claimed to have witnessed or participated in the trick, but they were firm in the belief that the whole thing had happened among seniors in their high school a year or two before the student folklorists graduated. Comparing the Anglo-Texan variants with Rubel's, we find that they agree in most important details: the elaborate put-on by a group of young conspirators; the legendary young woman married to an old and frequently absent husband; the eagerness and naiveté of the victim; the isolated farmhouse; the knock on the door by the "guide" answered by shouts of rage on the part of the fake husband; the bright light in the face of the victim, so he cannot recognize the "husband"; the shots fired; the fake wounding of the guide; the flight of the dupe into the woods; the search by the now-worried tricksters for the victim, who is found hours afterward, scratched, muddy, and scared out of his wits. Only in one detail do these student variants of the "Visiting the Widow" legend fail to jibe with Rubel's "Mabel Caper." In the stories collected by students, the victim is always a neophyte: a sheltered male virgin, a high school freshman, a newcomer to the town. Thus, the Anglo-Texan variants retain a verisimilitude that the New Lots narrative lacks.

By the 1950s several items of modern Anglo lore had entered border Mexican folklore and the folklore of interior Mexico as well. "The Vanishing Hitchhiker" legend, for example, was collected from Texas-Mexican informants by Ruth Dodson as early as 1942,[29] and it was current in Mexico City by the mid-1950s.[30]

It is within the realm of possibility that Homero and his friends did attempt the "Visiting the Widow" trick on someone, if not on Jaime. But the supposed results match the Anglo legendary anecdote so closely that they strain the limits of probability. It is much more probable that what Rubel witnessed was a folklore performance with a specific purpose. The attribution of the story to an unlikely protagonist (an experienced womanizer instead of a sexual neophyte) would seem out of place unless one knows that border Mexican performers often attribute standard jokes to absent members of their own group. Jaime, being not only absent but out of favor, would be a most likely candidate. The story then assumes in the ideal world of art the precise function that Rubel assumed it to have in ordinary, "real" experience. It becomes a kind of exemplum, warning *palomilla* members to remain faithful to the gang, and it collectively builds up the ego of the group.

With "The Mabel Caper," perhaps some acquaintance with items most familiar to folklorists might have been enough to alert the ethnographer. I am not recommending, however, that fieldworkers in Chicano anthropology memorize all available indexes of jokes and legends. For one thing, no such indexes exist. For another, not all performances involve such easily recognizable items or genres. Joking may take the form of complicated wordplay that sounds like serious discourse; or, as has been noted, it may be couched in a kind of banter that resembles gossip. This gossiplike banter is typical of young men who congregate in groups variously known as *pandillas, palomillas, gangas,* or just "the boys."

A favorite target, of course, is the individual who is in the process of separating himself from the boys for a more mature status as head of a family. A young man newly married or going steady with a girl is accused of regressing into an infantile state: *le pegan* (they spank him), *no lo dejan salir solo* (they don't let him out by himself), *lo traen de la mano* (they lead him around by the hand). The banter may occur when the individual is absent, but it is just as common when he is making one of his occasional visits to the group. Though the victim may be present, the imputations are usually in the third person as though he were somewhere else; and the sweetheart or wife is always "they." Sometimes the banter makes use of well-known humorous narratives to needle the victim. The following is an example from the Brownsville-Matamoros area circa 1940.

> After Alberto got married he rarely went out with the boys, and when he did he would never buy a round of drinks. He had other uses for his money. One night he did go out with his friends, and everybody bought rounds except him. The gang was gathered around the bar in a Matamoros *cantina,* when suddenly Alberto said in a loud voice: "*¡Éstas vienen por mí!*" (These are on me!)
>
> His friends cheered and said, "*¡Por fin disparó!*" (He's buying at last!)
>
> "Oh, no," said Alberto. "What I mean is that those two are coming for me." (Also said *Éstas vienen por mí.*)
>
> He had just seen his wife and his mother-in-law in the bar mirror.

So stylized and so well established as a rite of separation is this form of banter that it rarely causes offense. Other situations, however, may have more sting to them.

Dyadic relationships and *amigos de confianza* notwithstanding, there is a tendency to resent a close relationship between two members of a gang, as leaving out the rest of the group. If, for example, two individuals go on a trip together or take part in some amusement without the others, they are likely to face a roasting when they get back, in the form of much banter about their having a homosexual relationship. It should not be necessary to stress that the two individuals being raked over the coals are not by any means thought to be homosexuals. The imputation of homosexuality is the group's way of expressing resentment at being left out.

A similar situation may occur in regard to the ritual relationship of *compadrazgo,* which establishes a dyadic bond between two men. When individual A chooses individual B among all his friends as his *compadre,* the others may joke that B was chosen because he was getting pretty close to A's wife. To forestall any chance of becoming a cuckold, A chose B since sexual relations between *compadres* and *comadres* are considered incestuous. Because it casts aspersions on A's wife, the banter about A and B normally would take place when A is not present, though it is perfectly all right if B is there. If A is present at the kidding session, it may be acceptable to hint at the situation rather than to state it. Advice will be given to no one in particular to beware of *compadres,* or salacious stories about *compadres* and *comadres* may be told. Though A will understand, he usually will not take offense, since that would make him the loser in the game. Like the imputation of homosexuality, the whole thing is a joke. It may express some real resentment, or it may just be that the chance to fit an old joke to familiar names has come up, and one takes advantage of it during a kidding session.

Rubel notes that one way "in which Chicanos utilize ritual kinship as a means to restrain conflict occurs in the following: 'Sometimes when someone is afraid that you are going to sleep with his wife, he'll make you his compadre. That way you can't do it.'"[31] Rubel is not alone in this, however; he footnotes the well-known article on ritual co-parenthood by Mintz and Wolf, who state that "evidence from studies of two communities in Puerto Rico suggests that the *compadre* relation may be invoked to forestall sexual aggression."[32] There is nothing like evidence of geographical distribution to verify data scientifically. Puerto Ricans, by the way, share much of their humor with Chicanos and Mexicans, including jokes about American tourists.

Anthropologists have been aware of joking or teasing relationships since Radcliffe-Brown at least. They are also aware that *compadrazgo* is a relationship highly charged with tension and suppressed conflict, around which all kinds of jokes, dirty songs, and comic sayings have developed—

as one would expect in relationships demanding some degree of ritual avoidance or respect. Still, the supposed custom of making your *compadre* of a man who is trying to make your wife is allowed to stand as unchallenged fact. Again, it seems that a bit of common sense would have helped. Given the imputed image of the young Mexican male as a predatory, no-holds-barred Don Juan, one may well imagine the predicament of a man with a good-looking wife and a couple dozen male friends. He would be kept so busy producing offspring for his friends to baptize that he would have little time for anything else. Or perhaps that is the true reason for the high birthrate among people of Mexican culture. An additional bonus, of course, is that the wife would also be kept busy and out of mischief. An old Anglo farmer I used to know expressed the same sentiments in the advice he gave young husbands as to how to keep their wives out of trouble: "Keep them busy, barefoot, and with their belly full of kids." There may be a key to the Anglo character there.

Not always does performance of this sort occur within a joking frame; it may take place in other situations, where the conscious intent of the informant may be to communicate in a literal sense rather than to perform. Even in what appear to be obvious cases of direct communication, the message may not be the literal one that appears on the surface. Some factors related to the nature of conscious artistic performance, but operating less consciously than in joking, may be suggested here.

First is the obvious but still slighted fact that sometimes the informant selects the ethnographer rather than the other way around. This is especially a danger in participant observation, which is the most productive for anyone seeking data to generalize on such things as worldview, feelings, and general attitudes. Perhaps the danger is greater when working with Mexican Americans than with people in the villages of "Indian" Mexico, because there will be in almost every Mexican American community a certain number of acculturated or partly acculturated individuals with a better knowledge of English than the ethnographer's knowledge of Spanish. The chances are very high that it will be this type of person who will become the fieldworker's informants, not only because the fieldworker finds them the most useful for his purposes but—much more important—because these individuals feel a need to establish friendly relations with the visiting Anglo and to present their own image of the community to him. Until recently (the mid-1960s, let us say), these individuals were most likely to be rather conservative, with an excessive admiration for Anglo culture and a strong desire toward acculturation. Thus, a perceptive anthropologist like Arthur Rubel could spend months in New Lots and never suspect that a political revolution was taking place before his eyes, concluding on the contrary that Mexican Americans just were not interested in political issues. Conversely, some fieldworkers since the *movimiento* apply a supersynchronic bias to their work, ignoring even recent Mexican American history and describing the Chicano movement not only as a kind of unique phenomenon arising full-blown out of nothing but writing as if all Mexican Americans were part of the *movimiento*.

There are certain personality types who are most likely to attract the ethnographer's attention as potential informants because they are more approachable, seemingly more knowledgeable, and more articulate than others. These personality types, I would suggest, are most likely to be the better performers of the community—the jokers, the narrators of legends, the gifted role players. The informant who is a natural performer can very well make a performance out of what he intends as a simple act of factual communication. Reminiscence is embellished into legend, reality gilded over with a patina of romantic remembering.

Furthermore, such informants may very well be deviants, exceptions, or failures from the standpoint of the community, or special pleaders for or against their own group. Anthropologists are trained to watch out for the unrepresentative informant, of course; but the rules of thumb that work in an "Indian" village in Mexico may not operate in the more complex, fluid world of the Chicano *barrio*. The deviant may not appear so to the ethnographer if the deviant's ideas and behavior are much like those of the ethnographer, or if the deviant's assessment of his own culture confirms biases or stereotypes the ethnographer has brought with him into the field.

Under such circumstances, the informant may go out of his way to tell the ethnographer what he thinks the ethnographer wants to hear. This tendency of some informants to be pleasant to fieldworkers is sometimes noted in the literature, though ethnographies on Chicanos would suggest that it is too often ignored in the field. Lee Haring is one of those who has taken note of this particular fieldworker's pitfall, presenting evidence that some of his African informants told him what they thought he wanted or ought to hear.[33] In reading Chicano ethnographies one sometimes gets that same feeling, of the informant eager to please or to be polite to the Anglo. But this need not always be the case; it is possible that the informant is using what sounds like literal discourse in a rhetorical way, intending it to be interpreted as meaning more than it says on the surface.

For an excellent example we can step outside the Western Hemisphere, since the problem is not exclusively ours. In Norway the Lapps seem to occupy a position very much like that of the Mexican Americans in the Southwest. Norwegian anthropologist Harald Eidheim has made an interesting as well as sympathetic study of some groups of Norwegian Lapps, analogous to certain groups of Chicanos on the Mexican border. Eidheim notes that the Norwegianized Lapps "were bothered by not being fully proficient in Norwegian and by the spite and ridicule to which they were often exposed for this and other reasons in interactions with self-confident and arrogant Norwegians." Eidheim concludes that the Lapps suspect their backwardness might "derive from their being of an inferior race." His evidence? Quite often his Lapp informants remarked to him, "The Lapps must be stupid."[34]

One way of interpreting the above statement would be to assume that the Lappish informant was telling the Norwegian what he felt the Norwegian wanted to hear. But Eidheim's informant may not have been trying to please. It is much more likely that what we have here is the all too frequent case of an unconsciously arrogant majority member mistaking an agonized rhetorical statement by a minority informant for a declarative one. Eidheim had made friends with these Norwegianized Lapps, while local Norwegians looked on them with contempt. To Eidheim, the Lapp is basically an informant; making friends with him is a methodological tool—establishing rapport. But to the informant the ethnographer's friendship is real and of high value. So he confides in his new friend, and his words are, "Lapps must be stupid, we are so backward." But what he is saying is, "Other Norwegians look down on us and call us stupid because we are backward. You are Norwegian, but you are my friend. You don't really think I'm stupid, do you?"

The same question was posed to Rubel by a couple of young Chicanos, but in a different context, the difference being due mainly to the fact that they were not his informants but approached him drunkenly and with some truculence at a political rally.

> They asked whether I attributed to inherent biological differences the fact that "the Anglos are always ahead of us." I asked them whether *they* thought that to be the reason. They did not. Then both of the youths began to shake their heads from side to side. They continued to shake their heads negatively as if silently saying: What is it that we do wrong all the time?[35]

Several hours (and presumably many beers) later, one of the pair again approached Rubel and suggested that Rubel become a Chicano leader, adding, "Well, whatever we may not have, at least we're always happy."[36]

Madsen furnishes a clearer example of the tell-them-what-they-want-to-hear approach:

> I once asked a Latin if he thought the Anglos were in any way responsible for holding back the Mexican-Americans from their God-given destiny. "Of course not," he replied. . . . [37]

Rubel quotes an informant, "You know, sometimes I don't blame the Americans for discriminating against the Mexicans."[38] Rubel also tells us that "with rare exceptions, the Spanish-speaking peasants felt themselves the intellectual and economic inferiors of the more recently arrived Americans and Europeans."[39] Rubel is referring to a long period of Rio Grande Valley history, from 1850 to 1915, during which time he was not himself present to observe the "Spanish-speaking peasants'" attitudes. One wonders how he arrived at this conclusion, and we can only assume that someone told him this was so, and that Rubel found the assertion reasonable. One thinks of the tendency, for example, and especially among "Spanish-speaking peasants," to consider outsiders as one's intellectual inferiors, especially if the outsiders cannot speak Spanish. It is the acculturated town-dweller who is more likely to have doubts about himself and his culture, and who is likely to seek reassurance from his friendly Anglo ethnographer.

There is also the matter of what, for lack of a better term, I will call "expected behavior," in contrast to actual, observed behavior. The idea embraces the concept of ideal versus real behavior but is more inclusive, for while one thinks of ideal behavior as usually based on esoteric values, expected behavior may be an expression of either exoteric or esoteric representations, with positive or negative connotation. Expected behavior is often embodied in stereotypes. Some of the stereotypes (usually, though not always, regarded as negative) are those the ingroup thinks the outgroup holds about the ingroup, while others (usually regarded as favorable, though again not always) may owe their existence to the ingroup itself.

In the case of minority groups such as the Chicano, conscious or unconscious bias on the part of the majority, to which the ethnographer usually belongs, is an important factor; but other things are involved, including the ingroup's sense of the ridiculous and a kind of culture lag.

When the Chicano is the ingroup and the Anglo the outgroup, a common pair of stereotypes embodying opposite poles of expected behavior are the "stupid, naive, primitive Mexican peon" versus the "charming, urbane Spanish *caballero*." Their origins are at the core of the complex relationships that have existed between Mexicans and Anglos for the past 150 years or so. When the Anglo has looked with disfavor upon the Mexican, the Anglo has seen the Mexican as childlike and not endowed with too much intelligence, an excellent source of field labor if you know how to handle him. It is no accident perhaps that now that "greaser" is considered too inelegant for public conversation—especially if Mexicans are within earshot—the prejudiced Anglo Texan can achieve the same results by referring to a Mexican he does not like as a "peon," "wetback," or *bracero*. On the other hand, when the Anglo has wished to flatter the Mexican, the Anglo has looked upon the Mexican as a refined Spanish gentleman.

It has already been mentioned that Chicano informants may assume the Mexican peon persona in joking situations and that an unwary ethnographer may accept the performance as a straight communicative event, especially if it conforms with his latent biases. The Mexican peon persona, however, is usually intended as a transparent put-on. Its mirror image, the charming Spanish *caballero* persona, may be part of performances of different kinds and is not so easily identifiable generically. In some cases it may be a conscious put-on, but in others it may be at least partly unconscious or involuntary on the part of the performer. Usually, however, the performance is triggered by an Anglo outsider, whose own behavior requires the performance as a response. More than once have I observed this or that Chicano friend confronted by an Anglo with an exaggerated idea of Mexican courtesy, and how he will in spite of himself play up to the part of the courtly Spanish *caballero*. And indeed, it is hard to keep from falling into the genteel *caballero* persona when a strange, well-meaning Anglo drops in on you and proceeds to act as though he was Zorro paying a visit to Fray Angelo, or whatever the name of that good friar was. Unless you are careful, you unconsciously react and assume the expected role.

In but slightly different situations, the informant may not play the graceful colonial gentleman, but he may be led to describe his culture in terms reminiscent of Helen Hunt Jackson's *Ramona*. This use of "positive" stereotypes may occur—as mentioned earlier—because of an informant's abilities for or compulsion toward performance, which turns reminiscence into legend; or it may be the result of a kind of idealized culture lag, abetted by Anglo romantic literature about Spanish colonial times in Mexico and the Southwest. It is manifested in a tendency to describe current mores in terms of ideal patterns of behavior that may or may not have been true fifty or one hundred years ago, but which have become idealized as part of a past when there was order and beauty in the world. It is something like the general American habit of thinking about the contemporary United States as an individualistic frontier society.

Like the assumption of the charming *caballero* persona, this idealization of one's culture may be triggered from the outside—for example, by the ethnographer's request to an informant that he describe and assess his mores and his values. At times one gets the impression from ethnographies on Chicanos that these are studies made not in twentieth-century United States but in the Mexico of Porfirio Díaz, at the very latest. Young men go into bondage with their future fathers-in-law, like Jacob with Laban. Fathers are supreme despots in their families, feared by their children; women are meek, hardworking, and kept in seclusion. There is an extreme ritualization of daily life. Men willingly assume debts made by their relatives, so strong are bonds of the family—the rock that defies all the storms of life.

One would expect that such reports by informants would be checked against observed behavior, but apparently this is not often the case. In a couple of instances Rubel does compare idealized with observed behavior. For example, he contrasts the image given him by informants of the Chicano father as stern and domineering with what he saw in actual family interaction. He found fathers warm and affectionate with their children, sometimes more so than the mothers. In at least one case, the child refused to obey his father's command that he go to bed and was upheld in his refusal by the mother.[40]

My own experience is that informants, when asked to evaluate their culture in respect to the Anglo's, tend to see their own behavior with a lag of something like one or two generations. Much of my work has been on culture conflict, and one way of expressing such conflict is by moral judgments about the other side. One of the recurring criticisms of the Anglo on the part of the more traditional border Mexican is the "shamelessness" of Anglo women, who "go about half-naked or wearing pants, paint their faces, and go out with men all by themselves." Border Mexicans of the 1920s did have reason to be scandalized by Anglo women of the flapper era, because at that time border Mexican culture still was strongly traditional and few border Mexican women dared to bob their hair, paint their faces, or wear their skirts above the knee. The thing is that some informants were condemning Anglo culture in this fashion in the 1960s, when their own daughters were wearing brief shorts and going out on dates. By that time one could see women wearing blue jeans and miniskirts even in the *ejidos* on the Mexican side. Perhaps the continued performance of some traditional genres like legends and *corridos* has something to do with the discrepancy between ideal and actual behavior. These genres, for example, still mock the Anglos as "ham-eaters" (*jamón* usually meaning slab bacon or salt pork) when the border Mexican has made bacon and ham part of his own diet.

At times the process of painting an idealized picture of local behavior for the ethnographer may take the form of moralizing legends, memorates, or belief tales, which normally would be used within the culture as instruments to maintain the old ways in the face of rapid change. For example, narratives about miraculous cures by *curanderos*, which confound the Anglo doctors, are told to shore up the belief in folk medicine.[41] Some of the statements recorded by ethnographers about Chicanos tantalize us by their resemblance to legendary narratives. Madsen, for instance, mentions two interesting cases of "social outcasting and reacceptance."[42] José is single and in his mid-twenties; María has been married for five years before her troubles begin. Both sin against traditional group mores, both are punished, both repent through the offices of *curanderos,* and both are taken back into the fold. Rather than case histories, they read like what the conservative members of a rapidly changing society wish would happen to all those young people who no longer follow the rules—the young single men who no longer obey their fathers, the young married women who refuse to be docile. Who told these accounts? The principals? Their parents? The *curanderos* who are supposed to have effected the repentance and reconciliation with the family in each case? To really know what these stories say, we would have to know the circumstances in which they were performed; but we are told nothing about that.

Another way of using expected behavior in interviews, in this case a negative one, may occur when the informant feels compelled to justify his or her own inadequacies by blaming them on some stereotyped feature of the culture, in the confidence that the ethnographer will sympathize and agree. A graduate student in anthropology at the University of Texas, Austin, Solveig Astrid Turpin, reported this kind of situation while doing research with Mexican American women in San Antonio. She did extensive interviewing of three married women of various degrees of acculturation and compared their statements with her own observations and with interviews made of other persons. Her conclusion was that all three women used their husbands and their families as rationalizations for what they considered their own lack of advancement.

Particularly interesting was informant S.O., described by Turpin as an attractive thirty-nine-year-old housewife with a high school education, who painted a grim but standard picture (standard by the Anglo ethnographer's experience) of her husband as a jealous and domineering *macho.* According to her statements, her husband was extremely jealous of her and did not let her go out alone because like all Chicano husbands he was scared she would "find a better man." She had more formal education than her husband and would have liked to go to college—at night perhaps—so she could become a home economics teacher. Her husband, however, did "not want her to do anything because then she might be above him," and that would hurt his *macho* ego.

The researcher discovered some contradictions on talking to and observing the husband, a successful businessman. The husband appeared to be anything but a domineering tyrant. He indulged his wife in her every wish and wanted her "to emerge more into the world." Though born into a strict fundamentalist Protestant sect, he was at ease with all sorts of people, while the wife—born a Catholic—seemed "ill at ease in public places or private parties where liquor is served." Turpin made some other revealing observations. Though the husband had less formal education than the wife, he was "fluently bilingual while she feels more comfortable in Spanish." The husband had no memories of overt discrimination at the hands of Anglos. The wife, on the other hand, "vividly recalls being denied admittance to public restaurants in San Antonio. Her father admonished [his children] to be careful of their appearance and constantly polite so they could be accepted anywhere."

Obviously, the informant was presenting a special persona to the fieldworker, dramatizing stereotyped aspects of Chicano male behavior that she felt would interest the fieldworker. The description of her husband in stereotyped terms gave her the attention and the control over the interview situation that are achieved in a successful performance, while also furnishing an excuse for the informant's not having a college degree like the fieldworker. Looking at her three informants not as Chicanas but as members of another minority group—women—Turpin agrees with Eric Hoffer that "when certain individuals in a disadvantaged group begin to attain a degree of achievement, it creates pressure upon the rest to inquire into the reasons for their relative lack of advancement. The chief rationalization for women has been husband and family."

I would suggest that rationalizing performances of this sort are just as common among male informants belonging to minority groups such as the Chicanos, and that failure to recognize these as rationalizations may distort an ethnographer's data. Again, consider the type of informant that may make himself available to the Anglo ethnographer arriving to work in a Chicano *barrio*. He is likely to be bilingual (for the ethnographer's Spanish may be unreliable at best), relatively acculturated, articulate, conscious of his own position in his minority culture and also of the fact that his life might have been otherwise, that somehow he has missed his chance in this land of opportunity. This consciousness is made acute by the presence of the ethnographer, a representative of the great world beyond that the informant did not attain. The urge to justify himself before the ethnographer is pretty strong, and you can always blame things on the system, for which one must read culture: *envidia,* folk beliefs, fatalism, lack of orientation, a system of values that stresses cooperation and frowns on competition, and so on.

A couple of examples from the literature in question will perhaps illustrate the point. Madsen, for instance, gives us an example of the workings of Mexican *envidia,* or envy, in his account of Antonio and his wife, Lupe, who are members of the "upper-lower class." He works as a gardener, she in a cannery during the harvest season. They are paying for a house and own a second-hand refrigerator, a stove, and a washing machine. "Their second-hand car," Madsen tells us, "is battered but shining and well serviced. Antonio has often thought of buying a new car but knows that his friends would regard it as pretentious. Most of them do not even own second-hand automobiles."[43] Anyone not oversold on convenient stereotypes such as *envidia* might suspect Antonio of talking nonsense. Madsen himself notes that "the combined family income is sufficient to meet the payments on the house and furnish it adequately."[44] Barely sufficient, I would suspect, knowing something about wage rates in the Magic Valley, especially for gardeners and seasonal cannery workers. But it would be hard to convict Antonio of believing in the Mexican peasant doctrine of the limited good; in fact, he looks very much like a convert to the Protestant ethic. Good American that he is, he is in debt up to his eyebrows. One would suspect that under normal circumstances he is very proud of his house, his refrigerator, his washing machine, and his battered but shiny second-hand car. After all, most of his friends are not doing as well as he. It is the presence of the anthropologist that makes him draw comparisons unfavorable to himself, and to wish he had a new car to show off to the Anglo professor. Of course, the only reason he does not have one is because of the envy of other Chicanos.

"Direct action may be taken to halt the advancement of the person envied," Madsen says. He goes on to tell about two brothers who enlarged their *cantina* into a "small night club" and how they were boycotted by their friends. "Several times the screens on the windows were slashed and the window frames broken. One night a truck 'accidentally' rammed the wall of the establishment and the large crack had to be repaired at considerable expense."[45] One wishes that Madsen had told us something about the matter from the viewpoint of the club owners' former friends. Would a man ruin his truck—with which he makes a living, presumably—just to cause a crack in an enemy's wall? The wall must have been of some material more substantial than wood, if it cracked rather than splintered. And what people in Mexiquito go to *cantinas?* Which to nightclubs? Were the former friends nightclub goers, or did they stop coming to the enlarged *cantina* because it no longer was the type of place they liked to frequent? Too much is taken for granted by the ethnographer; the important thing, it seems, is to gather data to fit the *envidia* stereotype.

Border Chicanos also lack goal orientation, we are told. "A good many of the Mexican Americans who go to college don't seem to know what they want out of an education. This lack of purpose is particularly characteristic of Latins who are seeking a higher education than their parents received. . . . Latins from the lower and middle classes who go to college rarely come out qualified for a profession or well-paid occupation." Pete is given as an example; he went to the University of Texas, changed his major several times while there, "and graduated as a 'C' student in history. Today he is a clerk in his father's small store."[46]

All this was happening within the decade following World War II or immediately after, when hundreds of Chicanos from the Valley were going to college under the G.I. Bill. Chicano college graduates were already having an impact on American institutions by the end of the 1950s, when the Hidalgo Project was in progress. During this time also, I was teaching at the University of Texas and acting as adviser for a Mexican American student organization from the Valley. I met many students, including some Chicanos, who changed their majors a number of times. And there were many students, of various colors, who went from a bachelor's in history, or English, or anthropology to a job at the store with Dad or some friend of Dad's.

I also knew a number of Chicanos who were in pre-med or studying law; among the latter was a young man of *bracero* origins from Hidalgo County. But the interesting thing about the period of the 1950s and the early 1960s is the area where a great many Chicano students were concentrated at the University of Texas: they were in the School of Pharmacy. There were so many Chicanos from the Valley in pharmacy that people made jokes about it. Before the war it had been education, and probably there were just as many Chicanos in education after the war as before, but pharmacy was the new thing. And there was a good deal of foresight and goal orientation involved. These were the two kinds of degrees that Mexican Americans from the border could obtain that would give them decent jobs in their home area. And since pharmacy paid better than teaching and gave one an opportunity to set up in business by oneself, there was a veritable rush into the field at the time. The men and women majoring in pharmacy and education would be part of the entering wedge in the political movements of the 1960s and 1970s. It seems that they did know what they wanted. Had they been asked what their goals were, there is no telling what each of them might have answered. Their actions, however, spoke loudly enough.

More recognition must be given to the process that takes place when a fieldworker interviews an informant. This should be true of all situations, but it is crucial when an Anglo fieldworker is working with a minority informant, where the situation may become a highly self-conscious one. Both fieldworker and informant occupy varying roles in the same large society, and they are highly aware of each other's presumed position in that society. This can leave a large margin for the operation of stereotypes; even more, there is a great deal of opportunity for the kind of face-to-face interaction that may lead to self-deception on both sides. The more stressful the situation—and contacts between minority members and anthropologists seeking to understand them can be quite stressful—the more likely it is that the informant may assume a role the fieldworker does not expect.

The ethnographer should always be aware of the informant as a potential performer of folklore. A full study of performance as part of the border Mexican's verbal art still is to be done, and this essay does not pretend to any definitive treatment of the subject. Stylistic devices in oral performance need to be treated in detail, while only a few can be pointed out here. It is, after all, easier to point out the existence of performances than to give sure guides for their identification in specific instances. Following Gregory Bateson and Erving Goffman, Bauman notes the presumed existence in all speech communities of "keys," or meta-communicative devices, that identify the frame within which a performance will be interpreted. In Bauman's words, "Each speech community will make use of a structured set of distinctive communicative means from among its resources in culturally conventionalized and culture-specific ways to key the performance frame, such that all communication that takes place within that frame is to be understood as performance within that community."[47] These communicative means may be classified in several different ways, but for my purposes I will subsume them in two: linguistic devices that will remain part of a recorded text and may be identified and studied away from the performance event; and paralinguistic devices, dramatic in nature, such as voice quality, gesture, and facial expression, which usually are not part of a recorded text. Also important is the context out of which the performance emerges. With Texas-Mexican performers I have observed, this would include not only the larger context—such as whether a gathering is a wake, a beer bust, or a street-corner confabulation—but also the absence or presence, arrival or departure of certain individuals, which may trigger a particular type of performance. This is particularly important to our subject, since the presence of the ethnographer may in itself serve as the stimulus for a particular performance that—depending on other factors—may be a joke, a legend, or a self-justificatory bit of autobiography.

Gary Gossen's studies of the Chamula are justly celebrated for their detailed analysis of verbal behavior.* But not all cultures are as orderly and traditional about their canons of oral performance as the Chamula. Chicanos certainly are not. One can, of course, identify well-known textual markers usually found at the beginning of certain kinds of narratives:

Joke: "Oye, saben la de. . ." (Listen, do you know the one about . . .)

Joke: "Ésa está como el que. . ." (That's like the guy who . . .)

[Both of the above are likely to be followed by "A ver, cuéntala" (Let's see; tell it) or "Ándale, échatela" (Come on, out with it) from the audience.]

Märchen: "Éste era un hombre. . ." (This was a man . . .)

Legend: "Hubo una vez un hombre en. . ." (There once was a man in . . .)

Sage: "¿Conocen a X? Dicen que una vez. . ." (Do you know X? They say that once . . .)

* See especially Gary Gossen, *Chamulas in the World of the Sun: Time and Space in a Maya Oral Tradition* (Cambridge: Harvard University Press, 1974).

The problem is that the expert joke teller will parody the styles of other genres as part of his stock-in-trade. I have recorded jokes, told at regular joke-telling sessions, using the last three examples above as conventional openings. There will also be a parody of paralinguistic markers, such as tone of voice, that go with other genres. Of course there are differences, mostly paralinguistic and contextual, that distinguish the performance of a joke from that of a *Sage.* Though paralinguistic markers are parodied, how obvious the parody is depends on the skill of the performer.

In the end, knowledge of the total context is probably the most important factor in judging the "tone" of the performance, because it is tone, as defined by critics of literature, that makes the difference: "the attitudes toward the subject and toward the audience implied in a literary work."[48] Certain kinds of tone fit certain situations, and an extremely serious tone of voice in a performance situation involving joking and wordplay is naturally suspect. Knowing something about the performer and his normal behavior is also important. An unusually serious or innocent-looking countenance on an individual obviously presages a joke. On both of these counts, unfortunately, the ethnographer is at a disadvantage: he rarely gets the chance to know individual performers for very long, and he creates his own context by his very presence. Again, it is not a simple matter always to identify a serious tone of voice or a comic tone in any particular culture or subculture. Add to this the fact that certain tones or qualities of voice (and special words or phrases as well) may identify for members of relatively small ingroups certain characters, real or fictional, and that agreed-upon attitudes toward the character being imitated will decide how the text delivered will be interpreted by those witnessing a performance.

It seems almost too obvious to mention, but the ethnographer should have some previous acquaintance with the folklore of the people he is working with. One needs to know about *curandero* belief tales, for example, in order to understand *curandero* jokes that parody the belief tales. Some characteristics of border Mexican joking behavior have been pointed out: the tendencies toward parody of serious behavior, toward the imitation and attribution of roles in narratives, toward subtlety and indirection in wordplay. But only the awareness and the observation of performances in specific settings can give one an insight into a culture's verbal art.

With legendary material and with the self-justificatory kind of performance, it is even harder to distinguish the interpretative from the literal. The ethnographer must fall back on what he is supposed to know best, a rigorous checking of his data; but first he must be aware of the need to do such checking. He must be very conscious of the informant as a potential performer. He must also keep in mind the existence of mutual stereotypes in himself and the people he is studying, what Jansen has called the esoteric-exoteric factor in folklore.[49] The informant not only has his stereotypes about the Anglo fieldworker, but he also has some very definite ideas as to what stereotypes the Anglo holds about him. Sometimes consciously, sometimes unconsciously, the informant may seek to conform to the stereotype he thinks the Anglo fieldworker has of him, rather than expressing his own attitudes and opinions. And like the Norwegian ethnographer among the Lapps, the Anglo ethnographer may be too quick to accept as genuine the informant's persona that most nearly corresponds with the ethnographer's own unstated, consciously rejected prejudices.

Part Two

The Folklore Genres:
History, Form, and Performance

— 5 —

Some Aspects of Folk Poetry

Everyone is familiar with the song called "On Top of Old Smoky." Though it is not as hallowed by tradition as, say, "Barbara Allen," most of us would agree in calling it a folksong. But let us consider a parody of "On Top of Old Smoky" that is quite popular with schoolchildren in Texas and elsewhere:

> On top of Old Smoky,
> All covered with sand,
> I shot my old teacher
> With a green rubber band.
> I shot her with pleasure,
> I shot her with pride,
> I couldn't have missed her,
> She's forty foot wide.

Now this is not the sort of thing that was collected by Francis James Child back in the nineteenth century. George Lyman Kittredge would scarcely have approved of it. But times have changed, and we folklorists have widened our horizons considerably. Such a song has great possibilities from the psychosocial point of view. Consider, for example, what it tells us about the status of the teacher in our culture. Or take the Freudian viewpoint and reflect on the eloquence of a dream situation in which a tremendously steatopygic female authority figure is the object of violence by the pupil. All of which is well and good. But suppose we note the sequence of "pleasure" and "pride," of "forty" and "foot," and express delight over the parallelistic design of the whole composition.

Some folklorists are likely to look at us with annoyance, if not downright suspicion. And if we go so far as to ask questions such as "Why *green?* Why a *green* rubber band?" somebody is apt to growl, "Whatsa matter? Trying to be literary or somethin'?"

Nobody would have insulted Kittredge by calling him literary, first because few people would have dared to try, and second because Kittredge and other folklorists of his time were literary men and proud of it. Things are different now. There are of course critics who use folklore to support generalizations made about sophisticated literature, but few folklorists approach their subject from the critic's point of view. It is true that in 1959 a distinguished folklorist, MacEdward Leach, of Pennsylvania, made a plea for the literary approach to folklore in a paper read before the Texas Folklore Society in Austin.[1] His plea does not seem to have had much effect, because two years later, at a meeting of the American Folklore Society, another distinguished folklorist was verbally assaulted by his colleagues for attempting to establish some relationships between folklore and literature. Folk verse, he was told, is meant to be useful rather than beautiful. Most of it is extremely bad by the standards of any intelligent man, while those pieces that the cultivated scholar admires as beautiful may not be considered so by the folk. We should look on folk literature—if you'll pardon the expression—merely as one of the aspects of culture.

We cannot blame the social scientists for scorning the literary approach to folklore, especially when they have done so well with their own methods of study, though we may express some concern about a new generation of folklorists teaching in departments of literature and using "literary" as a term of reproach. There is, of course, no reason why folklore should not be subjected to critical analysis. Distinguishing between better and worse is the critic's task, not that of the singer or poet. But it is one thing to say that we may apply critical principles to folk poetry and another thing to do it. Most of the condemnation of the literary type of folklorist these days is directed at the kind of approach he uses.

There was a time when existing methods of literary criticism could be fitted to the study of folk poetry without great discomfort. Folklorists were preoccupied with the origins and diffusion of songs and tales, that is to say with their "biographies." They were good literary historians. When critics insisted on turning from the poet to the poem, folklorists trained in literature found it hard to follow suit. Obviously what we need is analysis of folk poetry on its own terms rather than on those of sophisticated literature, while maintaining some common ground with modern criticism. This is the position taken by MacEdward Leach. He advocates an intrinsic study of the esthetics of folksong, naming five elements which to him distinguish folksong from sophisticated poetry: understatement, the use of formula, presentation through concreteness and specifics, translation of idea and emotion into action, and conservation as a key to selection.[2] The fifth element refers to the folksong process rather than to style, while of the other four only the use of formulas is perhaps true of all folk literature. I shall try in these remarks to pursue the matter a little further, especially in regard to language, structure, and tone in folk poetry.

It is an undeniable fact that the language of folk poetry is conventional in the extreme; yet efforts have not been wanting to prove that it is or should be the same as the language of sophisticated poetry. Consider for example a recent article by S. J. Sackett, "Simile in Folksong," in the Spring 1963 issue of *Midwest Folklore*.[3] After studying eighty-two folksongs from the Fort Hays Kansas State College folklore collection, Sackett arrives at the not-so-startling conclusion that the simile is less common in folksong than it is in sophisticated poetry. The eighty-two songs yield only twenty-six similes, only eighteen songs having any similes at all. Of these twenty-six similes, seven are found to be proverbial comparisons. On the basis of the remaining nineteen, which include examples like "gay as the flowers in May," Sackett finds enough evidence to suggest "an effort on the part of folk composers to search for unhackneyed comparisons."[4]

This, I believe, is a most unkind libel on the folk poet. If in eighty-two attempts to be original and unhackneyed he can produce only nineteen similes, he is made of poor stuff indeed. Matters are not helped by Sackett's suggestion that a better selection of folksongs would yield a higher proportion of striking similes,[5] since any folk collection made up of poems with strikingly original diction would automatically be suspect. The real value of Sackett's analysis is in proving what it attempts to disprove: that the language of serious folk poetry is highly conventional, and that it is intentionally so. This does not mean that folk diction cannot be striking or original. Take the Mexican *albur*, for example. It is a kind of poetic double-talk based on a Joycean distortion of ordinary language, the result being an ironic repartee full of double and triple meanings. But the *albur* is used for banter and insult, never for serious poetry. Imagination and ironical wit also play a part in English folk speech—in the humorous simile and the comic song. The most striking of Sackett's twenty-six similes is "as free as a pig in a pen." It comes from a humorous song, "The Lane County Bachelor," and resembles in form and spirit proverbial comparisons like "as busy as a dog full of fleas" and "as ugly as homemade sin." On the other hand, the serious songs in Sackett's collection, such as "Patonio," give us similes like "as black as a crow" and "as white as the snow."

One of the fundamental rules of folklore is that the only license it consciously allows is the license of the clown. Change and innovation do occur, but they are part of a process. The ritual dancer who uses tissue paper and old tin cans in making his traditional costume merely responds to the known, the familiar, since tin cans and tissue paper have become part of his environment. Radical departures from the norm belong to the clown, who has the license to upset the order of things. And to the folk mind the strange and the novel are incongruous and therefore laughable. We must make a distinction, then, between so-called colorful folk speech, in which there is a conscious attempt to be different if not original, and folk poetry of high seriousness, which is expressed in the ritualized language of convention. If we are aware of this formal, inherently ritual character of language in folk poetry, we will not make the mistake of condemning it as trite. It is the tone that offends us in trite language when it is used in sophisticated literature; the writer flaunts all the worn-out metaphors in our faces with the air of a man who has just invented them. Such is not the case in ceremonial or ritual language, where freshness or newness would surprise and offend. I am not arguing for the ritual origins of poetry; I merely point out that the esthetic effect of conventional language in folk poetry is much the same as it is in the conventional language of ritual.

This kind of language lends itself to subdued effects, to contrasts that would not be contrasts in other contexts. What seems at first glance a vivid flash of color may prove to be pastel against a background of whites and grays. The effect may be achieved with an adjective, as in "Jesse James":

> He was born one day in the county of Clay,
> And he came from a solitary race.

Or it may be a conventional but unexpected simile:

> They let loose the bloodhound dogs,
> They followed him from afar,
> But trying to catch Cortez
> Was like following a star.

Or unexpected action in a conventional setting:

> Lord Thomas he had a sword by his side
> As he walked about the hall;
> He cut off her head from her shoulders,
> And he kicked it against the wall.

Or it may be a seemingly pointless detail. Thus in the *romance* called "Álora la bien cercada" an unnamed Spanish commander lays siege to the city of Álora and is shot through the head by a crossbow bolt. The narrative up to this point has been swift and panoramic, but now we move up close and see Pablo lead the commander out of the fighting, while Jacobillo holds his hand. They are his foster sons, whom he took into his household as children. This kind of detail gives the scene another dimension. Ernest Hemingway uses the same technique in "The Killers" in the passage about Nick and Mrs. Bell, who is Mrs. Bell and not Mrs. Hirsch.

Effects of this sort are not so much matters of language as of pattern and structure. Formal patterns are also found in sophisticated literature, of course, but rarely are they as prominent as in folklore. Whereas the sophisticated poet may disguise his structure, folk poetry works toward very evident patterns that stand out even more starkly because the lack of vivid imagery emphasizes them. This is necessary to give a sense of form to an oral performance. Sophisticated poetry is primarily written poetry; a good part of its formal effect is visual, the arrangement of black marks upon a sheet of paper. Oral poetry, on the other hand, must achieve similar effects in other ways—with the end-stopped line, for example, which is the only line possible in folk poetry because there is no other way to show that one has come to the end of a "line" except by stopping. It is only in sophisticated poetry, with its dependence on the visual reference of the printed or written page, that one can have run-on lines. But to the unsophisticated ear such lines, even when they are neatly apportioned into iambic pentameters, will be heard as long, rhythmical utterances of varying lengths, especially if the lines are not rhymed. That is why teachers complain that some of their students cannot tell verse from prose. When folk poetry is written down, however, the repetitions, the refrains, the strong parallelistic devices that hold it together may become too monotonous to an ear that is guided by the eye.

At some point in the composition of sophisticated poetry, the poet decides on the form he will give his poem. Once he has finished the poem it is done—except for those poets who are never satisfied. The same may be true of the folk poet if his group recognizes some rigid poetic pattern, usually borrowed from sophisticated sources—the *décima,* the limerick, the sonnet. As a more general rule, though, structure and design in folk poetry are a matter of evolution, of development from relative formlessness toward form. What Albert B. Friedman says about the Anglo-American ballad may apply to most folksongs. They are "the result of a process capable of remaking to pattern verse of diverse sorts and sources, adapting it to the needs of an oral art."[6] If there does exist some dominant pattern, or patterns, toward which the form of the folksong seems to evolve, there must be a structural principle, or principles, which are so fundamentally appealing to the folk poet as to guide his creation—and even more so his re-creation—of the folk poem. It would be something more than stanza form, refrain, and incremental repetition, features that do not apply to even all Anglo-American ballads, much less to European folksong in general.

It is commonplace knowledge to students of Spanish that a basic feature of the *romance,* a narrative and lyrical folksong form, is its balanced line. In its oldest form the *romance* is a variable series of sixteen-syllable lines, all making the same assonance, with a caesura in the middle of each line:

> Rey don Sancho, rey don Sancho, ‖ no digas que no
>   te aviso
> que de dentro de Zamora ‖ un alevoso ha salido. . .

Often the eight-syllable sections will in turn be divided into four-syllable subsections, as in the first line above, "Rey don Sancho, | rey don Sancho." By the time the *romance* reaches Mexico from Spain as the *corrido* it has carried the principle of balanced lines one step further and developed an octosyllabic four-line stanza, with lines 1 and 2 balanced against each other and forming a unit which is in balance against a similar one formed by lines 3 and 4:

> Por el lado Salvatierra
> se agarraron a balazos,
> unos tiran con metralla,
> otros tiran cañonazos.

In its longer forms the Mexican *corrido* can be rambling and circumstantial, but as shorter variants develop, the same balanced pattern we see within the stanza asserts itself in the sequence and arrangement of the quatrains. In one of the shorter variants of the Texas-Mexican *corrido* "Gregorio Cortez," for example, the first four stanzas constitute the first "scene" of the narrative and are divided into two subunits of two quatrains each, covering separate actions in the first scene, the discovery of a dead sheriff and the discovery of the identity of his killer. Next comes a two-stanza unit introducing the sheriff-killing hero, Gregorio Cortez, both stanzas being speeches by Cortez and both beginning with the line "Then said Gregorio Cortez." The next unit is made up of four stanzas and shows Cortez in flight. These stanzas begin respectively with the words *venían, tiró, venían, decía* (they were coming, he struck out, they were coming, he said). Again we have a balanced arrangement, this time effecting a rhythmic change in the point of view—from pursuers to pursued, from pursuers to pursued. The *despedida*, or conventional ending, is made up of two quatrains, each beginning with the word *ya* (now): "Now they have taken Cortez," "Now with this I take my leave."* An even better example is a variant of "El corrido de José Mosqueda" collected by John A. Lomax in Brownsville in 1939. Except for the opening stanza, which is the conventional opening, the whole ballad is made up of paired quatrains complementing each other by means of rhetorical devices, similarity of subject, or other kinds of repetition.[7]

The tendency toward a balanced pattern conforms to the essentially binary structure that students of structural linguistics find in most folk

* For a more complete discussion of the pattern of "Gregorio Cortez," see Américo Paredes, *"With His Pistol in His Hand": A Border Ballad and Its Hero* (Austin: University of Texas Press, 1958), 175–240.

literature. Why this balanced binary form is essential may be still another matter. In some cases it does result from a juxtaposition of opposites, as Lévi-Strauss, Köngäs, and Maranda say.[8] But not always do we find opposites paired against each other. This is not usually the case with the proverb, one of the simplest forms of folk literature, in which the two elements may complement or be equal to each other. It should be taken into account that the subordination of some ideas to other ideas in thought, of some clauses to other clauses in language, is a mark of sophistication, while the parallel arrangement of independent clauses of equal value is more typical of the folk and primitive mind. One need only compare the style and subject matter of Ernest Hemingway to that of Henry James to appreciate the fact.

Alan Dundes defines the most familiar type of proverb as a binary structure consisting of a topic and a comment:[9]

> A stitch in time | saves nine.
> Nothing ventured, | nothing gained.
> A friend in need | is a friend indeed.

The proverb presents conventional wisdom in a neat package, while its obvious binary structure appeals to our logical sense. But proverbs also appeal to the imagination by means of such things as rhythm, metaphor, and rhyme—not only through structure but also through texture. It is the adroit fitting of texture to structure that gives proverbs their attractive and enduring characteristics. Their fundamental quality is that of a rhythmical utterance, a one-line folk poem, divided by juncture or caesura into two balanced parts.

In the oldest proverbs the pattern is isochronous:

> A stitch in time | saves nine.

As the proverb accepts newer prosodic styles, however, it makes use of meter and rhyme:

> First come, | first served.
> A friend in need | is a friend indeed.

It seems plausible to relate the balanced pattern in such an ancient and universal poetic form as the proverb to the same thing in the *romance* and the *corrido;* furthermore, the same relationship may be made with

Anglo-American folk poetry. The question whether this is a universal characteristic of folk poetry is beyond the scope of this paper, though if it could be shown to be an important feature of both English and Spanish folk poetry the matter may warrant some attention.

The British ballad in its early forms already consists of rhyming, end-stopped couplets that soon pass into the better-known ballad stanza of four lines with alternate four and three stresses. That is to say, what we have noted in the Mexican *corrido* of the nineteenth and twentieth centuries is apparent in the British ballad long before. Some of the most memorable passages in Anglo-American folksong make use of a binary form for balance and contrast:

> The first line that Sir Patrick read
> A loud laugh laughed he;
> The next line that Sir Patrick read
> The tear blinded his ee.

Here the balance is one of contrasting moods, between laughing and weeping, emphasized by the parallel form of the first and third lines. The sharecropping American Negro has applied the same pattern to his own kind of tragedy:

> The fus' time I seen de boll weevil
> He was settin' on de square;
> De next time I seen de boll weevil
> He had all his family there.

In another stanza from "Sir Patrick Spens" the contrast is one of images. The Scottish nobles that accompany Sir Patrick are so fastidious that they do not even want to wet the heels of their shoes, but before the end of the story they have had too much of water, and only their hats remain, tossed about by the sea:

> O our Scots nobles were right loath
> To wet their cork-heeled shoon,
> But lang ere a' the play were playd
> Their hats they swam aboone.

One of the most striking examples of the use of balance and contrast in American folksong occurs in the "White House Blues," which is about the assassination of President McKinley. McKinley is dead and Teddy Roosevelt is president. The time is one of mourning and expectation, quite reminiscent of recent events:

> Roosevelt's in the White House, | doing his best;
> McKinley's in the graveyard, | taking his rest.
> Roosevelt's in the White House, | drinkin' out of
>   a silver cup;
> McKinley's in the graveyard, | never waked up.

One of the most admired passages in "Sir Patrick Spens" occurs toward the end, where balance is achieved by means of parallel stanzas:

> O lang, lang may their ladies sit,
> With their fans into their hand,
> Or eir they see Sir Patrick Spence
> Come sailing to the land.
>
> O lang, lang may the ladies stand,
> With their gold combs in their hair,
> Waiting for their own dear lords,
> For they'll see them no more.

The passage is so effective that it has been suspected of being of nonfolk origin; yet it uses exactly the same technique found in *corridos* composed by *ranchero* folk on the Texas-Mexican border, in which the leave-taking stanza is repeated in exactly the same way. "Mary Hamilton" is another old British ballad that has this kind of ending, one that covers four stanzas:

> Oh little did my mother think
> The day she cradled me,
> What lands I was to travel through,
> What death I was to dee.
>
> Oh little did my father think
> The day he held up me,
> What lands I was to travel through,
> What death I was to dee.
>
> Last night I washed the queen's feet
> And gently laid her down,

> And all the thanks I've gotten the night
> To be hanged in Edinbro town.
>
> Last night there was four Maries,
> The night there'll be but three;
> There was Marie Seton, and Marie Beton
> And Marie Carmichael and me.

It is significant that these four stanzas, aside from being the source for A. E. Housman's "The Culprit," are the ones most commonly remembered in oral tradition today. The tightly structured four-stanza ending has developed into a lyric song, while the rest of the ballad is forgotten, through the same process that works in the *corrido* to produce shapely and well-balanced variants out of long and rambling ones.

Trinities abound in our mythologies, and in our folktales things always happen in threes; there are three princes, three knocks on the door, three tasks. The ternary pattern, however, disguises a binary structure. The third time is always the charm; the two older brothers fail, the youngest succeeds. This can also be seen in the uses of threes in the folk poem:

> Some put on the gay green robes,
> And some put on the brown,
> But Janet put on the scarlet robes
> To shine foremost through the town.
>
> First time she shot him, he staggered,
> Next time she shot him, he fell;
> Third time she shot him, oh Lordy,
> There was a new man's face in hell.

The American "Riddle Song" is an example of the superimposition of a ternary pattern on a binary structure, reproducing in three highly repetitive stanzas the situation in which a riddle is posed. If one reads the first lines in succession, then the second lines and so on, the result is a curiously catechetical effect:

> I gave my love a cherry without any stone.
> How can there be a cherry without any stone?
> A cherry in the blossom has no stone.

I gave my love a chicken without any bone.
How can there be a chicken without any bone?
A chicken when it's pippin' has no bone.

One of the most structurally perfect folksongs in English is the American variant of "The Maid Freed from the Gallows," quoted by Kittredge in his introduction to the compendium of Child's *English and Scottish Ballads*.[10] Kittredge calls attention to the "inevitableness in both structure and diction" of this variant, though he prefers to believe that it is a survival from a ballad Golden Age rather than a development of the ballad process. The poem is made up of twelve stanzas in four three-stanza groups. Each group of three stanzas has the pattern of the "Riddle Song"—exposition, question, and answer. The structure of each group is binary: hanging is delayed to ask a question; | question is answered. Each stanza in the three-stanza unit has a set and balanced form: (1) Hold your hand, hangman; | someone is coming. (2) Have you come to help me? | Have you come to see me hang? (3) I have (not) come to help you; | I have (not) come to see you hang. The pattern of the whole poem consists of four units, but the structure is again binary. The first three units repeat the same situation: a succession of relatives will not or cannot save the maid from the gallows. In the last unit the erotic partner arrives and saves her. Repetition is so important a device that only thirty-eight different words are used in the whole composition, and this is counting such words as "the" and "o," and considering "come" and "coming" as two separate words. Of these thirty-eight words, thirty-two appear for the first time in the first two stanzas. Small wonder that a discerning critic like Kittredge chose this ballad for comment, though his comments lamentably enough were about the communal origins of poetry.

Kittredge was a Shakespearean scholar. One should expect him to point out the similarity in the general form of "The Maid Freed from the Gallows" and some of Shakespeare's sonnets, Sonnet 73 for example. This sonnet also consists of four distinct units, three quatrains and a couplet. The first three units repeat the same situation, the poet's statement that he is old. The last unit, the couplet, supplies the second leg to a binary structure. Kittredge, however, was too intent on showing that the ballad achieves its most typical effects through incremental repetition. But the repetition in the first three units of "The Maid Freed from the Gallows" is not incremental. That of Sonnet 73—a repetition of images—is more truly so.

It is the differences between Sonnet 73 and "The Maid Freed from the Gallows" that should interest us most. In the sonnet a poet's mind has selected both form and structure before or during the act of creation. It is true that in the choosing of the sonnet form and even in the choice of theme, he was following literary conventions, but his was a conscious choice. At all events, form is but one element in the poet's creation; it is the images, the arrangement of sounds, the whole texture which make the sonnet memorable. In "The Maid Freed from the Gallows" structure was dictated by some unknown poet's choice of theme, the traditional and almost universal contrasting of the blood relations against the erotic partner. Form, however, has been a matter of development. Continental variants of this same ballad, notably those of southern Europe, go into much detail to explain the heroine's plight. She has been captured by pirates and is being held for ransom. British-American variants have dropped everything except the central dialogue and substituted a judge or hangman for the pirates. Even so, not all variants in British-American tradition have the shapeliness of the one quoted by Kittredge. In that very successful variant, form and structure are almost everything. It is a triumph of the folk style, an almost complete subordination of language to form.

Conventional diction and a strongly parallelistic design founded on a binary structure give form and an illusion of permanence to a poetry that disappears as each word is spoken or sung. Underlying the folk poetic style one can see a dominant pattern—the balance of hemistich against hemistich, line against line, stanza against stanza, section against section—this being the chief formative influence in the development of the folk poem in oral tradition, one that we can see in the simplest type of folk poetry, the proverb, and that is characteristic of primitive song as well.

One thing remains to be said, that folk poetry is performed; it is chanted or sung. Because it is a performance, and one of a very particular type, the complete context of a folk poem is not taken into account without a consideration of three factors contributed by the performance itself. One is the influence of the chant or song on both rhythm and diction, an element separate from the purely musical dimension. Lines that look rough or unrhythmical on paper may not be so when they are chanted or sung, while the most singable lines are not necessarily the most readable ones.

Then there is the context in which a folk poem is performed. Folksong expresses group feelings and attitudes that are natural and implicit in their own milieu. Torn out of its natural context, folk poetry loses a good deal of its emotional and esthetic impact. But plays are also performances, yet we study them as literature. Nor can we ever hope to reproduce the cultural milieu of an eighteenth-century play, for example, or a seventeenth-century masque. We may say this, however: that the presentation of a folk poem as recorded literature, devoid of its original context, is more genuine than its presentation in a hootenanny—or even a folklore society singsong—where it is surrounded by an artificially created atmosphere. It is important, though, that when we *read* folk poetry we keep in mind one of the simplest observations made by dramatic criticism: some pieces are good reading, others are good theater; and it is a happy occurrence when we find one that is both.

Finally, there is the performer himself. He is an actor, a personality. In the comic song he may play the clown. In the folksong of high seriousness he will be serious; he will take a detached attitude toward himself as performer. But he is far from detached in respect to his subject. On the contrary, it is a supreme involvement that gives him the intense style that is often called impersonality. This is the performer's contribution to the tone of the folk poem, there being no more reason to interpret his seriousness as impersonality than there is to say that an actor in a play is impersonal because he uses restraint instead of hamming up his part. Yet, no matter how he submerges himself in his part, the performer will be effective to the extent that he is a personality in his own right.

Here of course is a fundamental difference between folk and sophisticated literature. Folk literature is always a vehicle for the performer, who supplies a feeling of immediacy—of passion and power—through his own performance. This is another reason why folk literature has never felt the need for the striking or the original. It is when written literature gets farther and farther away from the spoken word that we must invent devices to hold the reader's attention, to excite his emotions and his imagination, all with those little black marks upon a piece of paper. In fiction we move toward new narrative techniques, seeking to gain the sense of immediacy that was lost when the written word took the place of the living narrator, who acted as well as narrated. One may note, in passing, that at least one modern writer of fiction, William Faulkner, has attempted to capture the vividness of the oral narrator directly on the printed page, and much more successfully than authors of first-person narrator stories like Ring Lardner's "Haircut." In sophisticated poetry, on the other hand, the tendency is toward more and more subtle and individualized modes of expression once poetry has ceased to be performance and has become an act of private communication between poet and reader. In folk poetry, not only does the performer have the task of bringing the "part" assigned him to temporary life, but he can re-create the text at will. In the end, it is the performer who is the poet—for the brief moment that he performs.

- 6 -

The Mexican *Corrido:* Its Rise and Fall

It was the *corrido* of the Revolution that turned Mexican students to the collection and study of ballads. Except for brief mention in earlier works, Mexican interest in balladry began in the 1920s, toward the end of the revolutionary period. Most significant works on the subject appeared during the 1930s, though collection of *romance* survivals in America had been done before 1910 by Aurelio Espinosa in New Mexico, by Vicuña Cifuentes in Chile, and by Menéndez Pidal in Spain.

The obvious *romance* ancestry of the *corrido* led students to overestimate the antiquity of the Mexican form, as well as its predominance as a uniform ballad type. At first an unbroken line was seen between the *romances* of epic themes and the heroic *corridos* of the Mexican Revolution.

The *conquistadores* had arrived in Mexico when the *romance* tradition was still strong in Spain, bringing the *romance corrido* with them, and thirty years after the conquest the Indians were composing *romance*-like ballads of their own. Two hundred years after the arrival of Hernán Cortés, in 1745, the colonization of Florida had been celebrated in *romances corridos,* evidence of the persistence of the *romance* tradition in New Spain. Then, with the war for independence, the *corrido* had emerged as a truly native form—speaking for the Mexican rural folk, singing of victories and defeats in the struggle against the Spanish Crown.

But the war with the United States produced a sudden break. The attempts to oust Santa Anna after the American war, the War of Reform, and the French occupation produced no *corridos* which survived. The epic tradition ended, and the only *corridos* which people were singing in 1910 were broadsides about thieves and outlaws. With the Revolution the *corrido* again sprang into life and entered its second and its best epic period.

This theory about the antiquity of the Mexican *corrido* left some important questions unanswered, especially regarding the material collected in what had once been the frontier regions of New Spain: New Mexico, California, and the Lower Texas-Mexican Border—the old Spanish province of Nuevo Santander.

One question was the validity of the ballad hiatus supposed to have occurred after the war with the United States. Another was why the Lower Border *corrido* was in the ascendant during the period from 1850 to 1910 while in adjacent areas of Greater Mexico the *corrido* at this same time was supposed to have been at its lowest ebb. Still another question was why the *corrido* had not migrated into the frontier outposts in early colonial days, or why the *romance* tradition did not flower into the *corrido* in the provinces—in New Mexico especially, where the *romance* tradition flourished until very recent times.

Héctor Pérez Martínez explained the hiatus as the result of the shock of defeat and occupation during the American war, followed closely afterward by the French occupation—these events wiping away the memory of the heroic songs of the war for independence and stifling the ballad habit in the Mexican people.[1] Pérez Martínez's theory does not seem tenable if one considers that a folk may compose its best ballads in defeat. The Scots made ballads about the reverses they suffered at the hands of the English; on the Rio Grande, Mexican folk groups made *corridos* about their conflict with the victors of the War of 1846. Mexican ballad students themselves believed that the Indians had begun to compose ballads thirty years after their conquest by the Spaniards.

Nor was there a satisfactory explanation for the relative recency of the *corrido* in the frontier balladries. In New Mexico the *corrido* never was an important native form, most of the better *corridos* collected in that area being Greater Mexican importations. The *décima* and the *verso* were the dominant forms, while the old Spanish *romances* were preserved. Some New Mexican scholars attempted to answer the question by overemphasizing New Mexico's cultural and physical isolation from Greater Mexico. When New Mexico was settled toward the end of the sixteenth century by Spaniards, the argument went, the *romance* and the *décima* had not given way to the Mexican *corrido*. After its settlement New Mexico remained isolated from the rest of New Spain, thus remaining "Spanish," as could be seen by the predominance of the *décima* and the *romance* in its balladry.

That New Mexican isolation from Mexico has been greatly exaggerated is recognized by Arthur L. Campa in his *Spanish Folk-Poetry in New Mexico.*[2] The emphasis on the "Spanish" character of New Mexico is relatively recent, obviously a reaction against Anglo-American prejudice toward the term "Mexican." Some other explanation was needed for the lack of a *corrido* tradition in New Mexico.

The biggest question, however, was posed by the Lower Texas-Mexican Border, where a local *corrido* tradition did develop. The *corrido* could be relatively recent in New Mexico because of earlier isolation from Mexico. One could suppose a *corrido* hiatus in Greater Mexico between 1848 and 1910. But the Lower Border *corrido*, flourishing during the supposed Greater Mexican hiatus, should have had an unbroken tradition stretching back to colonial times. The Rio Grande settlements were founded in 1749. If *corrido*-like *romances* were being composed and sung throughout New Spain in 1745, the *corrido* should have arrived on the Lower Rio Grande with the first settlers.

But such is not the case. As one works back along the chronology of the Texas-Mexican *corrido*, one begins to lose sight of it in the 1860s. It is not the individual *corrido* that is lost when one goes back to the early 1850s, but the *corrido* tradition itself. I have collected *corridos* along the Rio Grande from men born in the 1860s and talked to other people of their approximate age. Persons born in the 1860s and 1870s learned their *corridos* when they appeared (when the informants were children), or from older men of their own generation. They learned no *corridos* from their fathers or their grandfathers. Their answer to the question whether they learned *corridos* from the preceding generations invariably has been, "People sang *décimas* in those days."

In his monumental study on the music of the *corrido*, published in 1939, Vicente T. Mendoza, Mexico's foremost ballad authority, was of the opinion that the *corrido* went back to the earliest Spanish times.[3] Coming back to the *corrido* in 1954, after a study of the *décima*, Professor Mendoza redefines his position as to the *corrido*'s age. The *corrido* as we

know it, he says, is a relatively modern form.[4] What students had identified as *corridos* of the seventeenth, eighteenth, and early nineteenth
centuries were compositions in other forms. "The informative press of
the people . . . during the whole of the first part of the last [nineteenth]
century," Mendoza goes on to say, was the *décima*.[5] He defines the effective life span of the Mexican *corrido* as fifty years, from 1880 to 1930.
The *corrido,* as an independent form in Mexico, falls into three distinct
stages: a period of ascent from 1875 to 1910 (during which time the ballad
heroes are Robin Hood–like outlaws in rebellion against Porfirio Díaz);
a culminating period from 1910 to 1930 (the epic period of the Revolution); and a period of decadence from 1930 to the present.

Mendoza's revised views on the *corrido,* applied to the evidence collected by other ballad students, make possible a clearer picture of the
history not only of Greater Mexican balladry but of the related balladries
of California, New Mexico, and the Lower Rio Grande. The rise and fall
of the *corrido* among the more important folk groups of Mexican culture
can be traced with much more certainty, even though some questions
still remain without an answer.

IN ITS EPIC PERIOD IN SPAIN the *romance* was sung to a sixteen-syllable
line, all lines making the same assonance for long passages, in the manner of the epic poem. Later the line was broken into octosyllables, and
still later into rhymed octosyllabic quatrains with a refrain taken from
the dance lyric. The *romance* without refrain continued to be sung, especially in Andalusia, where it was called the *romance corrido*—that is, a *romance* sung straight through, rapidly and simply. It was in its refrainless
form that the *romance* seems to have come to America in greatest numbers. Gradually *corrido* became a noun instead of an adjective and the
Spanish-American name for the *romance.* In Chile, for example, Vicuña
Cifuentes published in 1912 Spanish broadside *romances* collected from
oral tradition, which the Chilean people who sang them called *corridos.*[6]

In New Spain the *romance* appears to have arrived with the first Spaniards. It was carried up into New Mexico, and later to California and the
Lower Rio Grande colony of Nuevo Santander. Those preserved the best
were *romances* on universal or novelesque themes—about unfaithful
wives, incestuous fathers, stupid shepherds, and fabulous lands. There is

some evidence, however, that a few heroic *romances* were sung until recent times, perhaps until the rise of the true *corrido* among peoples of Mexican culture.

The *romances corridos* underwent more changes in New Spain than they appear to have suffered in Chile, if Vicuña Cifuentes's collection is a fair indication of the Chilean type. In form the *romance corrido* of New Spain became less like the Spanish *romance vulgar* and more like the modern *corrido*. The subjects were preserved, but names, language, and settings were Mexicanized. These changes probably took place early, as the language and the habits of New Spain changed in response to local conditions.

Thus it seems that the people of New Spain, the future Mexicans, very early created their *corrido* form. But they did not use it, as far as one can tell, in new ballads of their own for a long time to come. The picture of the *conquistadores* making *romances* about their conquests in between battles with the Aztecs must be radically modified. The men of Hernán Cortés must have sung the *romances* that were popular at the time. But it is doubtful that they composed any *romances* of their own or preferred the *romance* over other current forms. Early examples of Spanish verse written in Mexico are most often *quintillas, redondillas,* or *décimas.* Some broadside *romances* were written in Mexico City in imitation of the eighteenth-century Spanish broadside, the *romance vulgar.* But the popular colonial songs dealing with crimes and other sensational events were neither *romances* nor *corridos* but *coplas,* satirical stanzas in a form that commented on rather than told about events.

The Mexican folksong for a long time lacked a narrative turn of mind. The Mexican's tendency toward lyric sadness or biting satire has been explained as the result of social conditions.[7] It is true that except for isolated areas colonial Mexico was a land of extreme class differences. The corruption of colonial governments led to cynicism among all classes. Nor did the situation change much with independence, which brought its continual coups d'état and generals like Iturbide and Santa Anna, who switched sides and ideologies when it suited them. Even heroic events were treated in lyric *coplas* or satirical verse. Calleja, the grim royalist general who was heroically resisted in the siege of Cuautla, is remembered in *coplas* like the following:

Ya viene Calleja	Calleja is coming
con sus batallones,	with all his battalions,
agarrando viejas	seizing old women
por los callejones.	he meets in the alleys.

These were the first native Mexican ballads, it would appear. Behind the satire there is interest in events which were of significance to the whole population.

But already by Calleja's time another form was achieving hegemony over Mexican balladry. On the eve of his execution in 1811, the patriot Hidalgo wrote two *décimas* on the wall of his cell with a piece of charcoal.[8] The *décima*, a stanza of ten octosyllables with a rhyme scheme which usually is *abbaaccddc* (*décima espinela*), is found as a dominant native folk form in Spanish America from New Mexico to Argentina, from the Pacific coast to the Antilles. It now seems evident that the *décima* also was the dominant ballad form in Greater Mexico and on the Lower Rio Grande before the *corrido* superseded it.

The custom of glossing Christmas carols (*villancicos*) existed in Spain before the sixteenth century. Often these glosses were in *quintillas*, five-line stanzas. The Huastecan *trovo* of the Mexican hot lands still uses the five-line stanza as a gloss.[9] Manuel and Dora Zárate are of the opinion that the *décima* was being used by the Spanish folk before it was introduced into court in the sixteenth century, or that it was sometimes found in the form of two fused *quintillas*.[10]

In any event, the *décima* was introduced into court in the sixteenth century by Vicente Espinel, principally as a gloss for *redondillas*. It gained wide acceptance among literary men both in Spain and in America. By 1553 the University of Mexico, the viceroys, and the Church were fostering the glossed *décima* among the cultured of New Spain by means of prizes and competitions. By 1583 religious verse in the *décima* was being directed by the missionaries at the Indians. By mid-eighteenth century the *décima* was in common use in Mexico City, especially for political satire. By the end of that century there were men known as *decimeros*, popular makers and singers of *décimas*. The War of Reform and the French invasion (1858–1867) were celebrated by *decimeros*, the most widely known of whom was blind Pascual Mauleón, an Imperialist.[11]

Crimes and wonders formed a great part of the *décima*'s subject matter. The *copla*'s tendency toward satire and commentary was continued, fostered by the nature of the gloss itself, which is a commentary on the *redondilla*. There were brief flashes, however, in which the *decimeros* caught the heroic spirit that the *guitarreros* later would give to the *corrido*. These occasions took place not in connection with the petty squabbles between generals but during times of foreign invasion. The *décimas* about Jarauta, the fighting priest who was a guerrilla against Scott's forces and who was executed because he refused to recognize the Treaty of Guadalupe, are more purely narrative than most others of their time. Jarauta himself is cast in the pattern of the *corrido* hero. He reminds one of *corrido* heroes like the Greater Mexican Benjamín Argumedo and the Lower Border Gregorio Cortez.

The Mexican victory over the French at Puebla produced some *décimas* which among the chaff of commentary contain little hard grains of heroic narrative.

¡Adentro los escuadrones!	In with the squadrons!
¡Machetazos de a montones!	Pile on the machete strokes!
¡De frente, carabineros!	Forward, fusileers!
En seguida los lanceros. . .	And let the lancers follow . . .
¡Fuego nutrido! y ¡En guardia!	Heavy firing and on guard!
Qué batalla tan preciosa. . .[12]	Oh, what a beautiful battle . . .

Professor Mendoza, whose *La décima en México* is a definitive work on the printed *décima*, tells us almost nothing about the purely oral form among people of Mexican culture. But the works in *décimas* of Luis Inclán, the *charro* novelist and poet of the 1860s, indicate that in rural areas of Greater Mexico *rancheros* were celebrating their horse races and their roundups in *décimas*, as were the country folk in New Mexico, on the Lower Rio Grande, in Cuba, in Panama, and in Argentina.* Thus, for a period covering at least a century, the *décima* was the dominant ballad form among widely separated folk groups of Spanish America. Then, during the latter half of the nineteenth century, the Mexican *corrido* usurps the hegemony of the *décima*.

Mendoza believes that in Greater Mexico the *corrido* begins as a definitely individual form during the 1880s.[13] But before 1880 there were

* See, for example, Inclán's *Recuerdos del Chamberín* (1860) and *El capadero en la hacienda de Ayala* (1872), reprinted in Luis Inclán, *El libro de las charrerías* (Mexico City: Librería de Porrúa, 1940), 67–140, 141–172.

some signs of its emergence. The *décimas* about Jarauta had the spirit of the *corrido*. The War of Reform (1858–1860), with its basic issues of religion and social betterment, produced *corrido*-like songs. One, written from the point of view of the *cristeros* (soldiers of Christ), contains the following stanza:

Ese tuerto de Salcedo,	That Salcedo, the one-eyed,
con su infantería lucida,	with his brilliant infantry,
iba flanqueando la izquierda	came flanking us on the left,
para quitarnos la vida.[14]	to kill us all.

The Liberal side produced a ballad that is almost a *corrido*. It comes from Durango, one of the northern states, and was published by Vázquez Santa Ana as "El corrido norteño" (The Northern *Corrido*), apparently Vázquez's own title.[15] The "Corrido norteño" still uses the *redondilla* and is full of literary bric-a-brac. At times, however, it sounds like a true *corrido*. It even has the beginnings of the *corrido* formal opening:

Amigos, voy a contar	Friends, I am going to tell
una horrible desventura. . .	of a horrible misfortune . . .

One of its interior stanzas could have served as *despedida* or formal close:

¡Adiós, chaparral florido	Farewell, flowery chaparral
de la hacienda de Avilés!	of the Avilés hacienda!
donde peleó Regalado	where Regalado fought
con rifles de diez y seis.	with number-sixteen rifles.

The French occupation gave the Mexican people a number of popular heroes in the guerrilla leaders who fought the occupying forces. The end of the war found Mexico filled with independent-minded local chieftains, many of whom had descended into banditry. In their bandit-hunting expeditions, Porfirio Díaz's *rurales* committed outrages against the humble village folk. On the whole, the condition of the peon worsened under Díaz. It was the men who took to the hills to escape Díaz's repressive measures who furnished the first heroes for the Greater Mexican *corrido*.

Class distinctions, however, were extremely strong, and the Díaz economy drew class lines even sharper. Most of the "better" people wanted peace and order at any price, especially if someone else paid the price. So it was the rebellious peon, the transported Indian, and the city *lépero* who swelled the ranks of the outlaw bands, and the Mexican *corrido* began not with a heroic period but with a proletarian one. The first *corrido* heroes rob the rich and give to the poor, showing their class-conscious origins. In them, however, are the seeds of the Greater Mexican heroic period.

The *corrido* must have begun in the rural areas and then moved to the broadside printing shops. As far as one can tell, the best of the Greater Mexican *corridos* of the proletarian period come from the provinces and were collected from oral tradition. Such are "Lucas Gutiérrez" from Jalisco, "Demetrio Jáuregui" from the Bajío region of central Mexico, "Heraclio Bernal" from Durango, and "Rivera" from the Lower Border fringe area of southern Tamaulipas and Nuevo León.

The Mexican broadside press seems to have turned toward the *corrido* at the end of the century. At first *redondillas* were used to continue a ballad begun in *décimas*. Then the *corrido* form appeared, though even some of the early revolutionary broadside ballads were in *décimas*. The influence of the *décima* remained in the broadside *corrido* as a tendency to comment on events rather than to tell about them. The broadside press concentrated on broadside themes, of course—wonders, sensational crimes, and the like. When it treated the bandit or the insurrectionist it indulged either in extreme sentimentality or in condemnation expressed in particularly pejorative terms:

Parra ha pasado a la historia,	Parra has passed into history;
su tragedia ha sido triste,	his tragedy has been sad;
la sociedad ha ganado	it is a gain to society
que ese vándalo no existe.[16]	that this vandal no longer exists.

After 1910 (particularly after 1913, when the assassination of Madero plunged the country into general civil war), the epic period of the Greater Mexican *corrido* began. The old system crumbled, and Mexicans were divided into partisan factions in which class distinctions did not count. They became for two decades what the medieval Castilians were for generations—a warring folk in whom loyalty was seen as loyalty to a personal leader and rank was something achieved by bravery rather than by influence or birth. Broadside balladeers in the cities and rural *guitarreros* became absorbed in the same themes; their productions became less distinguishable from each other. Some ballads appear to have had a *guitarrero* origin, while others apparently were broadsides first and then were transformed through oral transmission.

With the revolutionary *corridos* the ballad tradition of Greater Mexico reaches its peak. In the best of them a comparison with the *romance* is justified in the compact drama of the narrative and in the epic tone. These "robust and sounding verses," as Pérez Martínez calls them,[17] contain the spirit of the revolutionary wars in greater measure than do satirical war songs like "La cucaracha" or sentimental lyrics like "La Adelita," both of which antedate the Revolution in any case. The figure of Pancho Villa weeping for his Adelita owes a great deal to literate sources. The Mexican folk have seen Villa, who is one of the principal figures of the revolutionary *corrido*, in the way he is seen in "La toma de Zacatecas." Here he resembles the epic hero who rides up and down before the drawn armies, challenging the enemy champions to single combat:

Gritaba Francisco Villa:	Francisco Villa shouted,
—¿Dónde te hallas, Argumedo?	"Where are you found, Argumedo?
¿Por qué no sales al frente,	Why are you not in the van,
tú que nunca tienes miedo?—	you who never are afraid?"

The value of the *corrido* had scarcely been recognized when various forms of pseudo-*corridos* appeared. Poets wrote local-color pieces in the *corrido* style, and musicians used *corrido* melodies as themes for their compositions. Some, hoping to do for the *corrido* what the Golden Age poets had done for the *romance,* produced verses that imitated both and had the spirit of neither. Those closer to tradition actually wrote some *corridos eruditos* about events that had happened twenty-five, seventy-five, or a hundred years before.* The *corrido* also lent itself to political propaganda.

After 1930, when Mexico's Tin Pan Alley took over the *corrido,* its decay was inevitable. At first radio and the movies employed folksingers and composers, and Mexican popular music had a brief golden age. But soon the demand for more and more new songs wore the folk material

---

* See, for example, "La toma de Papantla" in Vicente T. Mendoza, *El corrido mexicano* (Mexico City: Fondo de Cultura Económica, 1954), 34.

thin. A type of song was developed that is to the true *corrido* what American hillbilly music is to the British folk ballad. Perhaps the ultimate was reached when Mexico's double-barreled answer to Gene Autry and Frank Sinatra, the late Pedro Infante, groaned a pseudo-*corrido* into a microphone while a bevy of Mexican bobby-soxers squealed in ecstasy.

But the folk *corrido* has not completely disappeared. Phonograph record companies, which recorded much traditional music in the past decades, have helped keep it alive. Columbia's Mexican catalogue for May 1957, for example, has a large number of traditional *corridos* on its record lists, along with the currently popular pseudo-*corridos*.

So can one trace the rise and fall of the Mexican *corrido,* a form distinct from the *romance* or the *romance corrido,* though descended from them, a form peculiar to folk groups of Mexican culture. There are certain things that the history of the Greater Mexican *corrido* can tell us about the folk balladries of the Spanish-speaking groups in what is now the southwestern United States. For one thing, it is evident that there has been a much closer cultural relationship between Greater Mexico and the Spanish-speaking Southwest than was thought by earlier ballad scholars. The presence of the *romance,* the *copla,* and the *décima* in New Mexico and California (and the absence of the *corrido*), instead of showing a particularly "Spanish" culture in those areas, and their complete isolation from Greater Mexico, indicates on the contrary that before the war between Mexico and the United States the frontier colonies formed part of a Spanish-speaking ballad tradition that not only embraced Greater Mexico but the rest of Spanish America as well. This was a folk tradition in which the *décima* and the *copla* were the dominant native forms and the *romance* was handed down from European tradition. Isolation does not occur until the Southwest becomes American territory. The *corrido* appears in Mexico after this time.

That brings us to the phenomenon of the *corrido* itself, its almost sudden appearance and its rise to hegemony over other ballad forms. It has been noted that the best *corridos* of the Greater Mexican proletarian period came from the provinces. It should also be noted that the Lower Rio Grande area (the region now half in Mexico and half in Texas that once was the Spanish province of Nuevo Santander) was producing *corridos* of its own at the very beginning of the Greater Mexican *corrido* period. Where did the *corrido* begin its ascent, then? In Michoacán, as

Professor Mendoza suggested in *El romance español y el corrido mexicano*? In Durango, in Jalisco, or in Texas?

The oldest Texas-Mexican *corrido* preserved in a complete form is "El corrido de Kiansis," about the early cattle drives from South Texas to Kansas. It dates from the late 1860s or early 1870s, a decade before the rise of the true *corrido* in Greater Mexico. As "El corrido de los quinientos novillos" (The *Corrido* of the Five Hundred Steers), this Texas-Mexican ballad has been collected by Mendoza not only in the northern Mexican state of Chihuahua, but as far south as the state of Hidalgo. "El corrido de Kiansis" appears to be the oldest *corrido* published in Mendoza's *El corrido mexicano.*

It is the Revolution that impels the rise of the *corrido* in Greater Mexico. The first stirrings of revolt against Díaz in the 1880s bring about the first outlaw *corridos* of Greater Mexico, but it is not until 1910, with the outbreak of general revolt, that the epic period of Greater Mexican balladry begins.

Border conflict, a cultural clash between Mexican and American, gives rise to the Texas-Mexican *corrido*. The Lower Border produces its first *corrido* hero, Juan Nepomuceno Cortina, in the late 1850s. By 1901, ten years before the beginning of the epic period of Greater Mexican balladry, the heroic tradition is fully developed in the Rio Grande area in such ballads as "El corrido de Gregorio Cortez."

Professor Mendoza has suggested that the *corrido* began in musical Michoacán and spread from central Mexico to other folk groups of Mexican origin, carried by the *michoacanos* themselves, who have traveled all over Mexico and into the United States as *braceros*. From the evidence at hand, however, it is more plausible to believe that the *michoacanos* got the *corrido* from somewhere else, though they have enriched the music of the *corrido* through their undeniable genius. The same thing has happened in the history of European balladry; a musical, dancing people takes a simple narrative-song tradition and transforms it, the result being a kind of ballad that may sometimes be danced, a ballad with a refrain. In this respect it is interesting that the *corrido* with refrain is almost unknown on the Rio Grande, while it is pretty common in central Mexico.

That the Mexican *corrido* went through its first stages on the Lower Rio Grande Border—under the impulse of border conflict—is a thesis that could never be definitely proved. But it is one that is worthy of consideration. It has been noted that the Mexican *corrido* is a form with individual characteristics. Special conditions bring it forth out of a continent-wide tradition in which the *décima* and the *copla* were the dominant ballad forms. It would be little short of wonderful if the *corrido* had suddenly come into being at two different places and two different times. Either the Lower Border *corrido* owes its existence to the Greater Mexican form, or the Greater Mexican *corrido* is indebted to the more localized Texas-Mexican ballad. Until true *corridos* are collected in Greater Mexico that go back farther than Cortina's raid on Brownsville and the cattle drives to Kansas, the theory that the development of the Greater Mexican *corrido* has been influenced by Texas-Mexican balladry is a plausible one.

~ 7 ~

The Concept of the Emotional Core Applied to the Mexican *Corrido* "Benjamín Argumedo"

W<small>HEN THE STUDY OF FOLK POETRY</small> still retained traces of literary romanticism, scholarly fashion was to prize the shorter and more highly structured variants of ballads as the oldest—the original ones—while long and detailed versions were dismissed as vulgar redactions done by contemporary minstrels, blind singers, and other specialists in folksong who plied their trade in public places. Especially valued as survivals of a mythopoeic past were folksongs composed almost exclusively in dialogue, which in a few stanzas vividly depict a dramatic situation or imply a narrative without actually telling it.

Favorite examples in British balladry were "Lord Randal," "Edward," and "The Maid Freed from the Gallows," numbers 12, 13, and 95 in the Child collection.[1] In the Spanish *romancero*, texts like "El conde Arnaldos" seemed to exemplify the true and original form of the folk ballad. It did not matter that among other peoples the same songs told much more complete stories. Such for example was the Sicilian "Scibilia Nobili," which showed similarities to both "El conde Arnaldos" and "The Maid Freed from the Gallows." Also known was a more complete version of "El conde Arnaldos," which had been collected from Sephardic Jews in Tangiers.* But these were seen as recent re-creations, attempts to explain the unexplainable.

These notions were part of a theory of communal creation of the earliest ballads by a "dancing, singing throng." In his introduction to a

---

* See no. 143 in Ramón Menéndez Pidal, "Catálogo del romancero judío-español," *Cultura Española* 4 (1906): 1045–1077; and 5 (1907): 161–199. For "Scibilia Nobili" see Francis James Child, *The English and Scottish Popular Ballads,* vol. 2 (Boston: Houghton Mifflin, 1886), 346–347.

compendium of Child's *English and Scottish Popular Ballads*, George Lyman Kittredge lent his great prestige as a scholar to this point of view, using "The Maid Freed from the Gallows" as an example of communal creation, offering it as "a survival of an archaic type-specimen, in full vigor of traditional life, at a very late date."[2] Francis B. Gummere, the most ardent proponent of the "dancing, singing throng" theory, eagerly accepted Kittredge's dictum, remarking that in the example offered by Kittredge "one can really think himself with the earliest ballad-makers."[3] Longer, more circumstantial versions of ballads, being sung by contemporary folksingers, were harshly condemned as degenerate redactions done by incompetent, if not frankly dishonest, men. Kittredge's remarks about James Rankin, a blind singer who served as principal informant for Peter Buchan's *Ancient Ballads and Songs of the North of Scotland* (1828), is example enough. Kittredge calls Rankin a liar "who seems to have been paid by the yard, and who found his honest patron an easy man to cajole." Rankin's ballads have traditional origins, but "they are almost always the longest versions known, padded with superfluous details (often silly beyond expression), tricked out with pinchbeck finery, and thoroughly vulgarized in style and spirit."[4]

Scholars of the Spanish *romance* took a different view. As early as 1844, G. B. Depping in his *Romancero castellano* concluded that longer versions of *romances* were older than the shorter ones. Minstrels, in his opinion, jealously guarded their repertoires from their rivals. The latter could learn from an experienced minstrel only by hearing him sing. As a result, they learned only the most memorable parts of what they heard and made their own versions of what they had learned.[5] In 1939, William J. Entwistle, professor of Spanish studies at Oxford, praised "El conde Arnaldos," calling it the flower of the *romancero*, but he identified it as part of a much longer narrative song (probably the Sephardic version). "The charm of *Count Arnaldos*," Entwistle says, "is produced by a most fortunate forgetfulness." Depping's apprentice minstrels would not have called the forgetfulness fortunate, since they would have wanted to sing as complete a narrative as possible. But one can agree with Entwistle that "the cut . . . has added just that salt of lyrical emotion which is needed to make the perfect ballad; for though we have defined ballads as narratives, yet such narratives only reach exquisiteness when they have this lyrical touch."[6]

A year before Entwistle's *European Balladry* appeared, however, Ramón Menéndez Pidal, the most distinguished of Spanish ballad scholars, published a little book called *Flor nueva de romances viejos*. Though published in 1938, according to the author the book had been written several years before. Menéndez Pidal also discusses "El conde Arnaldos," among other shortened *romances*. But to him the "fragmentation," as he calls it, is not caused by forgetfulness—either fortunate or unfortunate. To him fragmentation in the *romancero* is the result of an esthetic process, which in a *romance* like "El conde Arnaldos" becomes "a truly poetic creation."[7]

In the United States the theory of communal origins of the ballad did not die easily. We cannot go into what North American folklorist D. K. Wilgus has called the "Ballad Wars," but his work *Anglo-American Folksong Scholarship since 1898* is recommended to the reader of English.[8] By the 1930s, however, the proponents of communal origins of the ballad were in retreat. Chief among their opponents was Phillips Barry, who maintained that each variant of a folksong was part of a process that could create short versions of esthetic value out of long pedestrian texts. His viewpoint differs from that of Menéndez Pidal in that Barry saw ballad change arising not from a one-time editing but from a continual process involving re-creation by individual singers. Given sufficient time, folksongs of North American origins could develop the traits that distinguished the best folksongs of Europe.

But Barry's examples, though presenting plausible evidence that ballads go through a process of change, are inadequate in supporting the argument that lyrico-dramatic songs such as "Edward" or "The Maid Freed from the Gallows" could develop from long narratives in North American folksongs. Such a song as the American "Bury Me Not on the Lone Prairie" is not so much a development from the English "The Ocean Burial" as a parody or imitation of it. Meanwhile, Tristram P. Coffin enhanced Barry's insights in his study of "Mary Hamilton" (Child 173).

"Mary Hamilton" has been in oral tradition for some two centuries and exists in many variants in both the United States and Great Britain. Almost all the variants are fairly long, narrating the sad story of a lady-in-waiting who is hanged for infanticide. Before she dies Mary Hamilton laments her misfortune in three or four stanzas of lyric beauty. In the

United States some variants exist that are made up only of those stanzas. Coffin postulates the concept of an "emotional core" as a dominant principle in the evolution of folk poetry in the process of oral transmission. Every ballad, Coffin says, contains an emotional core, essentially lyrical, which is more important to its evolution than are its narrative parts. With the passing of time, the narrative parts are forgotten and nothing remains but the emotional core, which finally becomes a lyric rather than a narrative song.[9]

This suggestive concept of Coffin's has been accepted as complementary to the postulate that ballads evolve in the process of oral tradition, passing from long and detailed narrative versions to short, lyrical texts. But little has been done to test the hypothesis in the field. In a recent book, Roger Abrahams and George Foss remark—in reference to "Mary Hamilton"—that concrete evidence of this sort, illustrating the change of a folksong from narrative to lyric, "is seldom encountered in the history of individual ballads."[10] The reason may lie in the nature of the folk ballad in Britain and the United States. The ballad corpus is made up of a moribund tradition on the one hand and on the other of more recent songs, still alive in oral tradition but which exist in only one version or at most in a very few.

Lacking sufficient data in the Anglo-American tradition, I have looked for such in the Mexican *corrido*: a lyrico-narrative genre like the Anglo-American and in stanza form as well, but a vigorous, living tradition that has existed about a century in its present form and that includes historical themes that make it easier to trace its evolution. I will concentrate on "Benjamín Argumedo," a *corrido* more than a half-century old that still is current in oral tradition in several variants and that has what I would identify as an emotional core. Perhaps it may shed some light on the process of evolution in folk poetry and on the way songs function among groups that we call folk.

"Benjamín Argumedo" is a historical *corrido* from the Mexican Revolution. The principal events that inspired it can be documented. Benjamín Argumedo, like many other revolutionary chieftains, came from northern Mexico. He was born in Matamoros, Coahuila, and first made a name for himself as a cavalry officer, as did another *norteño* of greater renown, Francisco Villa. Like Villa, Argumedo was famous for his horsemanship, his personal valor, and the daring of his cavalry charges. When

Villa attacked Torreón, Coahuila, in 1914, it was Argumedo's cavalry that offered the most stubborn resistance, defeating several of Villa's units in the battles that preceded the taking of Torreón by the *villistas*. That is why *corrido* singers, in some versions of "La toma de Torreón" (The Taking of Torreón), depict Francisco Villa as challenging Argumedo to single combat, in the manner of old epic champions before the walls of a besieged city.

Gritaba Francisco Villa:	Francisco Villa shouted,
—¿Dónde te hallas, Argumedo?	"Where can you be found, Argumedo?
¿Por qué no sales al frente,	Why are you not in the van,
tú que nunca tienes miedo?—	you who are never afraid?"

Because of his exploits Argumedo earned epithets such as "the Lion of La Laguna," "Brave among the Brave."*

The bravery and skill displayed by Argumedo on the battlefield were not reflected in his ideological behavior. Though it was not rare for revolutionary chieftains to change sides, Argumedo acquired a sorry reputation for the facility with which he went from one faction to another. When the rebellion against the Díaz dictatorship began, Argumedo was one of the first to support Francisco Madero. Once Díaz was deposed, however, Argumedo joined Pascual Orozco in a rebellion against Madero and was defeated by government forces under the command of Victoriano Huerta. In 1913 Madero was assassinated during a coup led by Huerta. Most of the revolutionary chieftains united to fight the usurper, but Argumedo joined Huerta and was a general in Huerta's army at the time he fought against Villa before Torreón. Once Huerta had fled Mexico, Argumedo went from the extreme right to the far left and joined Emiliano Zapata, the peasant leader. As a *zapatista* Argumedo had the same luck he had as a *huertista*. His military skills earned him a few limited victories, but Zapata was defeated by Carranza's armies and retreated into the mountains of his native state of Morelos. Argumedo tried to seek refuge in his own "little fatherland" of Coahuila. With a group of faithful companions he worked his way north, getting as far as Durango, where he fell ill and could no longer travel. He hid in the mountains close to the boundary between Durango and Coahuila,

* La Laguna (or La Comarca Lagunera) is in the southeastern part of Coahuila, bordering on Durango, and includes Torreón as well as Matamoros, where Argumedo was born.

and there he was surprised and taken prisoner by Carranza soldiers under the command of General Francisco Murguía on February 4, 1916. Carranza had invoked the Law of January 25, 1862 (enacted during the time of Benito Juárez to punish military men who had collaborated in the French occupation of Mexico), and he applied it to those of his former enemies who were captured by the *carrancistas.* That was Argumedo's lot. On February 29 he was sentenced to death by a military tribunal, and he was shot on March 1 inside the Durango City penitentiary. According to Daniel Moreno, Argumedo was so weak because of his illness that he had to be tied to a chair to make a satisfactory target for the firing squad.[11]

Oral tradition often forgets the faults of its heroes, while extolling their virtues. Such has been the case with Argumedo, as with many others. Less fortunate is the role assigned by folklore to Francisco Murguía, Argumedo's executioner. Different variants of Argumedo's *corrido* call Murguía a "tyrant," a "traitor," or simply "*that* Murguía." History shows us a somewhat different Murguía, the antithesis of Argumedo: faithful to a cause and to the man who represented it.[12] From first to last he was loyal to Carranza, even after most *carrancista* officers had abandoned Carranza in favor of Obregón. After Carranza was assassinated, Murguía fled to the United States, where he made plans to avenge Carranza's death. He crossed the border with a handful of men and immediately became a fugitive, was discovered hiding in a church, and was shot (ironically) in Durango.

But there was another side to Murguía besides his loyalty to Carranza. He was accused of enjoying to excess the role of executioner, preferring to hang his victims instead of having them shot with due ceremony. Because of his preference for the rope as an instrument of execution, he was known as "Pancho Reatas." So it seems that Murguía had a reputation as a cruel executioner before he had Argumedo shot.[13]

According to Armando de María y Campos, "Las mañanitas del general Benjamín Argumedo" were being sung by "anonymous minstrels" in Mexico City by mid-1916, some three or four months after Argumedo's execution.[14] We cannot be completely sure whether these *mañanitas* were composed in Mexico City or whether they had been brought south from Coahuila or Durango. It is reasonable to assume, however, that María y Campos refers to a broadside published in Mexico City. At the end of this chapter are six variants of "Benjamín Argumedo"—texts A through F—embracing the fifty-four years that the *corrido* has been performed, from 1916 to 1970. Text A is taken from a broadside published by Eduardo Guerrero in Mexico City, in 1916 without a doubt. Argumedo was not greatly popular in Mexico City, and his death would have caused interest for a few months only, as one sensational event among many. The Guerrero broadside is entitled "Mañanitas de Benjamín Argumedo." It is printed without illustrations or decorative borders, unlike many others of Guerrero's broadsides about executions, murders, and other such events. There is only a stylized bar down the middle of the sheet dividing two columns of stanzas. "Jorge Peña" is printed below, evidently the name or pseudonym of one of the popular poets who wrote for Guerrero.

Texts B, C, D, and E come from the oral tradition of the Texas-Mexican border, the area where Argumedo was best known. The first three are from my own collection, recorded on magnetic tape during a field trip to the border. Text B was recorded in Matamoros, Tamaulipas, on August 24, 1954, from Juan and Alfredo Guajardo, sixty-three and fifty-three years of age, respectively. Text C was recorded in Brownsville, Texas, opposite Matamoros, on August 8, 1954, from Ignacio ("Nacho") Montelongo, then forty-six years of age. Text D was recorded at El Ranchito, Texas, a small community some thirty kilometers from Brownsville, on August 1, 1954, from Leopoldo Montes, age twenty. Text E comes from the same area but was recorded sixteen years later by a graduate student, Jerald L. Abrams, in Piedras Negras, Coahuila, on March 21, 1970, as part of his fieldwork assignment. The performers were Rubén Castillo Juárez, thirty, and Hilario Gaitán, twenty-five. Text F appears in the second volume of *La Revolución Mexicana a través de los corridos populares,* by Armando de María y Campos.[15] It is evidently a broadside and is attributed to Luis Camacho Treviño, "El Popo," whose name and pseudonym appear below the text. In a master's thesis dated 1965, Marcela Ruiz de Velasco Padierna says that El Popo was a well-known *corridista* in Monterrey, Nuevo León. In the 1960s El Popo was active in Monterrey as a singer, composer, and remaker of *corridos,* which he published as broadsides at a popular press in Monterrey.[16] Evidently the text given us by María y Campos comes from one of El Popo's broadsides, no older perhaps than 1960. It is not, therefore, the same text that María y Campos tells us was sung in Mexico City in 1916.[17] El Popo's broadside is clearly related to the *corridos* about Argumedo then current in oral tradition in the northeastern states of Mexico and the southern part of Texas.

If we compare text A, the Mexico City broadside, to the texts current in northern Mexico and Texas, we can see that we have two distinct versions of "Benjamín Argumedo," so dissimilar that they might be considered two different *corridos* were it not for the fact that certain stanzas occur in all six of the texts. Text A must have had a short life in the oral tradition of interior Mexico. Several scholars from that area have dealt with Argumedo and printed a copy of his *corrido*. Invariably the text has been the Guerrero broadside, down to the "Jorge Peña" at the end. On the other hand, one can identify a different version of "Benjamín Argumedo" in texts B, C, D, E, and F, all from northeastern Mexico and southern Texas. Nonetheless, the Mexico City version, text A, seems to be the source of the other texts, which we could group as variants of a *norteño* version. Not only do the *norteño* variants include several stanzas found in the Mexico City version, but these stanzas contain what—following Coffin's lead—we could call the emotional core of the *corrido*.

Text A is twenty-three stanzas long, including the formal opening and the formal close, or *despedida*. The formal opening most often used in *corridos* gives the date or place of the action. Text A, however, uses a less common formula, in which the singer asks permission of his audience in order to sing. The kind of *despedida* used in text A is more common in interior Mexico than in the North, especially in broadsides: the "Fly, fly, little dove" convention in which the dove is told to alight on something that rhymes with the title of the *corrido*. Text A is entitled "Mañanitas de Benjamín Argumedo," but the word *mañanitas* does not appear in the titles of the variants taken directly from *norteño* oral tradition. The informants of B, C, and D called their variants "El corrido de Benjamín Argumedo," while the singers of E called it simply "Benjamín Argumedo." Only A and F, both products of broadside presses, are entitled "Mañanitas de Benjamín Argumedo." Nevertheless, the *norteño* variants taken from oral tradition use *mañanitas* in their formulaic opening and closing stanzas. This seems to favor the thesis that text A, the Mexico City variant, is the source of the *norteño* variants. For if we take a brief look at the way *mañanitas* or *mañanas* has been used in Mexican narrative song, we can see that only text A conforms to the type, and that this characteristic is what makes it different from the *norteño* texts.

Mañanitas refers not to a distinct genre but to a particular style used both in *décima* and *corrido* form to narrate sensational events.* During the Revolution it appeared in *corridos* commemorating the execution of prominent military figures such as Generals Felipe Ángeles and Benjamín Argumedo. But they were most often used to tell about the deaths of ordinary convicts. Very often they were called *tiernos despedimientos* (tender farewells) or *tristes súplicas* (sad supplications), in which the person about to die repents of his sins, makes philosophical remarks about life and death, and says good-bye to family, friends, relatives, mountains, trees, and just about everything in sight, in a long series of lines all beginning with *adiós* (good-bye). In short, folk poems of this sort are the Spanish equivalent of the English "last goodnight." Translated into Spanish, "Mary Hamilton's Last Goodnight" would become "El triste despedimiento de Mary Hamilton."

These were the models Jorge Peña used in composing his "Mañanitas de Benjamín Argumedo." After the formal opening the *corrido* begins with Argumedo a prisoner, moments before he is sentenced to death. Ten stanzas (2–11) describe Argumedo's trial and its outcome in sentimental language; seven more (16–22) are devoted to "sad laments and farewells" on the part of Argumedo, in which he bids farewell to his family, his friends, and even the penitentiary where he has been held. Stanza 23 is, of course, the formal close. In other words, out of twenty-one stanzas devoted to narrative, seventeen are of the type we find in *décimas* and *corridos* about executed criminals. It is evident that the composer of text A saw Argumedo not as a heroic revolutionary but as a common criminal. One cannot tell whether this reflects Jorge Peña's personal feelings or whether circumstances required that he portray Argumedo in this light. The products of the broadside press cannot always be taken as "the voice of the people." Like newspaper editorials, they may be intended to create rather than reflect public opinion. The folksinger can criticize the powerful as long as he is careful where he sings. Words are air and the air takes them away. But the author or publisher of a broadside is vulnerable to official retaliation. Mexico City in

---

* The term *mañanitas* is more often used in lyric songs with other functions, but we cannot elaborate upon that here.

1916 was no place to show open sympathy for Argumedo. It was under the thumb of a very vengeful Venustiano Carranza. And if it was dangerous to express sympathy for Argumedo, it was equally risky to criticize his executioner, since Pancho Reatas was held in high esteem by Carranza. So there was more than one probable reason why text A depicts Argumedo the way it does.

But we have four other stanzas (12–15), in which Jorge Peña transcends the feelings of the moment and sketches for us the outlines of a different Argumedo. Stanza 11 accentuates the "last goodnight" tone of stanzas 2–10. Argumedo says to Murguía, "Válgame Dios ¿qué haré yo?" *Válgame Dios* translates literally as "God help me," but in actual usage it is equivalent to "Good heavens." So we are shown Argumedo as panic-stricken, saying to Murguía, "Good heavens! What shall I do?" and then asking for a boon. At this point we expect him to beg for mercy.

Murguía's answer is meticulously courteous, and he addresses Argumedo as "mi general Argumedo" rather than simply as "general Argumedo." But Argumedo does not ask for mercy. What he wants is the customary honor extended to defeated generals who must die before firing squads: the pomp and ritual of a public execution in which the condemned man can exhibit his coolness and flair in the face of death. This Murguía denies, pleading superior orders, and Argumedo is shot inside the prison walls. The stanzas, then, become a discreet allusion to Murguía's reputation for vindictiveness toward his defeated enemies. They are a high point in text A, in sharp contrast to the rest of the text.

Text B, the longest variant of the *norteño* version recorded in performance, is only seventeen stanzas long, in contrast to A's twenty-three, but it contains more narrative than A. The sentimental details about Argumedo's trial have disappeared. Instead we are told about Argumedo's falling ill in the mountains, his capture, and his being brought to Durango City. When he is surprised and taken prisoner, Argumedo is resting by a lagoon while some of his men bathe his horse. The scene sets an affective tone much different from the beginning of A. Especially significant is the horse, symbol of all Argumedo was before his illness. For men like Villa and Argumedo the horse represented mobility and military power. "He was famous for his cavalry charges," Daniel Moreno tells us of Argumedo.[18] But the horse, so well tended by his companions, is of no use to Argumedo because he is too weak to ride.

Once Argumedo is a prisoner, text B has him recover from his illness so he can meet Murguía face to face, erect and dignified. In B, Argumedo does not ask for a boon; Murguía offers to grant him one. And the latter is not called "Don Francisco Murguía" as in A but "that Murguía." When Argumedo responds to Murguía's offer, asking for a formal execution, Murguía denies his request, making his courtesy a kind of cruel hypocrisy. Frustrated in his wish for an honorable death, Argumedo does not lament his fate. He smiles instead. At this point text B returns to what evidently was its model, text A, with its long list of good-byes. In B, however, Argumedo makes but one farewell (B14), based on A18 apparently, but it is to his life as a fighting man that he bids good-bye.

> "Good-bye, mountains and sierras,
> cities and towns,
> where I was surrounded by bullets
> that rained upon me like fire."

This is followed by another *adiós* stanza, but it is the narrator who speaks rather than Argumedo, and its tone is not that of the "tender farewells" type of stanza. It accuses Murguía of keeping for himself the gold eagle that was Argumedo's insignia as a general, rather than returning it with his other effects to Argumedo's family.

> Good-bye to the eagle of gold
> he wore proudly on his hat.
> Where did it end up?
> In Murguía's hands!

A final and important change that text B makes over text A is in the *despedida*. The formal opening in B is almost identical to A's, but in the *despedida* B discards A's "Fly, fly, little dove" stanza and replaces it with a formal close modeled on A's formal opening.

> Now I must say farewell
> because I can sing no more;
> gentlemen, these are the *mañanas*
> of Benjamín Argumedo.

"I must say farewell because I can sing no more" introduces an element of ambiguity into the *despedida*. It can mean "I can sing no more because I have nothing else to say" or "I can sing no more because I am overcome with sorrow." The latter interpretation is in accord with the melancholy flavor of the tune,* as well as the connotations of lament and homage aroused by the term *mañanitas.* The new *despedida,* so similar to the formal opening, plays still another role in the esthetic effect of B. It provides a balanced frame, a pair of auditory vignettes, in which the emotional core and its accompanying stanzas are enclosed. In the hands of *norteño* singers Argumedo becomes a heroic figure, and the artistic value of the *corrido* is enhanced thereby.

Comparison of texts A and B reveals important differences and similarities. We have seen how they might be considered different *corridos,* were it not for the similarity of their verbal frames and the presence in both of a group of almost identical stanzas that serve as an emotional core, even though the feelings expressed by the emotional core are quite different in each. We may now examine texts C, D, and E in relation to B to see how an emotional core may function in variations occurring in a living oral tradition.

Juan Guajardo, sixty-three years old and the principal informant for text B, prided himself on his good memory and his ability to sing his *corridos* "as they should be sung," complete in all respects. He had been a folksinger from his early youth and was considered a specialist in the field, though he also owned a small restaurant on the outskirts of Matamoros, Tamaulipas. When Argumedo was executed, Guajardo was already twenty-five years old and was singing for pay within the limits of his own region—Tamaulipas, Nuevo León, and Coahuila. By 1954 he had been singing "Benjamín Argumedo" for at least thirty-five years and claimed that he sang it "as it originally was," though this assertion may be doubted.

Nacho Montelongo was forty-six in 1954, when he recorded text C, accompanying himself on the six-string guitar. He also was a folksong specialist but of a sort different from Guajardo. Montelongo did not sing for pay. He was a small rancher and farmer. He knew many *corridos* that were also in Guajardo's repertoire, though Montelongo's variants usually were briefer than Guajardo's. He said he had learned "Benjamín Argumedo" more than twenty years before he recorded it. Text C is fifteen stanzas long, two less than B, and some of the stanzas in C are not

* An example of the melody for the *norteño* version is included at the end of this chapter, with the *corrido* texts.

found in B. But the formal opening and the *despedida* are identical in B and C, and the emotional core is the same, except for minor variations in diction.

Text D was recorded by Leopoldo Montes, twenty, when Montes was working in South Texas as a *bracero*. He was from Michoacán, deep in interior Mexico, but he had been on the border for a few years, where he had learned "Benjamín Argumedo." He did not know anything about Argumedo's history. He just liked the song and sang it in the fields while picking cotton. Text D is only five stanzas long and has passed from the narrative to the lyric genre. Except for the opening formula, it is a monologue by Argumedo, structured around a remnant of the emotional core. Montes uses a conventional stanza about condemned prisoners listening to the clock striking the last hours of their existence: D5. The same stanza appears as A21 and F17; both texts A and F are broadsides. Montes also includes a stanza, D2, that is not in any of the other texts but which eloquently expresses the feelings of people weary of civil war.

> "I fought so long, so long
> with my Mauser rifle in my hand,
> only to die before a firing squad
> in Durango's cemetery."

Montes forgot to sing the *despedida*, though it is clear that he knew it because as he moved away from the microphone he said, "I forgot the *despedida*." Apparently the formal opening and the *despedida* were not as important to him as the lyrical stanzas. There is more of the pathetic than the heroic in text D. Though Montes still thought of his text as a *corrido*, what he sings is a lyric song. All that keeps it from being purely lyrical is the presence of the formal opening. Had he omitted this first stanza, we would have a lyric without any historical reference, an expression of the feelings of any man about to die before a firing squad. Scholars, however, still could have identified it as an offshoot of "Benjamín Argumedo" because of the stanzas it shares with other *norteño* variants of the *corrido*. Very much the same seems to have occurred with "Mary Hamilton."

Less than forty years after Argumedo's execution, the *corrido* narrating his death had been shaped into a lyric song by a Mexican equivalent of the ploughboys and milkmaids so highly prized as informants by nineteenth-century folklorists in Britain and the United States. But the fact that "Benjamín Argumedo" was being transformed into lyric song by some performers did not prevent other singers from keeping the narrative form alive. In 1970, sixteen years after I recorded text D, Jerald L. Abrams recorded text E in Coahuila, Argumedo's native state. In keeping with post–World War II changes in *corrido* performance, Rubén Castillo Juárez and Hilario Gaitán substitute an accordion for the bass guitar as complement to the six-string guitar in accompanying their singing. Otherwise, performance and content are much like texts B and C, collected in 1954.

There are only eight stanzas in E, two of them constituting the "frame" marked out by the formal opening and the *despedida*. All six of the remaining stanzas are found in other *norteño* variants so far discussed, but only one of them, E5, is found in the Mexico City version. This is the fundamental stanza in the emotional core—the core of the core, one might say—(A13, B10, C10, D3) in which Argumedo asks for a public execution. Although E is almost as short as D, it is a true narrative, detailing in that short space Argumedo's capture while watching his horse being bathed, the treatment of his illness, his being brought before Murguía, and Argumedo's calm demeanor when he is denied the honor of a ritualized death.

Text F, as noted earlier, comes from a broadside printed by Luis Camacho Treviño in Monterrey, Nuevo León, about 1960. Camacho Treviño recast old *corridos* and composed new ones, and had them printed on broadsides which he sold to people who gathered to hear him sing in public places. His nineteen-stanza text either is based on another long version once in oral tradition, before Camacho Treviño's time, or it is a recasting of several of the shorter *norteño* versions being sung in the northeast Mexico–South Texas area in the 1950s. Except for F8, which is a variation on F7, all the stanzas in Camacho Treviño's broadside are found in one or more of the *norteño* variants, taken from oral tradition, that we have discussed. There is a serious flaw in text F, however, occurring in stanza 12, which should be the equivalent of A13, B10, C10, D3, and E5. In F12 Argumedo asks *not* to be executed in public. This may have been a printer's error. It vitiates the most important stanza in the *corrido* and the rest of the emotional core as well.

SUMMARY

The six texts at the end of the chapter are offered as representative variants of "El corrido de Benjamín Argumedo." The two broadsides were chosen as reference points in regard to the variants in oral tradition. The four variants from oral tradition were chosen because they were tape-recorded under well-documented conditions from traditional *corrido* singers. Since "Benjamín Argumedo" still is part of a vigorous living tradition, there are many more variants that could have been chosen. We do not need hundreds of variants, however, since this is not a historic-geographic study but a consideration of the process of change in style and content undergone by one example of folk poetry in oral transmission.

Text A is well known to students of the Mexican *corrido*, but it must have had a very short life in performance. On the other hand, the *norteño* variants are witness to the fact that this version enjoys a vigorous life in the oral tradition of a considerable geographic area, at the very least the Mexican states of Coahuila, Nuevo León, and Tamaulipas and the state of Texas. The *norteño* variants reveal sympathy for Argumedo and a strong antipathy toward General Murguía. Historical sources suggest that such sentiments did exist in this area in 1916, and interviews with performers and their audiences in 1954 show that such sentiments still existed up to the mid-1950s.

From a folkloric viewpoint the most important contribution of text A is that it made possible the creation of the *norteño* version. This was achieved with a seminal stanza (A13) that became an emotional core in the *norteño* texts, functioning in a manner analogous to the emotional core identified by Tristram Coffin in the British ballad. In oral tradition stanza A13 served as a catalyst for a configuration of emotions quite different from those expressed in the Mexico City broadside. Texts B, C, and D support the thesis that the narrative elements of a folksong may "wear away" in transmission until only a lyrical core remains. But we must remember also that texts B, C, and D were all tape-recorded during the same summer, in an area covering less than fifty kilometers, all three of them part of a living folk tradition. Lyrical versions were emerging, but the narrative forms showed no signs of disappearing. In this respect, one must take into account the character of the informant. The younger, the less specialized the singer and the farther he is removed from prose accounts that are transmitted with the song, the more likely it may be that his variant will be short and lyrical.

Juan Guajardo, the oldest and most specialized of the three informants in question, prided himself on the fact that he sang "complete" versions of his *corridos*. Furthermore, Guajardo had his own ideas about the way that shorter variants were produced from longer ones. We were talking about another *corrido* very well known on the Texas-Mexican border, "Mariano Reséndez," about a famous smuggler of textiles into Mexico who lived at the end of the nineteenth century. I had already collected four or five variants of "Mariano Reséndez" before visiting Guajardo. When I asked Guajardo whether he had ever heard of Reséndez, he replied that he had and that he knew a *corrido* about him. Then he asked me, "Well, has Machetitos already sung that *corrido* for you?" Machetitos was another singer in Matamoros, some thirty years younger than Guajardo. When I admitted that such was the case, Guajardo said, "Let me sing it for you. But I know the old version; it won't go into one disc." I assured him that the tape could record for half an hour without stopping, so he sang the *corrido* for me, in truth a longer and more complete version than the one Machetitos had recorded. When he finished the following dialogue took place.

P. That is the old *corrido?*
G. Yes, this is the old version.
P. And what is the difference between the way it was sung in other times and how it is sung now?
G. Now they sing four or five stanzas and then they throw in the flower of May . . . and "here is the end of the singing of the verses about Don Mariano."

In truth, Machetitos had recorded a variant seven stanzas long, ending with the usual *despedida:*

> Now with this I say farewell,
> plucking a flower of May,
> this is the end of the singing
> of the verses about Don Mariano.

Guajardo used the same *despedida,* but his version was thirty-eight stanzas long. I asked Guajardo where "they" had learned their four or five stanzas, and he answered, "From me, of course. Where else would they learn them?"

We see that Guajardo, who did not have the remotest idea about folkloristic theories, had the same concepts about change in the ballad as those held by Depping and Entwistle. Shorter variants are newer than older ones. The shorter ones come about when younger minstrels hear older ones sing; and they learn only the more memorable stanzas, which they recast into complete songs. In the *corrido* the *despedida* is a convenient device to give form to a fragment.

But there is more to change in the *corrido* than the wearing away of the more pedestrian stanzas by forgetfulness, fortunate or unfortunate. Another look at the variants of "Benjamín Argumedo" shows us that some pedestrian stanzas persist even in the shortest variants, while such admirable stanzas as B15 and D2 appear only once. This suggests that the process of re-creation is more complex than the simple wearing away of less memorable stanzas as the *corrido* is transmitted from one singer to another, until nothing is left but the lyricism of an emotional core. *Corridos,* it would seem, do contain groups of memorable stanzas that one can identify as emotional cores and that persist in variant after variant. But each singer also has a store of other stanzas in his memory, from which he can choose for any performance, depending on his state of mind at the moment of performance and the general ambience in which the folkloric act is set.

Coffin tells us about the Anglo-American ballad that "its whole life proceeds as a denial of its origin" as a narrative song.[19] That may be true of the British ballad in North America, where it is an imported tradition, preserved rather than vigorously active, and slowly disappearing, leaving us only fragments that sometimes produce miracles of folk lyricism. But such a process is not absolute as regards the *corrido.* Text E of "Benjamín Argumedo," recorded sixteen years after the lyrical text D, shows us that the Mexican *corrido* has not yet reached the point where it rejects the narrative genre. On the contrary, both the narrative and the lyrical forms coexist.

This suggests another possible function of the emotional core. In "Benjamín Argumedo" the emotional core functions as a focal point or constitutive principle that structures the total composition during the act of re-creation each time a song is performed in a folkloric context. In the variants at hand we can note a good deal of variation in the selection and ordering of stanzas before we arrive at the climax, the emotional core. But the stanzas that follow appear in the same order in all variants.

There is evidence, then, of a store of stanzas, both memorable and pedestrian, in the mind of the singer at the moment of performance. The same person can sing different variants of the same song under different circumstances. Other fieldworkers using tape recorders may have had the experience I had with one of my informants who recorded several songs for me. He decided to begin with "Gregorio Cortez" but insisted on singing the *corrido* once with the machine turned off, to get used to the microphone. When he did record it a few minutes later, the variant was quite different from what he had sung when the machine was off. He left off both the opening and closing formulas and substituted some of the stanzas in his first performance with others. Not only did the recorded text cease to be a *corrido* in the strict sense of the word, but it no longer was a coherent narrative. Though some stanzas contained narrative, the text as a whole reflected the feelings of Cortez rather than his actions.*

Not only may the emotional core function in the spontaneous variation of the same *corrido;* it may lead to the recasting of versions that may be considered as different *corridos* by the performer. Let us take another look at "Mariano Reséndez" as sung by Juan Guajardo, a *corrido* twenty-three stanzas long giving us a detailed story of Reséndez as the ideal smuggler. The emotional core contains two kinds of feelings: celebration of the deeds of Reséndez and condemnation of the authorities for shooting him, supposedly while he was trying to escape, when they were taking him to Monterrey. The variant recorded by Guajardo's young rival Machetitos is simply an abbreviation of Guajardo's, seven stanzas only but concentrating on the same emotional core as Guajardo's variant. But earlier that same summer I had recorded two texts of "Mariano Reséndez" in Brownsville from Jesús Gómez, who at sixty was only three years younger than Guajardo. Gómez, who sang without accompaniment, said he knew two different *corridos* about Reséndez, and he recorded both of them during the same session. His first text is seven stanzas long and is structured around that part of the emotional core in Guajardo's variant that censures the authorities for having killed Re-

---

* See variant 1 in Américo Paredes, *"With His Pistol in His Hand": A Border Ballad and Its Hero* (Austin: University of Texas Press, 1958), 173–174.

séndez. Gómez's second text contains eleven stanzas and is organized around the figure of Reséndez as the consummate smuggler, fighting and winning skirmishes against border guards.

Gómez said he had learned the two texts as different *corridos*. Guajardo, on the other hand, claimed he had learned his long version of "Mariano Reséndez" as one *corrido* many years before. Given Guajardo's long career as a folksong specialist, it is more probable that Guajardo's text antedates those sung by Gómez, though Guajardo's text may not be "the original," as he claims. In such case, some variant like that of Guajardo's broke in two, each segment taking part of the emotional core of the original and creating a different ballad around it. If Gómez knew only one text of the *corrido,* one might conclude that his variant was the result of forgetfulness, but he knew two texts that were for him two different *corridos.*

One may conclude that the singer of a *corrido,* at the moment of performance, has three constants that can structure his variant of the moment: the formal opening, the *despedida,* and the emotional core. The formal opening and the *despedida* serve as a frame in which the singer can form his verbal images. The emotional core—to extend the analogy with a painting—becomes the principal image, the focus around which the picture is organized. The variables are made up of all the other stanzas that are contained in the singer's memory, which he uses to fill out the details of his verbal painting, and which are chosen according to certain conditions: the place of the event (whether the singing occurs in a *cantina,* at home, or in the open); feedback from the audience and other variables of ambience; the emotional or psychological state of the singer at the moment of performance; and the singer's basic concept as to what constitutes the ideal *corrido.* Guajardo and Gómez, for example, differ in the esthetic of the *corrido.* Guajardo prefers long and complete narratives while Gómez seeks unity of effect.

From this point of view the act of singing a *corrido* involves an element of re-creation on the part of the singer every time he sings. One should emphasize that this is not the same process as that described by Albert Lord in regard to the performers of heroic songs in Yugoslavia, although there are analogies between the two.[20] The differences are obvious if one remembers that the *corrido* is in stanzaic form and sung to a melody of four to eight musical phrases, while the Yugoslav folk epic is made up of long series of lines sung to a simpler melody, allowing for a great degree of improvisation. But Coffin provides us with a useful insight into variation of ballad forms like the Mexican *corrido* in his essay about the emotional core in the British ballad, which shares significant characteristics with the *corrido* in spite of differences in culture and language.

THE BENJAMÍN ARGUMEDO TEXTS

The following is a typical melody for "Benjamín Argumedo." Variations occur, as is usual in oral tradition. The most common, shown below, is in the first line of a stanza, although to my knowledge it never occurs in the formal opening.

Variation

Text A

MAÑANITAS DE BENJAMÍN ARGUMEDO

1

Para ponerme a cantar	I ask your permission
pido permiso primero;	before I set out to sing;
señores, son las mañanas	gentlemen, these are the *mañanas*
de Benjamín Argumedo.	of Benjamín Argumedo.

2

Último día de febrero,	On the last day of February
novecientos diez y seis,	of nineteen hundred sixteen,
han sacado a Benjamín	they took Benjamín out [of prison]
entre las nueve y las diez.	between nine and ten o'clock.

3

Pues era un martes por cierto,	It happened to be a Tuesday,
presente tengo ese día,	I remember well the day,
cuando lo sacó la escolta	when the military escort took him
de la Penitenciaría.	out of the penitentiary.

4

Lo llevaron por la calle,	They led him down the street,
bastante gente acudió,	a good many people gathered;
se llenó la plaza de armas	they filled the main plaza
a ver lo que sucedió.	to see what was happening.

5

Dos lo llevaban del brazo,	Two men were holding his arms,
lo llevaban pie a tierra,	they were taking him afoot;
lo llevaban al palacio;	they took him to the [municipal] palace;
era al consejo de guerra.	the court martial was there.

6

Lo subieron al palacio	They took him up in the palace
donde fue su tribunal,	to the place where he was tried;
fue donde oyó su sentencia	that was where he heard his sentence,
que era pena capital.	which was capital punishment.

7

Su familia, que alií [*sic*] estaba,	His family, who was there,
estaba tan desolada	was so distressed
que al oir esa sentencia	that when they heard the sentence
hubo de caer desmayada.	they fell into a faint.

8

Lo bajaron del palacio	They brought him down from the palace,
por la calle en gran alarde,	down the street in great ostentation;
lo llevaban a su destino,	they were taking him to his fate,
serían las seis de la tarde.	it was about six in the evening.

9

Por la calle donde iba
aquel veinte de noviembre,
como iría su corazón;
seguro nadie lo entiende.

As he went along the street
that twentieth of November,
no one knows for sure
what was in his heart.

10

Cuando llegó a su destino
dijo: vengo en agonía,
pues hoy tengo que ser muerto;
Dios así lo dispondría.

When they came to the destined place
he said, "I am in anguish
for I must die today;
God must have so decided.

11

Válgame Dios ¿qué haré yo?
dijo al General Murguía
y le pidió una merced
a ver si se la concedía.

"Good heavens! What shall I do?"
he said to General Murguía,
and he asked him for a boon,
hoping that it would be granted.

12

Pues don Francisco Murguía
le contestó con esmero:
¿qué merced es la que quiere,
mi general Argumedo?

And Don Francisco Murguía
answered most courteously,
"What is the boon that you wish,
my general Argumedo?"

13

Oiga usted, mi general,
yo también fui hombre valiente,
quiero me haga ejecución
a la vista de la gente.

"Listen, my general,
I too was a courageous man;
I want you to execute me
where people can see."

14

Oiga usted, mi general,
yo no le hago ese favor
pues todo lo que yo hago
es por orden superior.

"Listen, my general,
I will not do you that favor
because all I am doing
is following superior orders.

15

En algunas ocasiones
también a Ud. le ha pasado,
pues jefe de operaciones,
ya sabe que soy nombrado.

"This must have happened to you
on some occasions,
for you know I have been appointed
chief of operations."

16
Ya que Dios me ha concedido
el no morir en la guerra
quiero que a mi alma en camino
animen [*sic*] Cristo en la tierra.

"Since God has allowed me
not to die in battle,
I want that Christ on this earth
should encourage my soul on its journey.

17
Adiós, todos mis amigos,
me despido con dolor,
ya no vivan tan engreídos
de este mundo engañador.

"Good-bye, all my friends,
I say farewell full of sorrow.
Do not become too fond
of this deceitful world.

18
Adiós, mi tierra afamada,
recintos donde viví,
adiós, mi querida esposa,
yo me despido de ti.

"Good-bye, my renowned land,
and places where I lived,
good-bye, my beloved wife,
I say farewell to you.

19
Adiós, mis padres queridos,
de toda mi estimación,
no me volveréis a ver,
volé a la otra mansión.

"Good-bye, my beloved parents,
whom I have esteemed so much;
you will see me no more,
I fly to the other abode.

20
Adiós, familia querida
que era toda mi alegría;
adiós, mi querida esposa;
adiós; Penitenciaría.

"Good-bye, my beloved family
that was my greatest joy;
good-bye, my beloved wife;
good-bye, penitentiary.

21
Adiós; también el reloj;
sus horas me atormentaban
pues clarito me decían
las horas que me faltaban.

"Good-bye also to the clock;
its hours tormented me
for they told me very clearly
the hours that I had left.

22
Amigo, no te señales
por riqueza ni estatura:
pues todos somos iguales
materia de sepultura.

"Friend, do not be proud
of your riches or your status,
for we are all equal,
matter for the grave."

23

Vuela, vuela palomita,	Fly, fly, little dove;
párate en aquel romero	alight on that rosemary shrub;
éstas son las mañanitas	these are the *mañanitas*
de Benjamín Argumedo.	of Benjamín Argumedo.

—*Jorge Peña*

Text B

EL CORRIDO DE BENJAMÍN ARGUMEDO

1

Para empezar a cantar (*bis*)	I ask your permission
pido permiso primero,	before I begin to sing;
señores son las mañanas (*bis*)	gentlemen, these are the *mañanas*
de Benjamín Argumedo.	of Benjamín Argumedo.

2

Cuando Rodríguez salió, (*bis*)	When Rodríguez went out,
que a Sombrerete llegó,	when he got to Sombrerete,
ese general ingrato	that ingrate of a general
dijo que se iba a la sierra	said he was going into the mountains,
y a Benjamín traicionó.	and he betrayed Benjamín.

3

En esa estancia del Sauz, (*bis*)	In the ranch of El Sauz,
camino pa'l paraíso,	on the road to paradise,
estaba Argumedo enfermo, (*bis*)	Argumedo lay ill,
enfermo que Dios lo quiso.	ill because God willed it so.

4

Como a las tres de la tarde, (*bis*)	About three in the afternoon,
de la tarde de ese día,	in the afternoon of that day,
aprehendieron a Argumedo, (*bis*)	they captured Argumedo
y a toda su compañía.	and all of his company.

5

Como a las tres de la tarde, (*bis*)	About three in the afternoon
comienza un tren a silbar;	a train's whistle begins to blow;

veinte soldados de escolta, (*bis*)
que lo fueran a bajar.

an escort of twenty soldiers
was sent to take him off.

6
En donde estaba Argumedo (*bis*)
tenían el camino andado,
donde se encontraba enfermo
a orillas de una laguna,
yendo a bañar su caballo.

Well did they know the road
to where Argumedo was,
where he was lying ill
by the shores of a lagoon,
while his horse was being bathed.

7
Otro día por la mañana (*bis*)
lo fueron a examinar;
le pusieron dos doctores (*bis*)
que lo fueran a curar.

The next morning
they went and examined him;
they assigned him two doctors
to see that he got well.

8
Cuando Argumedo sanó, (*bis*)
que se le llegó su día,
lo fueron a presentar (*bis*)
con el general Murguía.

When Argumedo recovered,
when his time had come,
he was taken
before General Murguía.

9
Y le dice ese Murguía, (*bis*)
y le dice con esmero:
—¿Qué merced quiere que le
haga, (*bis*)
mi general Argumedo?—

And that Murguía tells him,
he tells him most courteously,
"Is there a boon I can grant you,
my general Argumedo?"

10
—Oiga usted mi general, (*bis*)
yo he sido un hombre valiente;
quiero que usted me fusile (*bis*)
al público de la gente.—

"Listen, my general,
I have been a courageous man;
I want you to have me shot
in public, before the people."

11
—Oiga usted mi general,
mi general Argumedo,
yo no le hago ese favor;
pues todo lo que hago yo (*bis*)
es por orden superior.

"Listen, my general,
my general Argumedo,
I will not do you that favor
because all I am doing
is following superior orders.

12

—Como a usted le habrá pasado (*bis*)
en algunas ocasiones,
ya sabe que soy nombrado (*bis*)
general de operaciones.—

"As must have happened to you
on some occasions,
you know I have been appointed
chief of operations."

13

Cuando Argumedo ya vio (*bis*)
que no se le concedía,
él no demostraba miedo, (*bis*)
antes mejor sonreía.

When Argumedo saw
that his request would not be granted,
he did not show any fear,
on the contrary he smiled.

14

—Adiós montañas y sierras, (*bis*)
ciudades y poblaciones,
donde me vía yo en las balas (*bis*)
que parecían quemazones.—

"Good-bye, mountains and sierras,
cities and towns,
where I was surrounded by bullets
that rained upon me like fire."

15

Adiós el águila de oro (*bis*)
que en su sombrero lucía;
¡a dónde vino a parar! (*bis*)
¡a las manos de Murguía!

Good-bye to the eagle of gold
he wore proudly on his hat.
Where did it end up?
In Murguía's hands.

16

Ya se acabó Benjamín, (*bis*)
ya no lo oímos mentar,
ya está juzgado de Dios, (*bis*)
ya su alma fue a descansar.

Benjamín is no more,
people no longer speak of him;
he has been judged by God,
his soul has gone to its rest.

17

Ya con ésta me despido (*bis*)
porque cantar ya no puedo;
señores son las mañanas (*bis*)
de Benjamín Argumedo.

Now I must say farewell
because I can sing no more;
gentlemen, these are the *mañanas*
of Benjamín Argumedo.

Text C

EL CORRIDO DE BENJAMÍN ARGUMEDO

1
Para empezar a cantar (*bis*)
pido permiso primero,
señores son las mañanas (*bis*)
de Benjamín Argumedo.

I ask your permission
before I begin to sing;
gentlemen, these are the *mañanas*
of Benjamín Argumedo.

2
A donde estaba Argumedo (*bis*)
tenían el camino andado,
a orillas de una laguna, (*bis*)
viendo bañar su caballo.

Well did they know the road
to where Argumedo was,
by the shores of a lagoon,
watching his horse being bathed.

3
Señores tengan presente (*bis*)
que fue el veintiocho de enero;
aprehendieron a Alanís (*bis*)
y a Benjamín Argumedo.

Gentlemen, keep it in mind
that it was the twenty-eighth of January;
they captured Alanís
and Benjamín Argumedo.

4
Señores, ese Murguía, (*bis*)
ese caso superior,
dijo que se iba a la sierra (*bis*)
y a Benjamín traicionó.

Gentlemen, that Murguía,
that notorious character,
said he was going into the mountains
and he betrayed Benjamín.

5
De pronto comunicaron (*bis*)
al tirano de Murguía
que aprehendieron a Alanís (*bis*)
y a toda su compañía.

They quickly sent a message
to that tyrant of a Murguía
that they had captured Alanís
and all his company.

6
Se fueron todos al punto (*bis*)
y luego lo sorprendieron;
el pobre se hallaba enfermo (*bis*)
y por eso lo aprehendieron.

They all went instantly
and caught him by surprise;
the poor man was ill,
and that was why he was captured.

7

Echaron a Benjamín (*bis*)
en un carro como flete,
pasaron por San Miguel, (*bis*)
llegaron a Sombrerete.

They loaded Benjamín in a boxcar
as if he was a piece of baggage;
they went past San Miguel,
they arrived at Sombrerete.

8

Al llegar a la estación (*bis*)
comenzó el tren a silbar;
veinte soldados de escolta (*bis*)
lo vinieron a bajar.

On arriving at the station
the train's whistle began to blow;
an escort of twenty soldiers
came to take him down.

9

Le saludó ese Murguía, (*bis*)
le saludó con esmero:
—¿Qué merced quiere que le
        haga, (*bis*)
mi general Argumedo?—

That Murguía greeted him,
he greeted him most courteously,
"Is there a boon I can grant you,
my general Argumedo?"

10

—Oiga usted mi general, (*bis*)
yo también fui hombre valiente,
quiero que usted me afusile (*bis*)
al público de la gente.—

"Listen, my general,
I too have been a courageous man,
I want you to have me shot
in public, before the people."

11

—Mi general Argumedo, (*bis*)
yo no le hago ese favor
porque todito lo que hago (*bis*)
es por orden superior.

"My general Argumedo,
I will not do you that favor
because all I am doing
is following superior orders.

12

—Como a usted le habrá pasado (*bis*)
en algunas ocasiones,
bien sabe que soy nombrado (*bis*)
general de operaciones.—

"As must have happened to you
on some occasions,
you well know I am appointed
chief of operations."

13

Luego que Argumedo vio (*bis*)
que no se le concedía,
él no le mostraba miedo, (*bis*)
antes mejor sonreía.

Once Argumedo saw
that his request would not be granted,
he did not show him any fear,
on the contrary he smiled.

14

—Adiós montañas y sierras, (*bis*)
suidades y poblaciones,
donde me llovían las balas (*bis*)
que parecían quemazones.—

"Good-bye, mountains and sierras,
cities and towns,
where the bullets rained
down upon me like fire."

15

Ya con ésta me despido (*bis*)
porque cantar ya no puedo,
aquí dan fin las mañanas (*bis*)
de Benjamín Argumedo.

Now I must say farewell
because I can sing no more;
here end the *mañanas*
of Benjamín Argumedo.

Text D

El corrido de Benjamín Argumedo

1

Señores para empezar (*bis*)
pido permiso primero,
señores son las mañanas (*bis*)
de Benjamín Argumedo.

Gentlemen, I ask your permission
before I begin;
gentlemen, these are the *mañanas*
of Benjamín Argumedo.

2

—Tanto pelear y pelear (*bis*)
con el máuser en la mano;
vine a morir fusilado (*bis*)
y en el panteón de Durango.

"I fought so long, so long
with my Mauser rifle in my hand,
only to die before a firing squad
in Durango's cemetery.

3

—Y oiga usté mi general, (*bis*)
yo también fui hombre valiente;
quiero que usté me afusile (*bis*)
y en público y de la gente.

"Listen, my general,
I too have been a courageous man,
I want you to have me shot
in public, before the people.

4

—Y adiós montañas y sierras, (*bis*)
suidades y poblaciones,
donde me viá yo en las balas (*bis*)
que parecían quemazones.

"Good-bye, mountains and sierras,
cities and towns,
where I was surrounded by bullets
that rained upon me like fire.

5

—Y adiós también el reló, (*bis*)
sus horas me atormentaban;
pues clarito me decía (*bis*)
las horas que me faltaban.—

"Good-bye also to the clock,
its hours tormented me
for it told me very clearly
the hours that I had left."

Text E

BENJAMÍN ARGUMEDO

1

Para empezar a cantar (*bis*)
pido permiso primero,
señores son las mañanas (*bis*)
de Benjamín Argumedo.

I ask your permission
before I begin to sing;
gentlemen, these are the *mañanas*
of Benjamín Argumedo.

2

Doy esto y en realidad (*bis*)
que fue el veintiocho de enero,
aprehendieron a Alanís (*bis*)
y a Benjamín Argumedo.

I give you this as the truth,
that it was the twenty-eighth of January;
they captured Alanís
and Benjamín Argumedo.

3

A donde estaba Argumedo (*bis*)
tenían el camino andado,
donde se encontraba enfermo
a orillas de una laguna,
yendo a bañar su caballo.

Well did they know the road
to where Argumedo was,
where he was lying ill
by the shores of a lagoon,
while his horse was being bathed.

4

Cuando Argumedo sanó, (*bis*)
que se le llegó su día,
lo fueron a presentar (*bis*)
con el general Murguía.

When Argumedo recovered,
when his time had come,
he was taken
before General Murguía.

5

—Oiga usted mi general, (*bis*)
yo también fui hombre valiente,
quiero que usted me afusile (*bis*)
en justicia de la gente.—

"Listen, my general,
I too have been a courageous man;
I want you to have me shot
in justice before the people."

6

Luego que Argumedo vio (*bis*)	Once Argumedo saw
que no se le concedía,	that his request would not be granted,
él no demostraba miedo, (*bis*)	he did not show any fear,
antes mejor se sonreía.	on the contrary he smiled.

7

—Adiós montañas y sierras, (*bis*)	"Good-bye, mountains and sierras,
suidades y poblaciones,	cities and towns,
'onde viví entre las balas (*bis*)	where I lived among the bullets
que parecían quemazones.—	that rained upon me like fire."

8

Ya con ésta me despido (*bis*)	Now I must say farewell
porque cantar ya no puedo,	because I can sing no more;
señores son las mañanas (*bis*)	gentlemen, these are the *mañanas*
de Benjamín Argumedo.	of Benjamín Argumedo.

Text F

Mañanitas del General Benjamín Argumedo

1

Para ponerme a cantar	I ask your permission
pido permiso primero,	before I set out to sing;
señores son las mañanas	gentlemen, these are the *mañanas*
de Benjamín Argumedo.	of Benjamín Argumedo.

2

Se los digo en realidad	I tell you this as the truth,
que fue el veintiocho de enero	that it was on the twenty-eighth of January
que aprehendieron a Alanís	that they captured Alanís
y a Benjamín Argumedo.	and Benjamín Argumedo.

3

Cuando Rodríguez salió	When Rodríguez went out,
que a Sombrerete llegó,	when he got to Sombrerete,
dijo que se iba a la sierra	he said he was going into the mountains,
y a Benjamín traicionó.	and he betrayed Benjamín.

4

En donde estaba Argumedo
tenían el camino andado,
donde se encontraba enfermo
a orilla de una laguna,
viendo bañar su caballo.

Well did they know the road
to where Argumedo was,
where he was lying ill
by the shores of a lagoon,
watching his horse being bathed.

5

De pronto comunicaron
al tirano de Murguía,
para aprehender a Benjamín
y a toda su compañía.

They quickly sent a message
to that tyrant of a Murguía;
they were to capture Benjamín
and all of his company.

6

Echaron a Benjamín
en un carro como flete,
pasaron por San Miguel,
llegaron a Sombrerete.

They loaded Benjamín in a boxcar
as if he was a piece of baggage;
they went past San Miguel,
they arrived at Sombrerete.

7

Al llegar a la estación
comienza un tren a silbar,
veinte soldados de escolta
que lo fueron a bajar.

On arriving at the station
a train's whistle begins to blow;
an escort of twenty soldiers
was sent to take him down.

8

Como a las tres de la tarde
que lo fueron a bajar,
apenas podía dar un paso
ese pobre general.

About three in the afternoon,
when they went to take him down,
that poor general
could barely walk.

9

Otro día por la mañana
que lo fueron a examinar,
le pusieron dos doctores
que lo fueran a curar.

The next morning,
when they went and examined him,
they assigned him two doctors
to see that he got well.

10

Cuando Argumedo sanó
que se le llegó su día,
lo fueron a presentar
con el general Murguía.

When Argumedo recovered,
when his time had come,
he was taken
before General Murguía.

11

Ahí le pregunta Murguía,	Then Murguía asked him,
le pregunta con esmero:	he asked him most courteously,
—¿Qué merced quiere que le haga,	"Is there a boon I can grant you,
mi general Argumedo?—	my general Argumedo?"

12

—Oiga usted mi general	"Listen, my general,
yo también fui hombre valiente	I too was a courageous man;
quiero que no me fusile	I don't want you to have me shot
al público de la gente.—	in public, before the people."

13

—Mi general Argumedo	"My general Argumedo,
yo no le hago ese favor,	I will not do you that favor
pues todo lo que yo hago	because all I am doing
es por orden superior.	is following superior orders.

14

—Como a usted habrá pasado	"As must have happened to you
en algunas ocasiones,	on some occasions,
ya sabe que soy nombrado	you know I have been appointed
general de operaciones.—	chief of operations."

15

Luego que Argumedo vio	Once Argumedo saw
que no se le concedía,	that his request would not be granted,
él no demostraba miedo	he did not show any fear,
antes mejor se sonreía.	on the contrary he smiled.

16

—¡Adiós montañas y sierras,	"Good-bye, mountains and sierras,
ciudades y poblaciones,	cities and towns,
donde me veía yo en las balas	where I was surrounded by bullets
que parecían quemazones!	that rained upon me like fire.

17

—¡Adiós reloj de Durango	"Good-bye, clock of Durango,
que tanto me atormentaba,	that tormented me so much
que clarito me decía	because it told me quite clearly
las horas que me faltaban!—	the hours that I had left!"

18

Ya se acabó Benjamín,	Benjamín is no more,
ya no lo oirán mentar,	people will no longer hear about him;
ya está juzgado de Dios,	he has been judged by God,
ya su alma fue a descansar.	his soul has gone to its rest.

19

Ya con ésta me despido	Now I must say farewell
porque cantar ya no puedo,	because I can sing no more;
aquí dan fin las mañanas	this is the end of the *mañanas*
de Benjamín Argumedo.	of Benjamín Argumedo.

—*Recuerdo de*
  Luis Camacho Treviño,
  el popular "Popo"

—*Souvenir from*
  Luis Camacho Treviño,
  the popular "Popo"

- 8 -

José Mosqueda and the Folklorization of Actual Events

Since my early childhood on the Texas-Mexican border, I have been familiar with legendary accounts about José Mosqueda, who held up the Point Isabel train, and about his deadly little partner, Simón García. Many times in my youth I sat around campfires or at *ranchero* gatherings in the cool of the night, and when the conversation turned to subjects such as trains, sharpshooting with a .30-30 carbine, godsons and godfathers, buried treasure, or even casual reference to the Texas town of Point Isabel (now Port Isabel), someone would tell part of the story of José Mosqueda. During this same time—the late 1920s and early 1930s—there was also current on the border a *corrido* about Mosqueda. A variant of the *corrido* was collected in Brownsville in 1939 by John A. Lomax and Alan Lomax, who recorded it from José Suárez, a blind *guitarrero*. Suárez was perhaps the most celebrated *corrido* singer on the Lower Rio Grande Border during the first forty years of the present century, and he may have been the creator of many of the *corridos* of border conflict current during the same period.

The Lomax recording of "El corrido de José Mosqueda" is in the Library of Congress (no. 2609 A 1). Gustavo Durán published a transcription of it in *14 Traditional Spanish Songs from Texas*.[1] Durán added the following note to his transcription of the text: "Historical data relating to the life of the hero of this corrido were not available. However, the frequent mention of names of particular persons gives to the story the stamp of a true narration of a recent occurrence."[2] In 1951 and again in 1954 I made field-collecting trips in the Brownsville-Matamoros area, and following Durán's suggestion I collected what historical data were available on José Mosqueda, as well as legendary accounts about him. A summary of the legendary accounts and such historical data as were available up to 1954 were published in *Western Folklore*.[3]

Since publication of the article in *Western Folklore*, other data—both historical and folkloric—have become available to me, including the following: (1) documentary materials from the records at the Cameron County, Texas, courthouse not available previously;* (2) publication of the memoirs of William A. Neale of Brownsville, containing a chapter entitled "The Rio Grande Railroad Robbery";[4] (3) collection of variants of the Mosqueda *corrido* that include stanzas not found in the Lomax version; and (4) tape-recording in 1962 in Matamoros, Tamaulipas, of an especially interesting version of the Mosqueda legend. These new materials make the Mosqueda matter worth reconsidering from two viewpoints: as an example of the *corrido*-legend process and of what Latin American folklorists often call the "folklorization" of historical events.

THE CORRIDO

"El corrido de José Mosqueda" is played and sung slightly faster than most other Border *corridos*. There is a jaunty air to it. If singing it to guitar accompaniment, a staccato strum should be used.

El   die - ci - nue - ve   de e - ne - ro

el   pue - blo se al-bo - ro - tó - o

cuan - do fue el pri - mer   a - sal - to

que   Jo - sé Mos-que - da dio - o.

* These data were obtained through the kind assistance of Mr. Eddie Valent of Brownsville, Texas.

JOSÉ MOSQUEDA

1

El diecinueve de enero
el pueblo se alborotó,
cuando fue el primer asalto
que José Mosqueda dio.

On the nineteenth of January,
the people were all astir;
that was when José Mosqueda
carried out his first assault.

2

Decía José Mosqueda
con su pistola en la mano:
—Tumbamos el ferrocarril
y en terreno americano.—

Then said José Mosqueda,
with his pistol in his hand,
"We knocked over the railroad train,
and right on American soil."

3

Decían los americanos:
—Qué mexicanos tan crueles!
Dejaron el ferrocarril
bailando fuera 'e los rieles.—

The Americans said,
"How cruel these Mexicans are!
They have left the railroad train
jigging outside the rails."

4

En el rancho de La Lata,
donde se vio lo bonito,
en donde hicieron correr
al señor Santiago Brito.

It was at La Lata ranch
where some pretty things were seen;
it was there that they made
Mr. Santiago Brito run away.

5

Más allá, en El Calaboz',
donde se vio lo muy fino,
en donde hicieron correr
al diputado Justino.

Farther on, at El Calaboz',
where the finest things were seen,
it was there that they made
Deputy Justino run away.

6

Decía José Mosqueda
en esa Loma Trozada:
—Pues a correr, compañeros,
porque ahi viene la platiada.—

Then said José Mosqueda,
at that Broken-Off Hill,
"Comrades, it is time to gallop;
that pile of silver is coming."

7

Decía Simón García
en su caballo melado:
—Vamos a gastar dinero,
todos para el otro lado.—

Then said Simón García,
on his honey-colored horse,
"Let us all go spend our money
on the Mexican side of the river."

8

Decía Fabián García
en una voz y sin sueño:
—Vámonos tirando bien,
con rumbo a El Capitaneño.—

Then said Fabián García,
in an even and vigilant voice,
"Let us strike out directly
toward El Capitaneño."

9

El cobarde de Blas Loya,
que hasta el caballo cansó,
con dos bultos de dinero
hasta que el río cruzó.

That despicable Blas Loya,
he even wore out his horse,
carrying two bundles of money,
until he had crossed the river.

10

Decía don Esteban Salas
como queriendo llorar:
—Por haber hecho los hierros
también me van a llevar.—

Then said Don Esteban Salas,
as if he was going to cry,
"For having made the iron bars,
they are going to take me too."

11

Decía don Esteban Salas:
—Esto les voy a decir,
por haber hecho los hierros
dos años voy a sufrir.—

Then said Don Esteban Salas,
"I am going to tell you this;
for having made the iron bars,
I shall suffer for two years."

12

Decían los adoloridos,
debajo de los mesquites:
—Se va a poner en venduta
la fragua de Juan Benítez.—

All the aggrieved people said,
as they sat beneath the mesquites,
"They are going to auction off
Juan Benítez's blacksmith shop."

13

A Simón no lo aprehendieron,
pues no se dejó arrestar;
al estado de Sonora
se fue para vacilar.

They did not capture Simón,
for he would not be arrested;
he went to the state of Sonora
to have himself a good time.

14

Ya con ésta me despido
al salir a una vereda,
pues el que ha tumbado el tren
se llama José Mosqueda.

Now with this I say farewell,
coming out upon a trail;
for the man who knocked over the train
is named José Mosqueda.

15

Mosqueda, yo ya me voy,	Mosqueda, I'm leaving now,
mi compañero se queda,	my companion stays behind;
pues el que ha tumbado el tren	for the man who knocked over the train
se llama José Mosqueda.	is named José Mosqueda.

HISTORICAL BACKGROUND

Mosqueda's Great Train Robbery was no earth-shaking historical event, and historians may be pardoned for omitting it from their works. Enough sources are at hand, however, to give us a good idea of the historical data on which later folklorizations are based. These sources can be supplemented with nonlegendary materials collected in interviews with informants, some of whom were children or teenagers at the time of the events. Lt. W. H. Chatfield's *The Twin Cities of the Border*, published just two years after the robbery, is perhaps the most reliable source for general background on the Brownsville of Mosqueda's time.[5] Unfortunately, Chatfield scarcely mentions the robbery, though he does give valuable information on the Rio Grande Railroad and on some of the businessmen who were victims of the holdup. Other documentary sources do not always agree on details. William A. Neale's account is contradictory in some respects; it is obviously reminiscence set down some time after the events. Court records are in summary form and plagued with misspellings and other obscurities. Even so, there are enough data to reconstruct the principal events that were to be preserved in legend and song.

In the 1890s the southernmost tip of Texas—now commonly called the Rio Grande Valley—was almost completely isolated from the rest of the United States. The more important populated places were along the Rio Grande, on the border with Mexico. Between these towns and Texas north of the Nueces there were no means of communication except on horseback or by stagecoach along poor and dangerous roads. The area was more like an occupied section of Mexico than part of the United States. The greater part of the population was Mexican; Spanish was the language most commonly used; and Mexican currency was the regular medium of exchange in most business transactions. It was not until 1904 that the St. Louis, Brownsville, and Mexico Railroad connected this part of Texas with regions north of the Nueces. In the 1890s, however, there was one rail link with the outside world, the Rio Grande Railroad—a narrow-gauge road running twenty-two miles from Brownsville, the largest town in the area, to Point Isabel on the coast. On it were transported goods from South Texas and a large area of northern Mexico.

The Rio Grande Railroad had its troubles, among them frequent floods that tore up the roadbed and epidemics that quarantined the port and stopped the flow of goods to Point Isabel from Brownsville. In 1890, according to Neale, traffic between New Orleans and Point Isabel was interrupted by a quarantine due to a smallpox epidemic in Brownsville.[6] By the time the quarantine was lifted, there was a considerable amount of freight accumulated in Brownsville, waiting to be shipped to Point Isabel on the Rio Grande Railroad. There also was a considerable amount of gold and silver, both in coin and in bars, though it is difficult to estimate the exact amount. The total may have been as low as $20,000 or as high as $220,000. Neale's estimate of $75,000 is probably close to the mark.[7]

On the morning of January 1, 1891, the first train since the quarantine left Brownsville for the coast, carrying the gold and the silver coin as well as some U.S. money orders. Also on board were about a dozen passengers, one of them a woman, as well as a crew of four. At a point called Loma Trozada, some ten miles from Point Isabel, the train was held up and robbed by several masked horsemen. Loma Trozada had been a hillock rising some thirty feet or so above the plains between Brownsville and Point Isabel. The railroad cut right through it, leaving a mound of earth on each side of the line, a convenient place for an ambush. The robbers pulled out the spikes along one side of the line, using a clawlike iron tool made especially for the purpose. When the train was close to Loma Trozada, they came out of concealment and pulled at the rail with a rope, derailing the train. After the holdup they locked passengers and crew in a boxcar and rode away.

The site of the robbery was some thirteen miles from Brownsville and the sheriff's office. The Rio Grande and Mexico, on the other hand, were about six miles away. One would have expected the robbers to ride for the Mexican side of the river as fast as their horses could take them. On the contrary, they rode into the brush, where they divided their loot into several caches, buried them, and then left for Brownsville and other points in Cameron County. Two or three of the robbers did cross the river with their share of the loot (and perhaps with the share of others), but it is not clear when this took place—that is to say, whether they doubled back and dug it up as soon as their comrades rode off or whether they went into Mexico immediately after the money was buried and came back much later to dig it up. One reason for burying the money was that most of the men involved were Texas-Mexicans. They intended to let things blow over before they recovered the loot a little at a time. Another reason was that not all the conspirators involved in the robbery took part in the actual holdup of the train. A grand jury at Brownsville on June 13 of the same year indicted seven persons as the actual robbers of the train: José Mosqueda, Fabián García, Simón García, Blas Loya, Reyes Loya, Crecensio Saldaña, and Serviano Jiménez. Fourteen others were indicted as accessories; among these were Tomás Hinojosa and José Morelos (or Mireles), accused of having raised a signal flag over the courthouse in Brownsville when the train with the money left town; Juan Benítez, a blacksmith; Francisco Jaramillo, a sheepherder; and Esteban Salas, a farmer. It is impossible to know for sure how many of those indicted were captured, or how many others were arrested who were not involved with the crime. Evidently charges were dropped against some of those originally indicted, and most of those accused were never caught. Of those indicted, only three were brought to trial. José Mireles (or Morelos) was found not guilty on September 28, 1891, of complicity in the holdup. José Mosqueda and Fabián García were found guilty on June 19 of robbing the United States mail and were sentenced, respectively, to life imprisonment and to ten years at hard labor. Charges were dropped on September 28 against a Francisco Jaramio [*sic*], who the record says "is dead." This must have been the sheepherder Francisco Jaramillo, named as an accomplice in the original indictment. Neale mentions a Jaramillo as having been killed by Esteban Cadena, a sheriff's deputy, when Jaramillo resisted arrest. Neale gives his name as José, but unless the deputy shot the wrong man this evidently is our sheepherder Francisco.[8]

The holdup caused something of a stir on the border. As soon as word reached Brownsville, authorities organized an extensive manhunt, enlisting the aid of Mexican officials, who sealed off their side of the river with troops, police, and customs officers to prevent the culprits from crossing into Mexico. The hunt apparently was over in nine days' time, if one can use as evidence a letter to Mexican authorities in Matamoros signed by Thomas Carson, mayor of Brownsville, and Emilio C. Forto, Cameron County judge. The letter, dated January 28, 1891, gives effusive thanks to Mexican authorities for "guarding the Mexican bank of the river . . . with the laudable intention of intercepting the robbers if they attempted to cross into Mexican territory with the large sum stolen, while the search was being prosecuted on this side."* By the twenty-eighth, it would seem, authorities on the United States side of the river had captured all of the holdup men, or all those they had reasonable hopes of capturing. Among those taken was the leader, José Mosqueda. Legend, folksong, and oral report say that Mosqueda was captured by Sheriff Santiago Brito of Brownsville, who chased others of the gang in and out of the thorny chaparral. Brito, however, was not sheriff of Cameron County when the train robbery occurred.

Santiago A. Brito, prominent in Brownsville politics toward the end of the nineteenth century, was owner of *El Demócrata,* one of Brownsville's Spanish-language newspapers, at a time when border papers were primarily organs of political partisanship. In 1884, Brito was elected Cameron County sheriff, serving until November 1890, when Matthew L. Browne won the office. Less than a month later, on December 1, Brito applied for and obtained the post of Brownsville city marshal. The letters of recommendation supporting Brito's application are signed by many of the most influential men in Brownsville. Among them was Agustín Celaya, one of three members of the Celaya family associated with the Rio Grande Railroad. Brito had been city marshal of Brownsville some six weeks when Mosqueda and his men staged their train robbery. Since the act took place many miles outside the limits of Brownsville, it was in Browne's jurisdiction rather than in Brito's. The United States mail was rifled by the robbers, so the United States marshal was also concerned. But oral tradition seems to be correct after all. It was City Marshal Brito who captured Mosqueda.

According to Neale the robbery remained unsolved for "quite a number of days." Then Simón Celaya, general manager of the Rio Grande Railroad, "together with some of the leading merchants called upon

* Courtesy of Eddie Valent and Lorenzo Paredes, Sr., of Brownsville, Texas.

Don Santiago A. Brito and requested him to take a hand in arresting the perpetrator of such a dastardly crime."⁹ Celaya could not have waited many days before calling on Brito, since the hunt for Mosqueda and his men was over nine days after the robbery took place. Perhaps Celaya was understandably anxious to recover the stolen money; the Matamoros firm of Juan S. Cross and Son would later sue Celaya and other officials of the railroad for the loss at Loma Trozada of 10,500 silver *pesos* and a package of gold valued at $9,110. It also is possible that Celaya and his associates felt that Brito had a better chance of breaking the case than Sheriff Browne because of Brito's Mexican background. It may even be that by the time Celaya called on him Brito already was in possession of some of the clues that enabled him to solve the case. These are but conjectures. What is certain is that Sheriff Browne resented Brito's participation in the case.

As city marshal, Brito could not operate outside of Brownsville, but he had received some time before a special appointment from the governor as a Texas Ranger. On his authority as a state official, Brito organized a posse from his former deputies and began to scour the countryside around Brownsville, questioning farmers, ranchers, and sheepherders as he went. Sheriff Browne and his posse, presumably, were engaged in the same task. The robbers were being sought out by two separate and mutually hostile groups of lawmen. Oral reports speak of heated encounters on the streets of Brownsville between Brito and Browne, exchanges that came close to reaching the shooting stage. Two events seem to have broken the case open for Brito. While riding by Loma Trozada (where the holdup had occurred) on his way home from one of his scouting trips, Brito met "a half-witted boy who was herding a lot of sheep" and who told Brito his name was Librado Jaramillo.¹⁰ Brito asked the boy where his uncle was, and Librado answered that his uncle had gone away with Don José Mosqueda and Fabián García on the day the train was robbed, and that he hadn't seen them since. The uncle must have been Francisco Jaramillo, the sheepherder, later indicted as an accomplice of Mosqueda's and apparently shot to death by one of Sheriff Browne's deputies. Meanwhile a Mexican *vaquero* riding through the brush found an iron bar that proved to be the homemade spike-puller used to derail the train. The bar was brought to Brito, who proceeded to question all the blacksmiths in the area until he found the man who had made the bar. The blacksmith must have been Juan Benítez, since a blacksmith by this name was one of those indicted as accessories to the robbery. According to oral reports, it was through the blacksmith that Brito learned of Mosqueda's part in the robbery. Brito then went and arrested Mosqueda, it is said.

There are a few other relevant details in accounts about the Mosqueda case that have appeared in print. After Mosqueda and Fabián García were arrested, Mosqueda was "sweated," according to Neale, and he "sang."[11] Neale is careful to make clear what he means: "In other words, he confessed all that he knew of the affair." Neale gives Mosqueda's "full confession," covering some two pages in reduced type.[12] There is no reason to doubt Neale's assertion that Mosqueda was third-degreed in an effort to gain a confession, which was later read in court. But whether Mosqueda did make a full confession is doubtful. For one thing, the "confession" printed in Neale's memoirs reads like something written by an English-speaking amateur writer rather than a statement by a living Mexican. The Mosqueda in the confession speaks like the stock Mexican of North American dime-novel fiction. Again, if Mosqueda did make a full confession while in jail, it is strange that none of the other conspirators—except for Fabián García—was ever convicted. Finally, there is another passage of Neale's that directly contradicts the confession. The passage is based on accounts Neale heard from Mosqueda's jailer. After Mosqueda was sentenced, according to this other account, he asked the jailer where the sheriff got all the information used in court. The jailer answered that Fabián García had confessed everything, giving all the details of the robbery and the names of the participants. Mosqueda then remarked that "all this had happened by taking boys into their affairs." Mosqueda went on to say that he thought Fabián García had got out of the affair cheaply enough, considering his undependable and bloodthirsty nature.

> On the way to derailing the train, in selecting the best place, Fabián had wanted the bandits to derail the train at the black bridge [perhaps an error of Neale's for "El Puente de los Negros"] so that all the passengers and crew would be killed, Mosqueda revealed. Simón García had persuaded Fabián to leave the selection of the place to Mosqueda, who wanted to kill no one. His wish was only for the money. Mosqueda added that he had told Simón García that Fabián García should not have been enlisted as he

was too young and could not keep secrets, but Simón said that he was his relative, and he felt sure that Fabián would never betray them.[13]

At this distance, about the only thing we can be sure of is that if a confession was read in court it probably was not Mosqueda's. Evidently Fabián García turned state's witness against Mosqueda in return for a reduced sentence. Neale's account, by the way, agrees with oral tradition as to Mosqueda's end. He says that both Mosqueda and Fabián García died in prison.[14]

The hostility between Sheriff Browne and City Marshal Brito must have become intense after Brito captured Mosqueda and some of his accomplices. Brito refused to hand over the prisoners to Browne. According to Neale, U.S. Marshal John M. Haynes took charge of them as federal prisoners—since they had robbed the U.S. mails—thus ending the "fuss" between Browne and Brito.[15] At all events, there was only one jail in Brownsville—the county jail—so the prisoners ended up in Browne's custody after all. Chatfield reports that while the prisoners were in the county jail the local militia, the Brownsville Rifles, was mobilized "as it was feared a rescue would be attempted."[16] This may have been a case of jittery Anglo residents seeing Mexican guerrillas under every bed and in every closet. Again, it may have been a reflection of the tension developed by the conflict between the sheriff and the city marshal.

Less than a year after Mosqueda was sentenced, Sheriff Browne was dead, shot during a cattle drive. His old rival, Santiago Brito, was immediately appointed sheriff in his place. And less than six months later Brito was shot and killed from ambush as he was riding a coach on the outskirts of Brownsville. Only a small part of the stolen money was ever recovered. There is no reason to disbelieve, in substance at least, what oral tradition reports concerning the unrecovered loot: it remained hidden in the brush near Brownsville until it was dug up and smuggled into Mexico by some members of the band. Neale supports this view, saying it was "strongly believed" that Esteban Salas got away with two thousand Mexican silver dollars. He also includes Blas and Reyes Loya among those who went into Mexico with some of the money. Neale states he talked to one of the Loyas "often" in Mexico after that, but they never mentioned the robbery. Simón García gets special attention from Neale in the last two sentences of his narrative about the train robbery: "Simón

García made two trips to where he buried his four sacks containing 8,000 Mexican silver dollars. Eventually he was killed in San Nicolás, Tamaulipas, México, in a gambling den over a dispute of a debt."[17]

FOLKLORIZATION IN THE *CORRIDO*

Such are the historical data about Mosqueda's train robbery, few of which appear in the version of "El corrido de José Mosqueda" collected in 1939 by the Lomaxes from José Suárez, the blind *guitarrero*. An interesting feature of the Suárez text is its balanced structure. Except for the first stanza, the formal opening introducing the action, the whole ballad consists of paired quatrains complementing each other by means of various devices such as similarity of subject and repetition. Even the formal close, or *despedida,* takes up two stanzas. This strongly parallelistic form is not what one would expect of a *corrido* freshly composed to narrate events. It is more than likely that the *corrido,* by the time it was recorded by the Lomaxes in 1939, had undergone a great deal of revision at the hands of one or more *corridistas.* This is based on two assumptions: that the *corrido* was composed soon after the events (or at least some years before 1939, when the Lomaxes collected it) and that in its original form it was a loose, circumstantial narrative rather than a neatly structured song.

The first assumption is supported by statements from informants such as Ricardo Flores and José Garza, both in their mid-seventies when interviewed in 1951, and in their early teens when Mosqueda's band robbed the train. Their testimony is that "El corrido de José Mosqueda" was known on the border at least by the turn of the century. Exactly what the *corrido* was like in those early days we cannot tell, since Flores, Garza, and other informants could remember only a few stanzas. One cannot, of course, say that a *corrido* (or any other ballad) may not appear in shapely, dramatic, well-structured form at its very inception. The chances, however, are against it. People who listen to new *corridos* about recent events like to get all the details. They love background materials just as much as do present-day watchers of television newscasts. Furthermore, some stanzas collected from aged informants in 1954 are not found in the Suárez text, and they are closer to the facts as we know them than is the version sung by Suárez. Not only do they support the existence of versions previous to the Suárez text—something accepted as general knowledge by most informants—but they also indicate that those earlier versions were more detailed and closer to historical fact than the text recorded by the Lomaxes.

As the only member of the band aside from Mosqueda to be captured, tried, and convicted, Fabián García must have been something of a celebrity along the border—for a few years at least—even if he did become a witness for the state. The Suárez text does not mention Fabián, but other versions of the *corrido* did sing of him. He is shown (stanza 8, above) in a pose typical of the Border *corrido* hero, speaking words of encouragement or command to his companions. Furthermore, Fabián speaks in a special tone of voice, as do other Border *corrido* heroes. Gregorio Cortez speaks in a loud voice, "en alta voz"; Mariano Reséndez and Cortez (in other versions of his *corrido*) speak in a divine voice, "con aquella voz divina." Fabián García speaks in an even and "sleepless" (vigilant?) voice, marking him as one of the main protagonists of the *corrido*.

Blas Loya was one of those indicted as having been among the seven persons who took part in the actual holdup of the train, but he was never brought to trial or convicted. Apparently he eluded capture by crossing the Rio Grande into Mexico. Both oral accounts (Ricardo Flores, 1954) and the Neale memoirs say that Blas escaped into Mexico with part of the hidden loot.[18] Traditional accounts add that Loya later sent a friend of his, Esteban Salas, to dig up another share of the loot on the Texas side. The stanza about Blas Loya (stanza 9) has a condemnatory tone, in contrast to the one about Fabián García. *Cobarde,* by the way, in contexts such as this one may mean "despicable" rather than "cowardly." Loya is condemned for running off with the money while Mosqueda, Fabián García, and others were in jail. It seems to express feelings prevalent among some border people at the time of the events.

If the stanzas about García and Loya strike heroic and disapproving tones respectively, the one about Juan Benítez the blacksmith (stanza 12) strikes a comic tone. We have a mocking view of all the rich people who lost their money in the holdup. They are living out under the mesquites and hoping to get some of their money back by auctioning off Benítez's humble blacksmith shop. The amusement of the impecunious over the discomfiture of the wealthy is obvious here, and again one may guess that the stanza has preserved a joke current after the holdup. Court records name Juan Benítez, a blacksmith, as one of those indicted as accessories to the robbery, though charges against him seem to have been dropped afterwards. These three stanzas must have belonged to long, detailed versions of the *corrido*, current soon after the events, in which Fabián García, Blas Loya, Juan Benítez, Simón García, and José Mosqueda—as well as others of the band—were mentioned in typical Border *corrido* style, each speaking his piece in a sort of epic catalogue.

The version recorded by the Lomaxes from the singing of José Suárez was collected forty-eight years after the events, as the period of border conflict was ending along the Rio Grande. It obviously is different from what the Mosqueda *corrido* of the 1890s must have been. Gone in the Suárez version are Fabián García, Blas Loya, and others of the outlaws. Juan Benítez becomes Esteban Salas, who we are told is sentenced to a couple of years in the penitentiary for making the iron tool with which the train was derailed, though, according to Neale, Salas was exonerated by Mosqueda of complicity in the affair.[19]

In substituting Salas for Benítez and having the blacksmith convicted and sent to prison, the Suárez version departs from the known facts. This, however, is the only such departure occurring in Suárez's text, which otherwise follows factual accounts quite closely. In spite of this the Suárez *corrido* is not, as one would expect, a ballad narrating a train robbery but a *corrido* of border conflict emphasizing the clash of Mexicans and North Americans along the border. Elsewhere I have discussed at some length Suárez's "José Mosqueda" as an example of the outlaw ballad recast into the pattern of the *corrido* of border conflict by careful selection and arrangement of details.[20] Suffice it here to summarize those remarks. The Suárez version begins with a common *corrido* convention, a dating of the action. This most often is merely a convention, with no relation to actual events; but it is worth noting that Suárez's "José Mosqueda" has preserved the correct month and day, "On the nineteenth of January," half a century after the events. The rest of the first stanza, however, implies that Mosqueda's exploit was something more significant than just a train robbery. "The people" are stirred up because José Mosqueda has carried out his "first assault." This first assault seems to be against Anglo Americans, because it is they whom we

see in the second stanza complaining about Mexican "cruelty." In the
third stanza we see Mosqueda himself "with his pistol in his hand," like
the heroes of border conflict, boasting that he has derailed a train "right
on American soil."

As we have seen, Mosqueda's exploit was a simple act of robbery. The
derailment at Loma Trozada was his first and last "assault." He was himself a Texas-Mexican, operating on his home soil, and the men who later
put him under arrest also were Texas-Mexicans. Even the money he
stole for the most part belonged to Spaniards, Mexicans, and Texas-
Mexicans. But in the *corrido* as Suárez recorded it, Mosqueda is seen
more like heroes of border conflict, such as Juan N. Cortina and Aniceto
Pizaña, who rise in arms against U.S. authority, defending their rights
with their pistols in their hands and fighting a series of skirmishes
against deputies and Texas Rangers. Even the derailment of the train "on
American soil" sounds like an echo of Pizaña's exploit near Olmito,
where Pizaña's band of *sediciosos* derailed a train in 1915.

Stanzas 4 and 5 have retained the names of Santiago Brito and one of
his deputies. The impression given, however, is that of a lively skirmish
between Mosqueda's band and a posse under Brito, with the posse running away. Stanzas 6 and 7 return to the scene of the train robbery at
Loma Trozada, but since they are sung after the supposed skirmish between Mosqueda's men and Brito's posse, they seem to be still another
of Mosqueda's exploits against the Anglos. Then Esteban Salas speaks,
lamenting his fate in a weepy voice. Salas is cast in the role of the blacksmith, and he is lamenting his involvement in the robbery and the
prison term he supposedly faces. But in this context, he sounds very
much like the cowardly raider in the *corridos* of border conflict, who
serves as a foil to the hero and as an example of how men should not be-
have. The final stanzas tell us, truthfully enough, that Simón García was
not captured. He goes into Mexico to spend his share of the loot. But we
are not told that Mosqueda did fall into Brito's hands. On the contrary,
the *corrido* ends on a tone of triumph. By use of the formal close, or *despedida,* we are shown a Mosqueda who retires victorious from the field,
saying farewell through the person of the singer and leaving his calling
card, as it were, in the manner of the Francisco Villa of legend, "José
Mosqueda is the name of the man who did these deeds."

The *corrido* of border conflict was well established along the Rio Grande when the Lomaxes collected "José Mosqueda" from Suárez.* The border-conflict *corrido* begins along the Rio Grande in 1859, with the Texas-Mexican uprising headed by Juan N. Cortina. It reaches its peak with the *sedicioso* movement headed by Aniceto Pizaña in 1915. By 1939 the period of actual border warfare had passed, but the *corridos* composed about such events were still very much alive. In such *corridos* we have a Mexican or Mexicans up in arms against United States authority because their rights have been violated. There is a Mexican exploit, followed by flight and pursuit by the *rinches*, or Texas Rangers. The raiders are overtaken and a fight takes place, ending in the flight of the pursuers. At some point in the ballad the principal raiders speak, making their boasts. Often their horses are described. Then the clown among the raiders speaks up. He is afraid, and the conventional line "como queriendo llorar" is proper to him, just as the lines "con su pistola en la mano" and "en su caballo melado" are proper to the heroic characters.

Thus we can see that the actual events concerning the train robbery at Loma Trozada have been transmuted into folksong in a very special way. Enough fragments of earlier versions of "El corrido de José Mosqueda" exist to make it clear that in its early form the ballad was a fairly long, essentially factual account of the events as seen from the Mexican point of view. The distress of the rich men who had lost their money in the robbery, the fears of those who were accused of complicity in the holdup, local sympathies and antipathies for the outlaws who had been lucky enough to escape into Mexico with some of the loot—all these reflect the direct experience of actual events as they must have appeared to the border people in the 1890s. But by 1939 the pattern of the *corrido* of border conflict has asserted itself upon the original intent of the Mosqueda ballad, which had been to tell the story of Mosqueda and his band as the border people thought it was. An outlaw ballad is made into a border-conflict ballad by excision of some details and by the arrangement of what is left into the pattern typical of the *corrido* of border conflict. We have here an example of the way that folklore adapts all kinds of materials into generic patterns dominant in a tradition. In this case it is not a

* For information on the *corrido* of border conflict see Américo Paredes, *"With His Pistol in His Hand": A Border Ballad and Its Hero* (Austin: University of Texas Press, 1958), 129–150.

direct folklorization of historical fact but a secondary process: from a pattern accepted in the tradition (the outlaw ballad) to a form that has achieved dominance in the minds of the group (the *corrido* of border conflict). Content has given way to demands of form, a form held in high esteem among the groups where the *corrido* was sung. It is also pertinent, however, to take into account the individual characteristics of the informant, José Suárez. "José el Ciego," as he was known to all, was perhaps the best-known singer and *guitarrero* along the Lower Rio Grande Border during the first third of this century, that is to say during the last part of the period of border conflict. Suárez was known both as singer and as redactor of *corridos*. A good many of the ballads of the Pizaña era may have been his own compositions. When he sang "El corrido de José Mosqueda" for the Lomaxes, he also recorded "La batalla de Ojo de Agua," a *corrido* celebrating a raid by Pizaña and his men on the village of Ojo de Agua—near Mission, Texas—in September 1915. Both by tradition and by personal background, José Suárez had an inclination toward the *corrido* of border conflict.

THE *CORRIDO* LEGEND

Though José Suárez's personality and background must have been important in the shaping of his version of "José Mosqueda," other factors were involved in the transformation of the Mosqueda *corrido*. These are what in another context I have called the *corrido* legend.[21] These factors, however, operated in the Mosqueda *corrido* in a somewhat different way than in border-conflict *corridos* such as "Gregorio Cortez" and "Jacinto Treviño." In the latter ballads, variants become shorter as time passes, not because events have been forgotten but because they have been transformed into legend. The telling of the legend, by the way, often accompanies the singing of the *corrido*. As the legend grows, the ballad diminishes. The ballad is no longer intended as a narrative. Its function is to evoke the image of the hero in lyrical or dramatic form. Meanwhile the legend takes on more and more embellishments from the stock of universal motifs. If the process is continued indefinitely, one would expect to reach a point where the *corrido* disappears or is sung in such a fragmentary fashion as to be unrecognizable as the complete entity. Neither "Gregorio Cortez" nor "Jacinto Treviño" has reached this stage.

They are still sung along the border, though in shortened form, while the legends accompanying them are much more elaborate.

"El corrido de José Mosqueda," on the other hand, is an example of the *corrido* that has reached the end of the *corrido* legend process. In 1951, again in 1954, and several times since then, I have questioned informants along the border about this *corrido*. I have found dozens of people who could repeat variants of the legend, but not one who knew anything but isolated stanzas of the *corrido*. Most people questioned knew the legend but could not repeat even one stanza of the *corrido*. The transformation of "El corrido de José Mosqueda" into border-conflict form around 1930 or earlier must have been the last stage in its history. By the 1950s the Mosqueda *corrido* had disappeared, at least in the area where it had been created. The legend, however, is still alive today.

The legend ordinarily does not take a definite form, or perhaps it may be more correct to say that it takes many forms. Parts of it may be told independently or in various arrangements, depending on what brings it to mind: a reference to Loma Trozada, to the old Rio Grande Railroad, sharpshooting, or buried treasure. That is to say, the *corrido* legend is not identifiable, as are tale types, by a certain ordering of its principal motifs. It is made up of a cluster of motifs occurring in different sequences, and it is their association with the *corrido* hero that identifies them as a distinct entity. Characteristically, the *corrido* of border conflict is realistic in tone. It exaggerates what it takes for fact, but it always gives us scenes taken from real life. The *corrido* legend, on the other hand, is more romantic, though it does not often make use of the marvelous. A favorite theme of the *corrido* legend is that of the hero who has been made prisoner by authorities in the United States. He is sent to prison for life, but once there is visited by the daughter of the governor or of the president of the United States. She falls in love with the hero and asks her father to give him to her "for Christmas." The father accedes to his daughter's wishes and the hero gains his freedom, but he then rejects the love of the Anglo woman. This is motif P512.1, "Release from execution at a woman's request (by marriage to her)."

Mosqueda's legend, however, does not quite follow this pattern, usual in the border-conflict *corrido*. As it is more often told, the Mosqueda legend may be summarized as follows:

José María Mosqueda was the one who planned the train holdup, but it was his lieutenant, Simón García, who carried out the plans. Simón García was a little man, but he was really bad. More than bad, he was evil, the devil himself perhaps. He could make incredible shots with the .30-30 carbine, his favorite weapon. He was never seen without his rifle in the crook of his arm. After robbing the train, the band broke up, with Mosqueda taking all the money with him to bury it in the chaparral until the affair blew over. Simón García went with him. On the way García asked Mosqueda what he would do if they met someone on the road. Mosqueda did not answer. Then Simón proposed, and Mosqueda agreed, that they would kill anyone they met. As soon as the pact had been made they met a young boy herding goats. It was a godson of Mosqueda's, whom he had raised in his own house. Simón reminded Mosqueda of his promise, but Mosqueda refused to keep his word. The two outlaws argued for a while in front of the boy, until Simón García seemed to give in. They let the boy go, telling him that he should say nothing about what he had seen. But as soon as the men left the boy ran into town and told how he had met a very strange-looking man in the woods who wanted to kill him, but that his *padrino* José Mosqueda did not let the man do it. It was in this manner that Mosqueda's complicity in the robbery was known, and Don Santiago Brito went and arrested him. Mosqueda ended up in prison, where he soon died, thus giving up his life in exchange for that of his godson.

Most of the narratives concentrate on Simón García rather than on Mosqueda. One by one the train robbers were captured, or they died resisting arrest. But Simón García remained untouched by the law. He would wander through hidden paths in the chaparral, waiting for the best opportunity to get to the hidden money stolen from the train. Many times he was seen by posses who were pursuing him, within easy rifle range. But he would just keep on walking—calmly and insolently—until he was lost in the chaparral, while his pursuers just sat in their saddles, afraid to fire because they knew that the first man who did so would surely be killed by a bullet from Simón García's rifle. Don Santiago Brito was the one who pursued Simón the most, and finally Don Santiago was murdered by the same man who many times was his guide when he was looking for Simón García. Finally Simón got to the buried money and disappeared. Afterwards it was said he had been seen in Sonora, in Chihuahua, and in other parts of Mexico. He finally became a revolutionary soldier in Villa's army and was killed in battle.

Such, in summary form, is the legend associated with "El corrido de José Mosqueda" as it is most commonly told. It is worthwhile comparing it both with the *corrido* as José Suárez sang it and with the historical data as we know them. First, it must be pointed out that the makers of the *corrido* legend are not the composers and singers of *corridos*. They are the people who listen to the *corridos* when they are sung and who only occasionally sing themselves. To a fieldworker collecting *corridos* and taking Von Sydow's view about passive and active carriers of folklore, the people who listen to the singing of *corridos* would be "passive" carriers of folklore. In reality, they are quite active and creative carriers of folklore as far as the *corrido* legend is concerned. The perpetuation and elaboration of the legend is their contribution to the total process involved in the performance of the *corrido* in its natural context, in which both singers and audience take part. It may be necessary, then, to question Von Sydow's dictum about passive and active carriers of folklore when applied to cases where we know very little about the total situation in which folklore genres are performed. The distinction may really be one between the carriers of certain highly structured genres like the folktale and the ballad, requiring the performance of specialists, and less formal genres such as the legend, which depend on a relatively informal dialogue carried on by two or more participants as its natural context, and on constant variation and repetition for its vitality.

The creators of the *corrido* and the makers of the *corrido* legend did not always agree on the folk image cast by José María Mosqueda. Or to put it more precisely, the same people who were willing to accept Mosqueda as a border-conflict hero in the context of the *corrido* were not willing to give him the same status in a legend-telling situation. At all events, though "El corrido de José Mosqueda" as sung by José Suárez in the 1930s is a *corrido* of border conflict, the accompanying legend does not fit the same pattern. We can see this, for example, in the lack of motif P512.1, "Release from execution at a woman's request (by marriage to her)," one of the persistent elements in legends about heroes of border-conflict *corridos*. In the legend Mosqueda dies in prison, and it is not he but Simón García who becomes the most important character in the narrative. Furthermore, the legend emphasizes the supernatural and the marvelous instead of romanticized reality, as is usually the case in legends associated with *corridos* of border conflict.

Why Simón García was chosen as the sinister protagonist of the legend is not easy to determine, since at this distance it is hard to distinguish fact from legend in regard to the redoubtable Simón. Neale, it should be noted, gave special attention to Simón in his memoirs. But according to Neale's memoirs it was Fabián García, Simón's young, hotheaded cousin, who was the bloodthirsty member of the gang. Apparently the stories about Fabián's sanguinary nature were transferred to his cousin Simón after it became known that Fabián had acted in less than heroic fashion by becoming a witness for the state. Simón, after all, remained at large until he died from other causes, most probably killed in a gambling dispute as Neale says. Simón, furthermore, seems to have recovered a good part of the loot and enjoyed its benefits in Mexico, something that would raise his standing as an outlaw hero. And Simón was, from all extant accounts, a formidable man. The association of the whole affair with legends of buried treasure, most of which use marvelous or supernatural motifs, has done the rest in making of Simón García, guardian of the treasure, a character with diabolical attributes. Also contributing to the sense of the marvelous were the somewhat mysterious deaths of Brito and Browne.

In the legend Simón appears in Mephistophelean guise, tempting José Mosqueda, use being made of motif S241, "Child unwittingly promised: 'first thing you meet.'" The first living thing Mosqueda meets after his agreement with Simón is not Mosqueda's own child, but it is his *ahijado*, who according to Mexican customs of *compadrazgo* has strong claims of ritual kinship on his godfather. The relationship is further emphasized by making the boy a foster son of Mosqueda as well. The fearsome deadliness attributed to Simón García is not in itself supernatural, being an attribute of many a western badman. But Simón is more than a bad man; his is evil with a special malign quality that makes him not an *hombre malo* but *El Malo,* the Evil One himself. When he haunts the chaparral, seeking the best opportunity to carry off the stolen money, he takes on some of the qualities of the supernatural guardians of hidden treasures (compare, for example, motif N571, "Demon as guardian of treasure"). And in his woodland associations and his diminutive size the legendary Simón García reminds us of the malignant spirits of the woods (F441.1, "Elf-like, male, malevolent woodspirit"). It is dangerous to molest such spirits, or to pursue them too closely, and thus it is that the legend has Santiago Brito die by the hand of his own instrument, the guide he used in his attempts to track Simón García down. Only in one respect has the old border-conflict *corrido* legend influenced the usual variants of the José Mosqueda legend, and it is not Mosqueda but Simón García who is given this attribute. The legend has Simón dying in battle during the Mexican Revolution, thus associating him with the heroic tradition of the Mexican revolutionary *corrido*.

THE MATAMOROS TEXT

Not always is the legend told in a casual, relatively unstructured way. At times it is subjected to the creative imagination of men with special narrative talents, specialists in the art of narration. Such a man is the informant from whom I tape-recorded the variant of the Mosqueda legend reproduced below. This text was recorded in Matamoros, Tamaulipas, in 1962. It has been transcribed as recorded, except for a few repetitions, when the informant became confused and started a sentence all over again. The ellipsis points breaking up many of the sentences do not indicate omissions but pauses in the narrative. Dashes have been used to mark abrupt stops or changes. The informant is a *mestizo* male, about seventy-six years old when he made the recording, and a native of the Brownsville-Matamoros border area. His father was a cattle rancher, and he grew up on a ranch, receiving only a primary education. Though he has lived in Texas for short periods, he speaks no English. While in his forties and fifties he served in various capacities with the Tamaulipas rural police. He has a reputation for being a man of great severity and rectitude, and of unassailable honesty. Proof of his incorruptibility is that he was extremely poor when interviewed, although he had occupied in years past several influential posts that could have made him rich had he been amenable to bribes. His is a patriarchal, almost a biblical, character. In his family, the old customs that were general in the region in past generations still prevail. He retains paternal authority over his married sons, to the point that they do not dare smoke in his presence. Among his children the younger look upon the elder brothers as substitute fathers and address them with corresponding respect. For the informant, the ideal woman is the submissive woman who "never goes around stirring up trouble and gossip" but stays home all the time and occupies herself with her household.

JOSÉ MOSQUEDA

There [in Brownsville, Texas] we met Librado Castillo and Ricardo Castillo. I was—I didn't count, I was a child. But they would sit down there to talk; they were Texans. There Librado Castillo told the story of José Mosqueda. José Mosqueda and a few others—a Ramírez, a Vázquez— Antonio Vázquez, an Aguirre—José Aguirre, and some talk about another one named Gutiérrez, and a few others over there—they robbed the train. They derailed the train from Brownsville, the one that went to Point Isabel, in '95 or '94. On the train was some money that was to be shipped somewhere, Mexican money so it is told. This I heard from that man. I heard it myself, that is why I am telling it to you. This is what he disclosed, later when his conscience tortured him . . . Librado, Librado. Not Ricardo. I knew Ricardo too. He was short, while Librado was dark and somewhat sad-looking. Ricardo was older.

There is a place known as Loma Trozada, which once, a long time ago my father told me, used to be called El Rincón de las Viejas. It was a corral that used to be there, around there. That is, a cove against the hill, and there was a gate. And they would drive horses into it and leave them there overnight. Very high. It turned out that the train went through there, and it cut through the hill. So they called it Loma Trozada. They posted themselves there.

In Brownsville there was a man—I don't remember his name—who was to raise the flag just as the train left. They already knew that the shipment of money was going that way. And he was in on the plot; his name was Joaquín, I think. [*suddenly decisive*] He raised the flag. All of them were ready over there, the men on horseback. They took out a rail from each side. Well, so there it comes and there it comes, the little train. You never saw them? Little things. You never got to see them, you were too small. They were tiny, with little engines.

And there it comes. Then they got to the rail. It came up to that place and it tumbled off right there. They robbed all of them on the spot, women and everybody aboard. They put the women with their faces over that way [*gesture toward the wall*]. Four men only. And they were . . . [*gesture across lower part of face, indicating kerchief as mask*]. Well, then [*gestures, hasty stuffing into sacks*] . . . and they took off. There was money scattered . . . ! They used to say you could find it anywhere, along the side of the road, ten or five *pesos* at a time in the *zacahuiste* grass. That's what they used to say, that people would find money. They would go looking, and they would find rolls this size [*roll-that-would-choke-a-horse gesture*]. [*tone of pleasurable excitement*] It was a regular riot!

Well, then . . . So they searched, and they searched, and they searched, and they searched. Who was it? And who was it? And who was it? And who was it? And well, who knows? And who could it have been? And who could it have been? [*roaming index finger showing trackers spreading out to look for signs*] And here goes this one, and here is that other one. And over here another one, and over here another one. [*decisive*] And nothing!

When they went out very early that morning—they were already going from the job—they agreed that whoever they came across they would kill him. This was an oath they swore. Who do they run into but Librado. Herding goats, poor little boy. He was about—it must have been in '95—about fourteen, fifteen years old. Wandering around there, with his little flock of goats.

[*Mephistophelean*] "Go ahead," he said.

[*pity, pleading*] "But man," he said, "he's my godson. How do you want me to kill my godson? [*firmly*] I won't stand to see him killed either. He's just a child, a very good boy. My very own godson, I baptized him. How do you want me to kill him?"

"Well . . . kill him, somebody."

He said, "No, no."

"You are the one out of the whole bunch who has to kill him."

"No, man, no. You all ride ahead." So then he rode up close to him and said, [*firm voice, careful instruction*] "Listen, if anyone asks you if you saw anybody around here, day before yesterday or yesterday or a week ago, from a week ago to this date, don't tell anyone a thing about seeing anybody."

[*humbly*] "Yes, *padrino*."

"But don't say anything. To nobody, nobody, nobody, nobody."

"Yes, *padrino*."

"You be very, very careful."

They took off then . . . [*voice drops*] they went away. [*louder, marked emphasis*] That's where he made his mistake.

And so, it happened. There was a woman whose name was—I don't remember what her name was—Leonor or Cecilia or I don't know what . . . Benigna! Benigna. A woman named Benigna Something-or-other who had sent some money somewhere or other because it wasn't very safe here. Well . . . it was quite a lot of money. And she offered five hundred *pesos* if somebody would say who had done the job, who they were. The days passed, and a month passed. After a month and a half had gone by, Ricardo was talking to Librado. Ricardo was married and Librado was a boy, as he used to tell it. For this was related by Librado. And he says, "Well, I wonder who it could be?"

"Well," he said, [*diffident*] "well, but . . . I know who it is, but don't say anything about it."

[*Rest of conversation between the brothers is told in a low, toneless voice such as might be used to discuss secret matters without descending to whispers.*]

"Who was it?"

"It was my *padrino*."

"Who?"

"Don José Mosqueda."

"José Mosqueda?"

"Yes, but don't tell anybody. Anybody. Don't go tell anybody about it. For my *padrino*'s sake. Afterwards they told me they had sworn to kill anyone they met up with, and he saved my life, man. Don't tell anybody about it."

"But you know," he said.

"Just keep it quiet."

"All right." He left.

At the house of a certain . . . he was an American, but I don't remember what his last name was, and I don't want to lie . . . He was a *cherif* or did the job of a *cherif*, a deputy isn't it? On a ranch. In that house was working Librado's sister-in-law, Ricardo's wife. The hag would go and mix in their affairs, as their cook.

"They offer this sum of money." The wife of the *cherife* of the county.

"And that-that whoever tells! And that-that whoever this! And that-that such! And that so!" [*By intonation, sentence rhythm, and seven uses of the word* que *narrator effectively imitates the cackling of hens.*]

So the hag comes home that night and she lets her husband know, and she says, "Listen. They will give so much money."

[*mild, confidential, almost sanctimonious*] "Yes . . . but no . . . It isn't right. No, no, no. [*suddenly firm*] What good would it do you to go and say . . . or me. What good will it do me to say 'It was so-and-so,' and then they kill some unfortunate wretch?"

"No, but look at it this way. And this and the other. And they are making it known—they say—"

"No, no, no."

[*sly*] "No . . . You know!" said the hag. A clever hag she was.

"Yes, I know. But it must not be told."

"Tell me! I won't tell, anyway, I won't!"

[*gravely*] "Well . . . it was Don José María Mosqueda."

"Librado's *padrino*."

"Librado saw him. He told Librado this and this, and he did not wish to kill him, according to what they say." Ricardo stood there thinking. He said, "Let them each keep his money." Three or four ended up on this side, in Mexico, because they were after them. "Very well," he said.

[*sibilant*] "Ah, yes!" she said. "So it was Don José Mosqueda!"

"Don't go tell. Poor man! He spared my brother's life. Don't be wicked."

[*airily*] "No, man! What makes you think I would tell?" No . . . ? These cursed hags! As soon as she got there, "All right now! I found out who it was."

"Who was it? Tell me!" the old woman said.

"Don José María Mosqueda was their captain."

Well, immediately the old man went out and arrested him, since he was a policeman. He was a very brave prisoner . . . brave! According to what they say, because I did not see it. I was a child. They say they would catch hold of him with pincers, here in the testicles. Here [*pinches lip*], his eyes, his nose.

"Tell us who was with you!"

"No, sir. I don't know anything."

They pulled out his fingernails. And the man never said a word! He never informed. They left him . . . well! The man was sick. But he was brave, there are few men like him. They left him scarred and crippled, and they put him in prison.

They tell—this was also told to me there—that during this time there was a new president. McKinley it must have been, or it may have been . . . No, it wasn't Taft either. I don't know who the president was. He had a daughter, and then the daughter learned about all this, as was natural since they had tried him already. She asked as a favor that he give her this man as a Christmas present. As *aguinaldo* or *Nochebuena,* we would say; for *Crismas,* as you would say. She wanted him for her gardener. And she took him away, and it is said that he died over there. He died after a year or two, he was already sick. But he never told who the others were, he informed on no one.

This happened. I heard Librado Escamilla tell about it when I was sixteen years of age. That is the truth.

COLLECTOR: And the five hundred *pesos?* Did they give them to the sister-in-law?

INFORMANT: Of course not! The *gringo* kept them for himself.

★

Allí conocimos a Librado Castillo. . . y a Ricardo Castillo. Yo era. . . contaba nada. Era menor. Pero. . . allí se ponían a platicar. Eran tejanos ellos. Allí platicó Librado Castillo la historia de José Mosqueda. José Mosqueda y otros cuantos, un tal Ramírez, un Vázquez—Antonio Vázquez, un Aguirre—José Aguirre, y unos dicen que otro, que Gutiérrez. Y otros cuantos allá. Robaron el tren, descarrilaron el tren que salía de Brónsbil, el que iba para Punta Isabel. El 95 ó 94. En ese tren iba un dinero que iba a embarcarse quién sabe para donde, dinero mexicano. Según cuentan. Eso lo oí platicar a ese hombre yo. Eso yo lo oí, por eso te estoy diciendo. Cuando acordaron— Según lo que descubrió el hombre después de que le remordía la conciencia. A Librado, a Librado. Ricardo no. Ricardo también yo lo conocí. Era romito y Librado era trigueño y medio mustio. Y el otro, Ricardo, era romito. Más viejo Ricardo.

Cuando acordaron estos hombres, que salieron en la mañanita— Hay un lugar que le dicen la Loma Trozada que entonces, más antes, me decía mi papá que se llamaba El Rincón de las Viejas. Era un corral que había allí, por ahi, que es un rincón y hay una puerta allí. Arrinconaban las caballadas en la noche y allí las dejaban. Muy alto. Tocó al tren ir por allí y trozó la loma. Y le pusieron Loma Trozada. Allí se pusieron.

En Brónsbil había un hombre, no me acuerdo como se llamaba, de acuerdo de izar la bandera cuando ya salía el tren. Ya sabían que iba esa carga de dinero para allá, según contaba el hombre ese, ese Librado. (Si Librado viviera. . . yo creo que no vive porque yo estaba joven. . . muchos años, desde el 1902.) Y él estaba de acuerdo, se llamaba Joaquín, yo creo, el hombre. [*with sudden emphasis*] Alzó la bandera. Todos estaban listos, ya allá, hombres a caballo. Sacaron un riel de cada lado. Pos que allá viene y allá viene el trenecito. ¿Tú nunca los viste? Chiquitos. Tú no los conociste, estabas muy niño. Chiquitos, maquinitas chiquitas.

Y allá viene. Cuando ya llegaron al riel. Allí se saltó y allí se aplanó. Allí los robaron a todos, mujeres y todos ellos allí. Pero nadie se dio cuenta, como era poca gente. A las mujeres las pusieron con la cara para allá [*gesture toward the wall*]. Cuatro hombres nada más. Y ellos andaban. . . [*gesture across lower part of face, indicating kerchief mask*]. Pues ahi [*gestures of hasty stuffing into sacks*]. . . y se pelaron. ¡Hubo dinero regado. . . ! Decían que por ahi se hallaban dondequiera, en la orilla del camino, de a diez y de a cinco pesos juntos, tirados en el zacahuiste. Eso contaban, que se hallaban dinero. Iban a buscar y encontraban rollos de este pelo [*roll-that-would-choke-a-horse gesture*]. [*pleasurable excitement*] ¡Hubo desgarriate!

El caso es de que. . . pues a buscar y a buscar y a buscar y a buscar. Quién fue, quién fue, quién fue y quién fue. Y pos quién sabe y que quién sería y quién sería [*roaming index finger showing trackers spreading out looking for signs*]. Y por aquí anda éste y por aquí está el otro, y acá el otro y acá el otro. [*decisive*] ¡Y nada!

En la casa de un tal. . . que era cherif, que la hacía como cherif. Diputado, ¿verdad? En un rancho, estaba trabajando la mujer de Ricardo, hermano de aquél. En la salida que dieron, en la mañanita, iban ya del trabajo, habían acordado que al que encontraban. . . matarlo. Ése era un juramento que hicieron. Encuéntrense a Librado, de pastorcito, como de unos—sería el 95—tendría unos catorce, quince años. De pastor, con un atajito de cabras que andaba por allí.

[*Mephisthophelean*] —Ándele —le dijo.

—Pero, hombre —le dijo—. [*pity, pleading*] Cómo vo'a matar a mi ahijado. [*firmly*] Ni verlo que lo maten tampoco. Es una criatura, un muchacho muy bueno. Mi ahijado carnal, mi ahijado de bautismo. Cómo lo vo'a matar.

—Bueno. . . mátenlo.

Dijo:

—No, no.

—Usted es el que lo va a matar de todos.

—No, hombre, no. Váyanse caminando.

Ya fue y se arrimó y le dijo:

—Oye, [*firm voice giving careful instructions*] si te preguntan a ti si viste alguna gente por aquí, antier o ayer o ocho días antes, de ocho días para acá, no digas a nadie nada que vistes a nadie.

[*humbly*] —Sí, padrino.

—Pero no le vayas a decir a nadie, a nadie, a nadie, a nadie.

—Sí, padrino.

—Tenga mucho cuidado.

Se arrancaron luego, [*voice drops*] se fueron. [*then with marked emphasis*] Ahi 'stuvo el mal.

Entonces, pasó el caso. Y había una señora que se llamaba. . . no me acuerdo como se llamaba, Leonor o Cecilia o quién sabe como. . . [*sudden recall*] Benigna, Benigna. Una señora Benigna quién sabe de qué, que había mandado un dinero quién sabe para dónde porque aquí no estaba muy seguro. Bueno. . . era bastante dinero. Y daba quinientos pesos porque dijeran quién había hecho el trabajo ese, quiénes eran.

Y ese señor, no me acuerdo, era un americano pero no me acuerdo como se apellidaba, y no quiero echar una mentira. Pero allí había un americano que tenía un tendajito y vivía, como la hacía de cherife allí hizo un capitalito. Pero no me acuerdo como se llamaba, no me acuerdo ahorita. Y en esa casa trabajaba la cuñada de Librado, la mujer de Ricardo.

Pasaron los días y pasó el mes. Al mes y medio platica Ricardo con Librado, Ricardo casado y Librado muchacho, catorce años poco más o menos según decía él, pues esto lo platicó Librado. Y dice éste:

—Hombre, ¿quién será?

—Hombre —dijo—, [*shy, diffident*] pos hombre, yo sé quién es pero no digas nada.

[*Rest of conversation between the two brothers is in a low, toneless voice in which secret matters might be discussed without descending to whispers.*]

—¿Quién fue?

—Fue mi padrino. Andaba mi padrino en la bola también.

—¿Quién?

—Don José Mosqueda.

—¿José Mosqueda?

—Sí, pero no digas a nadie, a nadie. A nadie le vayas a decir. Por mi padrino. Después me dijeron que habían jurado matar al que encontraran y él me salvó la vida, hombre. No le vayas a decir a nadie.

—Pero tú sabes —le dijo.

—Nomás calla la boca.

—'Sta bueno.

Se fue.

La vieja, que iba y se metía allá, de cocinera.

—Y que ofrecen tanto —la señora del cherife del condado— ¿Y que-que el que diga, y que-que el que esto, y que-que fue y que vino [*intonation imitates cackling of a hen*].

Y viene la vieja y le dice al marido en la noche, a avisarle:

—Oyes, ofrecen tanto.

—Sí [*mild, confidential, almost sanctimonious*], pero no conviene. No. No, no. [*suddenly firm*] Qué ganas tú con ir a decir. . . o yo. ¿Qué gano con decir yo "Fue fulano" y matan a un infeliz?

—No. Que mira que acá y que más allá, que mandan decir, que dicen.

—No. No, no.

—No [*sly*], tú sabes —dijo la vieja.

Vieja muy larga.

—Sí, yo sé. Pero no hay que decir.

—Dime, al cabo no digo, no digo.

[*gravely*] —Pues. . . fue don José María Mosqueda.

—El padrino de Librado.

—Librado lo vio. A Librado le dijo esto y esto, y no lo quiso matar, según dicen ahi.

[*thoughtful expression*] Y ahi 'sta Ricardo. Dijo:

—Que se queden con su dinero, cada cual.

Tres o cuatro vinieron a dar a este lado, a México, porque andaban detrás de ellos.

—Bueno —dijo.

—Ahi, sí! —dijo—. [*sibilant*] Con que don José María Mosqueda fue.

—No vayas a decir. Pobrecito. Le salvó la vida a mi hermano. No seas mala.

—No, hombre, [*airily*] qué voy a decir.

¡No. . . ! ¡Las viejas condenadas! Pero nomás llegó:

—Ora sí! Ya supe quién fue.

—¿Quién fue? ¡Dígame! —dijo la vieja.

—Don José María Mosqueda fue el capitán de ellos.

Pos luego-luego el viejo fue y lo arrestó. Si era empleado. Preso muy hombre, ¡hombre! Según cuentan porque yo no vi eso, 'staba chico yo. Dicen que lo agarraban con las tenazas de aquí [*touches crotch*], de los compañones, de aquí [*pinches lip*], de los ojos, las narices.

—Diga quién andaba con usted.

—No, señor; yo no sé nada.

De las uñas. Se las sacaban. Le sacaron las uñas de aquí [*puts out hand*]. Y *nunca* dijo *nada* aquel hombre. Jamás descubrió. Lo dejaron. . . ¡bueno! . . . enfermo el hombre. Jamás descubrió. Él fue hombre, de ésos pocos hay, hombres de esa clase. Jamás. Lo dejaron cicatrizado, lo dejaron inútil. Lo hicieron preso.

Cuentan, eso me lo contaron también allí, que entonces había salido presidente, la mujer de un presidente. Es decir, un presidente. No me acuerdo qué presidente era. Sería Miquenle o sería. . . no era Taft tampoco. No sé quién sería el presidente. Que tenía una hija y entonces la hija supo de esto todo, naturalmente, juzgado estaba ya. Le pidió de favor que le diera de aguinaldo o es decir de Nochebuena. De aguinaldo, como decimos nosotros. De Crismas. A ese hombre de jardinero. Y se lo llevó y dicen que allá murió. Al año o dos años murió el hombre. Ya iba enfermo. Pero nunca descubrió a los demás. A nadie descubrió.

Esto pasó. Lo oí platicar a Librado Escamilla. Cuando yo tenía dieciséis años de edad. Eso es positivo.

COLLECTOR: ¿Y los quinientos pesos? ¿Se los dieron a la cuñada?

INFORMANT: ¡Qué se los iban a dar! Se quedó el gringo con ellos.

WE HAVE STILL TO SEE a thorough study of the stylistic and structural differences that exist between the legend and the folktale. One general statement is that the legend usually takes the form of motif clusters that may be arranged and rearranged at will, while the folktale is recognized as a "literary whole," in which the different parts are arranged according to a definite pattern. Most folklorists, I believe, would accept the foregoing as it regards the wonder tale, but many would not agree that the legend always is a freely arranged bundle of motifs. Legends about hidden treasure, for example, have easily recognizable patterns based on underlying structures that may be quite uniform. Such is not the case, however, with usual tellings of the *corrido* legend, to which genre the Mosqueda story belongs. As has been said, the *corrido* legend usually exists in its totality only in the memories of the people who hear it and re-create it in every telling. Any part of it may be told at any one time, in any order. When told in this manner, in a natural context, the narration of each episode is a complete performance, with full verbal detail, gestures, and tone of voice—not to mention audience participation. But the only way to elicit the "total" legend from an informant is by interviewing him. Then he will give the collector a connected and fairly complete account, but it will be in summary form and in the tone of voice he would use to convey ordinary information. Our Matamoros text, then, is an exception. Its well-patterned form suggests the folktale rather than the legend. Interestingly enough, the informant would have been offended had I told him I considered him an artistic narrator of folktales. He considers it beneath his dignity to tell *cuentos*, or folktales, though he listens to others tell them. What he claims to narrate is unrecorded history. He presents his text as fact and not as fiction. This can be seen in some of the expressions he uses to give authority to his text: "This I heard from that man. I heard it myself, that is why I am telling it to you." And in reference to the name of an actor in the story: "I don't remember what his last name was, and I don't want to lie [by inventing a name]."

But the Matamoros text is a well-constructed whole, a unified narrative developed around a single theme. And it is precisely this feeling of unity that distinguishes it from the less patterned narratives forming most *corrido* legends. Without a doubt it is an artistic elaboration of materials found in the *corrido* legends about Mosqueda, in the *corridos* themselves, and in accounts taken from oral history. The process by which this elaboration takes place is apparently traditional and unconscious on the part of the narrator, but the result is art nevertheless. In usual legendary accounts it is Simón García who is the main actor, but our narrator has put José Mosqueda back into this role—a change in accord with historical fact. Mosqueda is made the hero so the narrative action may develop with him as its center; and this action is motivated by a series of prohibitions. As each prohibition is violated—by Mosqueda or by others—the resulting consequence affects the fate of Mosqueda as central character and carries the narrative one step further toward its resolution.

Simón García almost disappears from the story as told in the Matamoros text. His name is not even mentioned, though (when questioned after the recording) the narrator was quite familiar with Simón's identity and reputation. Nonetheless, Simón plays an important role, since he is the agent used to bring about the first and most important prohibition—not to allow anyone met on the road to live. This detail is found in all variants of the Mosqueda *corrido* legend, where it is the central motif. In the Matamoros text, however, it becomes the first link in a chain of violated prohibitions leading us to Ricardo's wife—the talkative, greedy, and inquisitive woman, source of all the ills of man. The evil character of Simón García is not completely lost, even though his name disappears from the text. There is a feeling of malignity not only in Simón's insistence that Mosqueda kill his godson but also in the tone of voice adopted by the narrator when he is playing the role of Simón. But Simón, the Evil One, seems soft and reasonable compared to the perverse malevolence of Ricardo's wife, who appears to be worse than the devil himself. This is motif G303.10.5, "Where the devil can't reach, he sends an old woman," and it—rather than the vow to kill the first person met—gives the Matamoros text its focus. One need not emphasize the fact that the evil old gossip, the *alcahueta*, has been a major figure in Spanish folktales since medieval times.

The folktale, we often hear, uses few details in describing setting or characters. Our text includes some fairly detailed description, but it should be noted that it occurs where the narrator is drawing directly from his own experience. The place called Loma Trozada is described not only as it appeared when the train was robbed but as it had been before the railroad right-of-way cut through the hill. Here the informant is drawing from his own memory and from what his father told him. Librado, whom the informant once met, is described as "dark and somewhat sad-looking" and contrasted with his brother Ricardo. Most of this description, in what one might call a legendary style, occurs during the early moments of narration, before the plot really starts moving, giving background details that are not really essential to the central situation of the story. This central situation involves two simply drawn characters contrasting with each other, one good and one evil, in the manner of Olrik's "law" of contrast.

The two extremes are represented by José Mosqueda and Ricardo's wife. Mosqueda, in spite of the fact that he is a train robber, is represented as a man in whom courage and fortitude are combined with compassion for the weak. He puts his own life in immediate danger when he saves Librado's life, and later he suffers torture rather than reveal the names of his confederates. Ricardo's wife, as we have seen, is evil incarnate, far surpassing in this respect both Simón García and the treacherous North American sheriff who cheats her out of the reward money. The brothers Librado and Ricardo also are simply drawn—basically good men but somewhat foolish and trusting. According to the values held by the narrator and his community, Librado is the less guilty of the two. He violates a promise made, it is true. He had promised his godfather Mosqueda to tell no one what he had seen. But it is to his older brother that Librado confides his secret. According to the patriarchal values of the narrator, an eldest brother is like a second father to the younger ones; the younger should keep no secrets from the older brother. Ricardo, on the other hand, has no such excuse; he represents an extreme of his own—the most extreme kind of foolishness a man may be capable of, according to the narrator's own values. He allows himself to be ruled by his wife. He violates a prohibition central to many a folktale, implicit in our text although never directly expressed: "Never confide a secret to your wife" (J21.22, "Do not tell a secret to a woman: counsel proved wise by experience"; T274, "Wife cannot keep secret").

Most of the usual folktale formulas are absent from our text. The formal folktale opening is lacking, for example; instead we have an opening in the style of the legend, giving names, places, the narrator's credentials, and other data "documenting" the narrative to follow. The ending also documents the narrative: "This happened. I heard . . . tell about it. . . . That is the truth." But it also resembles the formal endings used in mythical narratives among some Native American groups: "It happened that way. That is all." And it also bears resemblance to some closing formulas used in Mexican folktales, such as one collected in Mitla, Oaxaca, by Elsie Clews Parsons: "I was witness to that. After it all happened, I came back."[22]

More important to any comparison of our text with the folktale is the highly structured style of narration, the use of repetition in certain passages, as well as mimicry, gesture, and tone of voice, as part of the narrator's style. We noted that the text begins more in the style of the legend than of the folktale. The narrative is located as to actual time and place; the narrator identifies himself as a competent witness; places like Loma Trozada are described in what one might call a legendary style. But the style begins to change, until by the fourth paragraph (in the transcription—the narrator, of course, does not necessarily speak in paragraphs) we can identify the stylistic influence of the folktale. For one thing, the narrator begins to make greater use of gestures, to the point that the last part of the fourth paragraph would be unintelligible if we had the text alone, without some indication as to the gestures that accompany it.

From this point on the narrative style becomes much more dramatic. There is more dialogue, often without the use of introductory phrases like "he said." The narrator changes his tone of voice according to the character speaking. There is much repetition of words and phrases, not only for the sake of structure but to point up the feelings of the characters. There is also repetition to emphasize a scene or to give a feeling of tension, with gesture also being added. The confusion of the lawmen when they arrive at the scene of the robbery is vividly shown in this manner. And when the wives of the sheriff and Ricardo talk about the robbery, the narrator combines a series of *que*'s with repetition and intonation to make the women's conversation sound like the cackling of hens. It is also interesting that, though the narrator is acting within a basically European tradition, he has a tendency to repeat words and phrases in series of four rather than three.

Finally we should note the escapist functions of this text, which resemble those of the folktale rather than the legend. It is true that legends have their functional and dysfunctional features, but it is in the jest and the wonder tale where human fantasy loves best to challenge the values and rules of conduct consciously held by society, because these are fictions and set no limits to the imagination. Our text does reflect quite faithfully some of the values of the narrator and of the culture in which he grew up. Most important of these is the concept of manly courage, and the emphasis placed on this concept explains the presence of a motif not usually found in legendary accounts about Mosqueda, but almost indispensable in similar accounts about other Texas-Mexicans who are truly heroes of border conflict—the freeing from prison of the hero when a "great" North American lady falls in love with him.

The use of this motif turns Mosqueda into a hero more like the one pictured for us in the Lomax variant of the *corrido*. But there is a difference. We are not really told that the president's daughter falls in love with Mosqueda. She asks her father to free Mosqueda, not so as to marry him but to make him her gardener. This may be the fantasy of the narrator, a man almost eighty years old, who identifying himself with Mosqueda tends to see the relationship between the hero and the young daughter of the president from a paternal point of view. But the last picture we are given of Mosqueda—as a gardener charged with bringing things into life—coincides with the man's character before he was sent to prison, as the narrator has drawn it for us: the compassionate man who puts his own life in danger to save that of his godson, the stoic captive who suffers torture rather than inform on his companions. The other side of the cult of manhood is the attitude toward women; and here also the text reflects the values of the narrator and his society, especially in their patriarchal attitudes. For the narrator the only good woman is the submissive and silent wife whose only interest in life is to take care of her home and children.

There are other values, however, that are unconsciously rejected by the fantasy of the narrator. In him we have a man known for his strict probity, but he constructs a complete model of manly virtue around a train robber, not only elevating him to the status of border-conflict hero but making him a kind of martyr as well. The narrator, who in his years as police officer must have interrogated many a wrongdoer, clearly takes sides with Mosqueda when Mosqueda is third-degreed by his captors. Note also the indignation shown by the narrator when Ricardo's wife informs on Mosqueda, a reaction one would scarcely expect in a former policeman. But the fantasy of the narrator is most clearly revealed in the scene depicting the stolen money strewn about in great heaps out on the plain, within easy reach of anyone who might pass by and find it. There is something here of the wonder tale describing marvelous riches, and of some dream fantasies much favored by psychiatrists, in which the subject dreams he finds money scattered everywhere, in sizable heaps. This may also be an involuntary expression of regret on the part of a man who in his youth handled many such sums of illicit money, and who may feel that his honesty in not helping himself has brought him to an impoverished old age.

CONCLUSION

We have in the life and deeds of José María Mosqueda, train robber and multifaceted folk hero, a good example of what Latin American folklorists call the "folklorization" of actual events. In his case, the transmuting of actuality into folklore is especially interesting because there exist enough data to make comparisons. Even more interesting about the folkloric Mosqueda are his many aspects, and the way his story has moved about from genre to genre. Beginning with the same actual events, within the same folk groups, the José Mosqueda story has been "folklorized" in at least four different ways. From stanzas recollected by old people in the 1950s, we have evidence that there once was a ballad of the outlaw type, with some comic passages, recounting Mosqueda's exploits in a more or less factual way. The variant of "El corrido de José Mosqueda" collected by the Lomaxes in 1939, on the other hand, takes the pattern of the *corrido* of border conflict. Related to the *corridos* are a series of legendary accounts in which, contrary to the usual *corrido* legends, there are definite elements of the supernatural. Finally, in the hands of a gifted narrator—a man temperamentally adjusted to narrating wonder tales but who considers such tales beneath his dignity—the legendary accounts about Mosqueda assume much of the form and function of the wonder tale.

The different paths taken by the process of folklorization with the story of Mosqueda may be attributed to several causes. The sensational nature of the holdup assured its long life in the traditions of the area and allowed for changes to occur in retelling. Various patterns of folk performance preexistent among the people who retold Mosqueda's exploit supplied the different molds into which the Mosqueda story was cast by different folk performers. Such patterns were determined to a certain extent by the cultural and political conditions on the border. But, as can be seen from the Matamoros text, the personality of the narrator, his own background, and the conditions of performance had a great deal to do with the form he gave to the Mosqueda story. Much the same thing may be inferred from what we know about the *corrido* text collected by the Lomaxes. It was recorded from José Suárez, a well-known singer and re-creator of *corridos* of border conflict; so Suárez's version resembles a border-conflict *corrido* rather than an outlaw ballad, as one would have expected.

– 9 –

The United States, Mexico, and *Machismo*

O<small>NE OF THE MOST WIDELY DISCUSSED</small> Mexican national types is the *macho,* the superman of the multitude. He has preoccupied psychologists, sociologists, philosophers, historians, poets, and even folklorists. Some, like folklorist Vicente T. Mendoza, have explained him as a phenomenon caused by the climate, or as a result of tendencies inherited by the Mexicans from the people of Andalusia.[1] On the other hand, many others have explained *machismo* in terms of Freudian theories. *Machismo*—so they tell us—has its origins in the conquest, when Hernán Cortés and his conquistadors arrived in Mexico and raped the women of the Aztecs. From this act of violence is born the *mestizo,* who hates and envies his Spanish father and despises his Indian mother—in both cases as a result of his Oedipal complexes. Various Mexican writers have taken this line, but Samuel Ramos may be singled out as the initiator and Octavio Paz as one of the most eloquent defenders of this theory. In Argentina, too, Ezequiel Martínez Estrada applied a similar point of view to the *gaucho.*[2] The characteristic traits of *machismo* are quite well known: the outrageous boast, a distinct phallic symbolism, the identification of the man with the male animal, and the ambivalence toward women—varying from an abject and tearful posture to brutal disdain. The Mexican *macho,* Santiago Ramírez tells us, "is terribly fond of all articles of clothing symbolizing masculinity: the hat (either the fancy *sombrero* or the wide-brimmed Borsalino), the pistol, the horse or automobile are his pleasure and his pride."[3] *Machismo* finds expression in Mexican folklore, especially in the folksong. As Felipe Montemayor states, "The folksongs of Mexico are openly tearful and addressed to the woman who has gone away with another man 'who is no doubt more of a man than I am,' . . . in which he openly admits his frustration and failure; as for the rest, they are strings of phrases typical of one rejected, who tries to conceal his humiliation or the scorn directed at him by resorting to aggressive or compensatory forms."[4]

If all this has resulted from the rape of some Indian women by the soldiers of Cortés, then Mexican *machismo* is very ancient indeed. It has existed some four centuries at least, if one is to suppose that effects follow soon after causes. It should be possible, then, to make an interesting study of the folkloric expressions of Mexican *machismo*, from the time of the first *mestizo* up to the present. Such a work cannot be expected from either psychologists or poets, to whom we owe but superficial references to Mexican folksong and other folkloric genres. We would expect it from a folklorist, a Vicente Mendoza for example. And in truth, there is at least one study by Vicente T. Mendoza on this subject, "El machismo en México al través de las canciones, corridos y cantares," published in Buenos Aires in 1962.[5] In this essay, one of the last left us by the late Mexican folklorist, we are told that "there are two kinds of *machismo:* one that we could call authentic, characterized by true courage, presence of mind, generosity, stoicism, heroism, bravery," and so forth, and "the other, nothing but a front, false at bottom, hiding cowardice and fear covered up by exclamations, shouts, presumptuous boasts, bravado, double-talk, bombast. . . . Supermanliness that conceals an inferiority complex."[6] Mendoza goes on to cite more than thirty Mexican folksongs as examples of what he calls "authentic" and "false" *machismo*.

There are at least three points of interest in this study of Mendoza's. The first is his definition of the two kinds of *machismo*. Mendoza's false *machismo*—with its "presumptuous boasts, bravado, [and] double-talk"—is what all other writers on the subject would call the real *machismo*, that configuration of attitudes which has so preoccupied writers as divergent as Samuel Ramos and Octavio Paz. What Mendoza calls authentic *machismo* is no such thing. It is simply courage, and it is celebrated in the folksongs of all countries. Admiration for the brave man who dies for the fatherland, for an ideal, or simply because he does not want to live without honor or without fame is found among all peoples. It is the heroic ideal in any time and in any country. Furthermore, the examples of boastful songs that Mendoza gives us date from the last third of the nineteenth and the first third of the twentieth centuries. That is to say, they belong to the period of the Revolution or to the times of Porfirio Díaz, immediately preceding the revolutionary period. Finally—and this is the most surprising thing of all—in all the examples Mendoza gives us of folksongs illustrative of Mexican *machismo*, not once does there occur the word *macho* or any of its derivatives. The heroes of the folksongs cited by Mendoza "die like men"; they are said to be "real men," and they are "valiant" or "brave." But they are never *machos*. The words *macho* and *machismo* occur repeatedly in the essay, but only in Mendoza's discussion of this supposedly Mexican phenomenon.

If the reader believes that the examples given by Mendoza are not representative, he can consult the major collections—those of Vázquez Santa Ana, Rubén Campos, and others including Mendoza himself.* The reader will find no traces of *machismo* in the songs of the colonial period, the war of independence, or even the Reform. He will encounter many brave men in those songs, but rarely will he find the bully. The Mexican bully as a folkloric type begins to appear in the *décimas* printed in the last two decades of the nineteenth century, in leaflets from presses like that of Antonio Vanegas Arroyo and with titles like "El guanajuateño," "El valiente de Guadalajara." Let us emphasize that these boastful *décimas* of the last part of the nineteenth century are of a decidedly comic character. They abound in humorous sayings and proverbial phrases. A *décima* from "El guanajuateño" (The Man from Guanajuato) may serve as an example for the whole genre:

No se arruguen, valentones,	Don't back down on me, you bravos,
traigan dispuestos sus fierros	and carry your blades at ready;
que aquí está "El Guanajuateño"	here's a man from Guanajuato,
para darles sus lecciones.	to teach you a thing or two.
Acérquense los matones	Come a bit closer, you bullies;
que yo no les tengo miedo,	I am not afraid of you.
firme y parado me quedo	Here I stand, firm and erect,
esperando cuchilladas;	awaiting your thrusts to parry;
me parecen enchiladas	to me they're like enchiladas,
que me trago las que puedo.[7]	and I'll guzzle all I can.

* It is necessary to include the collections of *décimas* as well as those of *corridos, canciones,* and *cantares.*

One must be extremely ingenuous to think that we have here a faithful picture of the Mexican bravo in real life. The man who is convinced that life is not worth living does not waste time on well-turned phrases and colorful words. Artistic boasting is found among Mexican males, but almost always it is the buffoon of the group who cultivates this genre. Usually he is the drunkest and least courageous member of the group, whose lack of valor and manliness gives him a certain minstrel-like license. It is this type, and not the bravo, who is described in the *décimas de valientes.* And let us also keep in mind: the boastful protagonist of these *décimas* says he is "a real man," "valiant," and "brave." He may compare himself with the tiger and the panther, or he will say that he is "a fever on stilts." But he never calls himself a *macho.*

The Mexican boast turns serious once the Revolution begins, and then it passes from the *décima* to the *corrido.* The idea of manliness existed in the Mexican *corrido* before the Revolution, as Mendoza shows in his study, for example in the *corrido* of "Demetrio Jáuregui":

Le contestó don Demetrio:	Don Demetrio replied,
—Yo no me vine a rajar,	"I didn't come to back out of a fight;
yo vine como los hombres	I came here like a man,
aquí a perder o ganar.—[8]	either to win or to lose."

Now the *corrido* picks up the kind of boast seen earlier in the *décima,* no longer in jest, however, but with all the seriousness of spirits inflamed by the Revolution. For example, in the *corrido* "De la persecución de Villa," the singer pokes fun at the efforts made by Pershing's forces to capture Pancho Villa:

Qué pensarán los "bolillos" tan patones	What did these bigfooted *gringos* think, that they scare us with cannon.
que con cañones nos iban a asustar;	They may have piles of airplanes,
si ellos tienen aviones de a montones	but we have the thing that really counts.
aquí tenemos lo mero principal.[9]	

"The thing that really counts" is, of course, courage—concentrated in the testicles of the Mexicans—what will give them the advantage over all the cannon and airplanes of the United States. Here we come much closer to what is usually meant by *machismo.* Another *corrido* of the same era presents the same attitudes even more explicitly, this one being "Los ambiciosos patones":

> Se va a mirar muy bonito de gringos el tenderete,
> después no quedrán la gorda; les sudará hasta el copete.
>
> La verdad, yo les suplico que traigan a sus gringuitas,
> porque estamos enfadados de querer a las inditas,
> sé que las tienen bonitas, gordas y bien coloradas,
> ahora es tiempo, camaradas, de pelear con muchas ganas,
> que les vamos a "avanzar" hasta las americanas.[10]
>
> It will be a pretty sight, to see all those *gringo* corpses;
> they will flinch from the tortilla, and they will sweat up to here.
>
> In truth, I hope they will bring their *gringo* women along,
> because we are getting tired of loving our Indian girls.
> I know that they have some nice ones, plump and with red faces.
> Now is the time, my comrades, to fight with a will;
> there will be lots of plunder, even American women.

This last song has the melody of a *corrido,* but the text is composed in *décimas.* Moreover, the influence of the braggart type of *décima* may be seen in the number of proverbial phrases it contains, such as "they want to scare us with the dead man's pallet," "they are going to stake out their hides," and "go slow in reaching in there, or you'll get your hand full of thorns." It must be noted it is in the *corridos* about United States intervention in the affairs of Mexico where we find these examples of what could be called the "boast taken seriously." Nevertheless, the word *macho* does not occur in these *corridos* either. Not until the 1940s, during World War II, do we begin to run across it. Mendoza published a *corrido* entitled "De pistoleros y moronistas" (About Gunmen and Partisans of Morones), collected in 1949 but dating from the period between 1940 and 1946, the administration of President Manuel Ávila Camacho. The last stanza goes like this:

> ¡Viva el pueblo siempre macho! ¡Agustín el general!
> y ¡Viva Ávila Camacho y la vida sindical![11]
>
> Long live the people, always *machos!* Long live Agustín, the general!
> Long live Ávila Camacho and the labor unions!

In another *corrido*, very popular in the 1940s, the protagonist brags about Mexican courage, and how the Mexicans are going to wreak havoc on the Axis once Mexico decides to join in the war, adding that their president is "Ca . . . macho!" In still another song of the same period, threats are hurled at the Axis nations, as the singer says:

Yo soy puro mexicano	I am a true-blue Mexican,
y me he echado el compromiso con	and I have an obligation to the land
la tierra en que nací	where I was born,
de ser macho entre los machos,	to be a *macho* among *machos;*
y por eso muy ufano yo le canto a	and that is why I proudly sing to
mi país.	my country.

In these *corridos* of the 1940s, where we do find the word *macho*, we almost always see it in association with other well-defined factors. One of these is the grim figure of the *pistolero*, one of the most dismal products of the postrevolutionary period. This is the man of the Revolution projected into peacetime, and therefore out of his element: the pistol-toting bully who sates his brutal impulses by trampling on the common citizen, and who can do it with impunity because he has money or political influence or simply because he is the bodyguard of some congressman or governor. Another factor is World War II, in which Mexicans took almost no part, in which they were not threatened by danger, desolation, or death—as they were during the Revolution. This is why the boasts ring so false in the *corridos* of the 1940s as compared to those of the Revolution. The revolutionary boasts directed against the United States arose from a situation both dangerous and real, and they expressed the sentiments of a majority of Mexicans. The boasts against the Axis during the 1940s sound like those of a little man who hurls threats while hiding behind a protector much larger than he. And let us remember that in this case, the "protector" was the traditional enemy, the United States. A third factor is the accident that in this period the last name of the Mexican president included the sound "macho." I am not suggesting that the word *macho* was not used in Mexico prior to the 1940s, or that *machismo* would not have appeared in Mexico if Ávila Camacho had not been president. But we must remember that names lend reality to things. The name of Camacho—because it rhymes with *macho* and because it was well known when other factors favored *machismo*—gave to both word and concept a popularity they did not have before. Before that time *macho* had been almost an obscenity, and consequently a word less used than *hombre* or *valiente*. Now it became correct, acceptable. After all, wasn't it in the name of the president himself?

Then appear the *corridos* for which Mexico is known abroad, the same ones cited repeatedly by those who deplore *machismo*. The following stanzas exemplify the style:

¡Traigo mi cuarenta y cinco	I'm wearing my forty-five
con sus cuatro cargadores!	with its four cartridge clips!
¡Y traigo cincuenta balas,	And I carry fifty bullets;
las traigo pa' los traidores!	they are for renegades!

And another one, even more foolish:

¡Caramba, yo soy su rey	*Caramba,* I am your king,
y mi caballo el segundo!	and my horse is second only to me!
¡Ora se hacen a mi ley	Now you will bow to my law,
o los aparto del mundo!	or I'll send you from this world!

Such *corridos* were disseminated in Mexico and abroad by the voice of popular singers like Pedro Infante and Jorge Negrete. That is to say, these were moving-picture *corridos*. And when one says moving-pictures, one says middle class. These have been the songs of the man from an emergent middle class, a man who goes to the movies, has enough money to buy a car, and enough political influence to go around carrying a gun. During World War II, it was this middle class that became emotional hearing Pedro Infante sing:

¡Viva México! ¡Viva América!	Long live Mexico! Long live America!
¡Oh pueblos benditos de Dios!	Oh, nations blessed by God!

The feelings of the common man are revealed in a well-known anecdote. The news that Mexico has just declared war against the Axis reaches a little Mexican village. The authorities lead the people in the execution of various "vivas" to Mexico. In a pause a voice is heard yelling, "Viva México, and death to the *gringos!*" "Shut up, stupid!" they tell him. "The *gringos* are our allies." "But how?" he says. "If it isn't the *gringos,* then who are we fighting?"

It seems, then, that Mexican *machismo* is not exactly as it has been painted for us by people who like to let their imaginations dwell on the rape of Indian women. *Machismo* does not appear in Mexican folklore until very recent times. In a more-or-less comic form, it was characteristic of the lower classes in prerevolutionary times. In a more sentimental and meretricious style, it is identified today with the Mexican middle class. We note, furthermore, a certain influence of the United States. All this makes us ask: How Mexican is *machismo* and to what degree is it a Hispanic, a New World, or a universal manifestation?

We know that courage and virility have always been identified as the ideal traits of the male, and that both primitive and modern man often have equated the coward with the homosexual. Among some groups it has been the custom to dress in woman's clothes any man who did not show sufficient courage in battle. There is no lack of examples making direct identification between courage and manliness. In an Eskimoan song published by C. M. Bowra, an old man remembers his youth, when he was a great hunter. And he sings:

> I remember the white bear,
> With its back-body raised high;
> It thought it was the only male here,
> And came towards me at full speed.
> Again and again it threw me down,
> But it did not lie over me,
> But quickly went from me again.
> It had not thought
> Of meeting other males here,
> And by the edge of an ice-floe
> It lay down calmly.[12]

Let us take a second example from the Nordic peoples, of times past but not very remote, from the *Volsunga Saga*. Two heroes, Sinfjotli and Granmar, prepare to duel to the death; and as a preamble Sinfjotli says to his opponent:

Dim belike is grown thy memory now of how thou wert a witch wife on Varinsey, and wouldst fain have a man to thee, and chose me to that same office of all the world; and how thereafter thou wert a Valkyrie in Asgarth,

and it wellnigh came to this, that for thy sweet sake should all men fight;
and nine wolf-whelps I begat on thy body in Lowness, and was the father to
them all.[13]

Except for the archaic English, this might be a *pelado* doing the Mexican
equivalent of the "dozens" with another of his type. But let us move to
the eighteenth century, to the classical English poet John Dryden and his
famous ode on Alexander the Great, which includes a kind of refrain
that has become proverbial: "None but the brave, None but the brave,
None but the brave deserve the fair." That is to say, the most valiant and
vigorous *macho* wins the coveted female, a poetizing of the natural selection of the species before Darwin was even born. Yet, this is also the
theme of many *Märchen,* and of numberless plots in our popular literature, movies, and television.

The ingredients of *machismo,* then, are found in many cultures; however, what has been observed in Mexico is a whole pattern of behavior, a
popular philosophy, so to speak. Is Mexico unique in this respect? Martínez Estrada would have said no, since he thought he had found the
same thing in the Argentine *gaucho.* But let us look in the opposite direction, and we will find a country—the United States—where something very similar to Mexican *machismo* took place, with lasting influences on folklore, literature, and even politics.

The North American *macho* first appears in the 1820s and 1830s. This
was for the United States a time of revolution, the age of Andrew Jackson. Earlier the country had been dominated by the aristocrats of the Atlantic Coast, the big landholders of Virginia and the rich merchants of
New England. They talked, dressed, and lived in the English manner;
their poets and fiction writers were mediocre imitators of the Europeans. The age of Jackson brings radical changes; the country openly enters its nationalistic period. The man of the forest—the frontiersman
dressed in animal skins—becomes a political force, and the aristocrats of
the coast look with horror at the vulgarity of the new leaders. In letters
we have the dawning of a truly North American literature, which goes
from the humorists of the 1820s to the novelist Mark Twain, and from
him to the modern North American writers.* In folklore, the North

---

* We must remember that there is another literary tradition, oriented toward Europe, that of
Henry James.

American nationalistic movement is expressed in the tradition of the man from the backwoods, dressed in animal skins and armed with knife and long rifle. This figure—at the same time hero and buffoon—is expressed folkloristically in the tall tale, the humorous anecdote in which the stranger or Anglicized aristocrat from the coast is ridiculed, and the boast. Above all in the boast. The North American bully boasts of his vulgarity—the one thing the European and the easterner held most against him. He thinks of himself as the bravest and most ferocious man in the world; he can fight more men, love more women, and drink more whiskey than any other man alive. He compares himself to the bear and the tiger, to the alligator and the hurricane. He challenges the whole world with rowdy yelling; he leaps in the air and then struts around. In short, he is the spitting image of the Mexican *pelado* making out as the bravo from Guadalajara or the panther from Guanajuato.

We need not stress that the North American *macho* expressed feelings of inferiority in respect to European culture. The North American was trying to attain a true independence within his own country, to fashion a culture of his own. In order to reach his goal, he would boast even of his weaknesses. On the other hand, he could not completely ignore the technological superiority of Europe and his own East. He could laugh at English literature, at Italian music, and at French dancing masters; but he knew that the English navy ruled the seas, and that his rifle had been made by eastern craftsmen. Technology enabled him to conquer the West, although he always tried to deny it, giving the credit to his own manliness. Then came the Civil War, after which the United States began its march toward industrial and military world power. On the national level, Anglophobia gave way to Anglo-Saxonism, the glorification of a supposed Anglo-Saxon type.* During the period from 1870 to 1914, North American *machismo* undergoes some interesting changes. The *macho* becomes civilized, at least part of him. In folklore the frontiersman remains a comic character. The tall tales and the jokes in which the frontiersman appears as a boor continue to be told. That is to say, as a historical figure the *macho* persists in his role of buffoon. But the hero takes on new types (or stereotypes). In movies and dime novels, the *macho* becomes the cowboy. In serious literature he reappears as protago-

---

* Locally, especially in the center of the country, where there are many people of Germanic and Scandinavian ancestry, Anglophobia persists even today.

nist in the novels of Frank Norris, Jack London, and other writers of the naturalist school.*

In passing from folklore to the naturalistic novel, the North American *macho* loses not only his comic character but also his sexuality; that is to say, he becomes a Puritan *macho,* adjusting to the novelistic tradition of the times. He is all muscle and virility, but he releases his energy in orgies of violence against his enemies. The female still is the reward of his exploits, but all he does is show off in front of her—seriously now, and not in jest as the frontiersman had done. When he is not committing acts of barbarism against other men, he is a model of sobriety, filial love, and courtesy. In sum, he bears a surprising resemblance to the *charro* of recent Mexican movies, who—after shooting down half a dozen men— goes into church all loaded down with his guns, to sing a pious song to the Virgin of Guadalupe.

Aside from his asexual character, the *macho* of the naturalistic novel differs from the frontier *macho* in another respect: his nationalism turns into racism. The protagonist is always Anglo-Saxon, of course, and the cowardly, bad types are men darker than he—Italians, Portuguese, Spaniards, Mexicans, or Indians. The plot shows us that the blond *macho* is more of a *macho* than the dark ones; and therefore, he is Nature's chosen, according to the law of the jungle and the struggle for existence. This is nothing less than the superman as "blond beast," some forty years before Hitler. Furthermore, only the Anglo-Saxon blond is superior; the German, the Scandinavian, and the Irishman appear in the role of comedians or well-intentioned simpletons. This is a result, on the one hand, of Darwin's theories and, on the other, of the North American impulse toward empire and world power during this time. The pattern has its parallels in politics, and it is here that we find a historical figure, one single man, who symbolizes this second stage of North American *machismo.* This is Theodore Roosevelt—politician, cowboy, cavalry colonel, undersecretary of the navy, president, and a devotee par excellence of novelistic *machismo.* Not only in politics but in his personal life, Roosevelt made a determined effort to present before the public the figure of the *macho,* with all its strengths and weaknesses. Sickly as a child, myopic as to be almost blind, Roosevelt made it his business to

* See Maxwell Geismar's *Rebels and Ancestors: The American Novel 1890–1915* (New York: Hill and Wang, 1963) concerning *machismo* in these authors.

show the world that, in spite of his physical deficiencies, he was just as good as any other man. It was this preoccupation that led him to try the most dangerous tasks of the hunter, the cowboy, and the soldier.

After World War I, a decided shift from *machismo* to feminism occurs in the United States, but it is not immediately apparent in literature. On the contrary, it is at this time that a figure analogous to Roosevelt appears in North American literature, this being the novelist Ernest Hemingway—the most hallowed interpreter of the *macho*. The popularity of Hemingway's works in the period between the two world wars—as much among the critics as with the general public—shows us the attraction the *macho* still had for the North American, although in real life the man of the United States made less and less of a show over his masculinity. Hemingway himself understood this, and almost all his novels and short stories develop the theme of *machismo* in Spain, Mexico, or Cuba. Today Hemingway is scorned by the critics. This is not surprising, since the protagonist of the novels now acclaimed by the critics no longer is the *macho* but the homosexual—the other extreme, or perhaps the same thing seen from another point of view. And although Hemingway has not been rejected by the general public, his works no longer are as popular as are novels of the type begun by Mickey Spillane. These are an exaggeration of the Hemingwayesque theme: the *macho* heroes are fierce, sexual, and brutally sadistic with the female. They do not stop with a simple beating, as might the "primitive" man. They riddle their women with bullets, a favorite target being the woman's belly. In North American folklore also, *machismo* is not completely a thing of the past. The boast and the tall tale still are cultivated among white folk groups. In the cities, meanwhile, the North American Negro has developed a genuinely *macho* folklore, with heroes that are bad men of insatiable sexual appetites. Their feats are narrated in folk poems and stories of an exaggerated obscenity. In the poetry are many boasts such as the following, taken from Roger Abrahams's book about the Philadelphia Negro:

> I live on Shotgun Avenue, Tommygun Drive,
> Pistol Apartment, and Room 45.[14]

This brings to mind what Santiago Ramírez has to say about the Mexican's fondness for pistols, big hats, and automobiles—above all for the pistol, symbol par excellence of *machismo*. A sexual symbol, the disciples of Freud would tell us; and in truth, *pistola* is one of the many terms that the Mexican uses for "penis." But the pistol has other meanings for the Mexican, historical meanings related to the clash of cultures in the West, especially in the region of the Great Plains. The Spaniards arrived at the borders of the Great Plains centuries before the North Americans appeared, but they never occupied these areas. One of the obstacles they encountered were mounted Indians like the Comanches, who gave a lot of trouble to the Spanish garrisons on the edge of the plains. Then come the North Americans; and in less than fifty years they totally subdue the Indians, occupy the Great Plains, and civilize the whole area. To what did the North American owe the ability to do in half a century what the Spaniard did not even begin in three? In a work on the subject, entitled precisely *The Great Plains,* the well-known Texas historian Walter Prescott Webb has explained it very simply: the North Americans were racially superior to the Spaniards. The Spaniards, being Europeans, were able to conquer inferior races like the Mexican Indians, in whose veins—Webb tells us—flowed ditchwater instead of blood. But the Comanche was too fierce to be overcome by Spaniard or Mexican. Only the Anglo-Saxon could be a manlier man than the Comanche; and in subduing the Comanche the Anglo-Saxon proved his superiority over other Europeans like the German, the Scandinavian, and the Italian. As Webb tells it, the men who conquered the Great Plains all had English or Scottish names.[15]

No better examples exist of the influence of *machismo* in the academic world than the books of Walter Prescott Webb, in which we find an almost infantile admiration for the man who totes a gun and wears boots and a big hat. The explanation by this distinguished historian of the conquest of the Great Plains in terms of manliness—and exclusively of Anglo-Saxon manliness—ignores well-known facts: all classes of men participated in the conquest of the West, including Negroes, and the technology of the eastern United States was a decisive factor in the superiority the North American of the West gained over Indians and Mexicans.* The surprising thing is that these facts were well known to Webb himself, since he discusses them with erudition and insight in other chapters (especially 5, 7, and 8) of *The Great Plains.* It seems to have

* See Walter Prescott Webb, *The Great Plains* (Boston: Ginn, 1931), vi, where the author considers the conquest of the Great Plains as "a new phase of Aryan civilization."

been necessary for Webb, the man of the West, to reveal his personal feelings, boasting of the manliness of his region and its independence with respect to the East. Then Webb the historian gives us a careful study of the role played by the technology of the East in the conquering of the Great Plains: the importance of the repeating rifle, barbed wire, windmills, the revolver, and machines for large-scale agriculture. What he says about the revolver is of special interest for us.

The old long rifle was the North American's ideal weapon while he conquered the forests east of the Mississippi, where he fought in the woods on foot. But when he emerged on the plains, the North American found himself at a great disadvantage. His rifle, which he had to load through the muzzle with a ramrod, was an ineffective weapon against Indians and Mexicans, who were men on horseback. Once he fired his rifle, the North American had only his knife to defend himself with, and in the use of this weapon he found the Mexican a dangerous adversary.[16] The Indian was even more formidable, since he could discharge twenty arrows in the time necessary to load a rifle.[17] Furthermore, both Mexicans and Indians used the lance as well. Confronted with this problem, the North Americans in the West seriously considered two solutions that were not at all heroic. One was to build a series of forts on the borders of the Great Plains to contain the Indians—that is to say, precisely what the Spaniards had done. The other was the settling of French colonists in these same areas, to serve as a buffer between the Indians and the North Americans.[18] But it did not become necessary to carry out these projects, and the reason was the technology of the East. In New Jersey an artisan from Connecticut, Samuel Colt, began to produce the first revolvers in 1838. The North American army showed little interest in them, but the Texans and other men of the West received them with enthusiasm.[19] In 1844 the revolver was put to the test for the first time in a battle between Texans and Comanches; each Texan was armed with two revolvers and a rifle. The Indians fled in disorder; the revolver had changed the balance of power on the Great Plains in favor of the man with the two pistols.[20] A quarter of a century later, the Winchester rifle replaced the revolver as the preferred weapon in the Great West, but the revolver—as a result of its initial impact—remained the symbolic weapon as much in folklore as in popular literature, and later in the movies and on television.

The revolver not only changed the character of conflict with the no-madic Indian, but it also revolutionized the North American concept of manliness. Let us not forget that, before the arrival of the North Ameri-can in the Great West, the Mexican had faced the Indian armed only with lance and knife, as did the Argentine *gaucho* against the Indian of the pampas. The North American, Webb tells us, recognized the Mexi-can as an "artist with a knife."[21] Webb says it not in admiration but in a contemptuous tone, since it is part of the tradition of *machismo* in the United States to scorn the man with the knife, who is always given the role of coward and traitor.* It was not always this way, for there was a time when the North American boasted of his skill with the knife and held it in such high esteem that he gave personal names to his favorite blades, as did the medieval knights to their swords. This was, naturally, before the revolver, in the days of the backwoodsman, typified by Davy Crockett, who died in the defense of the Alamo against the troops of Santa Anna. Another of the defenders of the Alamo was James Bowie, whose name became a synonym for knife, because Bowie was a virtuoso in what Martínez Estrada calls "the art of cutting throats."[22] Considering the derogatory associations later given the knife in the folklore of the United States, it is truly ironic that legend should picture Bowie at the Alamo, knife in hand against the Mexican muskets. And in truth, if we imagine a confrontation between two men—one armed with a rifle or revolver and the other with a knife—which of the two would we say is taking the greater risk? Let the Knight of the Sad Countenance give us the answer, in the celebrated disquisition on arms and letters that Don Quijote makes in the chapters dealing with the Captive of Algiers.

> Happy the blest ages that knew not the dread fury of those devilish en-gines of artillery, whose inventor I am persuaded is in hell receiving the reward of his diabolical invention, by which he made it easy for a base and cowardly arm to take the life of a gallant gentleman; and that, when he knows not how or whence, in the height of the ardour and enthusiasm

---

* Note, for example, this passage from a so-called history book. The famous bandit Billy the Kid has captured several Mexicans and taken their weapons:
> The Kid examined the knives, lying on the ground beside the fire. They were of the finest steel and workmanship. He admired the knives and had an impulse to keep them, but he gave another order. "Throw these on the coals. Only renegades use knives" (William Lee Hamlin, *The True Story of Billy the Kid* [Caldwell, Idaho: Caxton Printers, 1959], 209–210).

that fire and animate brave hearts, there should come some random bullet, discharged perhaps by one who fled in terror at the flash when he fired off his accursed machine, which in an instant puts an end to the projects and cuts off the life of one who deserved to live for ages to come.[23]

Cervantes reveals his own sentiments, no doubt, since he was maimed as a result of one of those "accursed machines." But he also expresses the feelings of most soldiers of his time. This is also the point of view in *Martín Fierro*, where we see the valiant *gaucho*, with "the one that never misfires" in his hand, facing cowards and scoundrels armed with revolvers and muskets.[24] But if we are gun-toters ourselves, we cannot accept such a judgment. We must change the situation, and thus it was in the North American tradition. The knife was made the weapon of the renegade, of the coward; the pistol became the weapon of the *macho*, the brave man. A paradox? It is, in truth, but it agrees with the tendency to change an unpleasant reality by inverting it, the very thing that is at the base of *machismo*.

Understandably, the Mexican did not immediately accept the North American's point of view. In much of Mexican folklore the steel blade retained its character as a suitable instrument for admirable deeds, and it was considered a very Mexican weapon as well. In a *corrido* from central Mexico of the 1930s, "Conversation between Two *Rancheros*," we hear of a migrant worker who returns to Mexico from the United States, full of *gringo* ways and saying insulting things about Mexico. His *compadre*, who had stayed home on the farm, takes out his huge knife to punish him. Seeing the knife, the Americanized migrant falls on his knees and begs forgiveness for having offended the fatherland.[25] By this time, however, the Mexican had learned to use the revolver. The *norteño*, the Mexican from the border, recognized its worth at an early date by having been on the receiving end of more than one revolver. It is through the Border *corrido*—in *norteño* folklore—that the revolver enters the folklore of Mexico, as the Mexican folk hero first abandons the knife for the gun. This corresponds with actual fact, for the border Mexican was a man with a pistol in his hand by the end of the 1850s. In 1859, when Juan Nepomuceno Cortina rebelled against North American authority in Texas, he did so after a shootout with a North American city marshal who had beaten one of his mother's farmhands. From Cortina on, the protagonists of the Border *corrido* are men "pistol in hand." That is to say, they fight "American style," as we are told in a *corrido* from Sonora, "De Cananea":

Me agarraron los cherifes	The deputies arrested me,
al estilo americano—	in the American style—
como al hombre de delito—	as they would arrest a criminal—
todos con pistola en mano.	all with pistols in their hands.

"With a pistol in his hand" or "with his pistol in his hand" becomes a conventional phrase in the *corrido* of the border between Mexico and the United States, distinguishing it from the *corrido* of southern Mexico, where this formula rarely appears before the 1930s. The man with pistol in hand is rarely a bully in the *corridos*. He pursues other goals, as did Cortina, defending himself against the abuses of an oppressive authority.

In a *corrido* from Coahuila, as late as the 1930s, a young man named Arnulfo and a state policeman gun each other down after the policeman slaps Arnulfo, simply because Arnulfo did not lower his eyes when the policeman looked at him. After the two are dead, the singer tells us in a fit of enthusiasm:

¡Qué bonitos son los hombres	How beautiful it is to see two men
que se matan pecho a pecho,	gun each other down, standing face
cada uno con su pistola,	to face!
defendiendo su derecho!	Each with his pistol,
	each defending his right!

Something remains of the *corridos* on the clash-of-cultures theme, but this also sounds like *machismo*—presented in a situation like that of a Wild West movie. And there is good reason for the resemblance, since there is a very close relationship between Hollywood and the gun-toting *macho,* the *pistolero.* Let us return to the North American *macho* with his pistol in hand, and we will find him converted into the cowboy. Why the cowboy became the type chosen to synthesize the *macho* is another question, but let us look at these two figures—the *macho* and the cowboy—in relation to that great North American *macho,* Theodore Roosevelt. Roosevelt's admiration for cowboys was excessive, almost childish. He lived with them, working at their tasks, in order to prove his manliness. Later, during the Cuban war, he formed a regiment of cowboys, putting into practice his conviction that the cowboy was the best soldier possible because he was the epitome of all the austere, manly virtues. Nothing speaks more emphatically—Mody C. Boatright tells us in a study entitled "Theodore Roosevelt, Social Darwinism, and the Cowboy"—of Roosevelt's delight in the life of the cowboy than the fancy and expensive clothes he wore. Boatright quotes from a letter written by Roosevelt to his sister:

> I wear a sombrero, silk neckerchief, fringed buckskin shirt, sealskin chaparajos, or riding trousers, alligator hide boots, and with my pearl-hilted revolver and my beautifully finished Winchester rifle, I shall be able to face anything.[26]

The cowboy was taken almost totally from the Mexican tradition, but the North American made some important contributions, among them the pistol, the Stetson hat (an adaptation of the Mexican *sombrero*), and in our days the substitution of the horse with the Cadillac of the rancher-turned-millionaire. The pistol, above all—first the revolver and then the .45 automatic with its four cartridge clips. A phallic symbol perhaps, but in a much more direct sense a symbol of power—and of the abuse of power as well. A symbol of the manliness of the bully, the *macho* of the movies, who guns his rival down in the middle of the street, lifts the girl to his saddle, and rides into the sunset on his faithful horse. Or on his Cadillac, heading for Houston, or Austin, or Washington. The pistol above all—symbol of the overbearing bully. The Mexican knew this well enough, from the day the first Colts arrived on the border. Harassed, dispossessed by the man with the gun, the Mexican lost no time in wishing to be a man with a gun also. And so it was that the Mexican took back from the North American something he had lent him, the figure of the *vaquero;* but he received his loan with interest, since the *vaquero* returned as cowboy—a *pistolero* and a *macho* among *machos.*

It would be an overstatement to say that the Mexican *macho* is merely a mirror image of the North American cowboy (although it is not much more extravagant to claim that he originates in Oedipal complexes caused by the conquest). But any evaluation of Mexican *machismo* will not be complete if the following point is ignored: The fundamental attitudes on which *machismo* is based (and which have caused so much distress to those wishing to psychoanalyze the Mexican) are almost universal. What might distinguish Mexican *machismo* is not the presence of those attitudes but their undeniable exaggeration; yet, this is not peculiar to the Mexican, since something very similar has occurred in a modern and neighboring country, the United States. There is no evidence that *machismo* (in the exaggerated forms that have been studied and condemned in Mexicans) even existed in Mexico before the Revolution. Available evidence suggests that it is a phenomenon dating from the 1930s to the present, that is to say, from the period after the Revolution. There is an intriguing parallel between North American and Mexican *machismo*. In the United States the sense of manliness is exaggerated during the 1820s and 1830s, because of a growing sense of nationalism, resulting in greater participation by the common man in the democratic process of the country, as well as in a marked feeling of hostility and inferiority toward Europe, especially toward England. During this period the idea of North American manliness is mainly unconscious and expresses itself generally in folkloric forms, especially in the boast and the tall tale. Nor is this supermanliness completely divorced from reality, since it occurs at a time when the North American male becomes an explorer and conqueror, extending the borders of his country farther and farther to the west.

An analogous period in Mexico is the Revolution and the years immediately preceding it. The boundaries extended by the Mexican during this time are not geographic but of the spirit. Nevertheless, the attitudes are more or less the same: a growing feeling of nationalism accompanied by sentiments of distrust and inferiority toward outsiders, particularly toward the United States; and a movement toward democracy and equality. As with the North American during the 1820s and 1830s, such sentiments in the Mexican were for the most part unconscious; and they were expressed in folkloric forms—in the artistic boast during the final years of the Díaz regime and in the *corrido* during the Revolution. Again, it may be said that the Mexican sense of manliness had a firm basis in reality during the Revolution, when struggle and death were accepted as daily occurrences.

North American *machismo* becomes artificial and grotesque when the frontier ends, when the Wild West disappears and men no longer live in the midst of conflict and danger. Then comes on scene the cowboy, fabricated by the cheap popular writers, the *macho* of Theodore Roosevelt's

234 — *The Folklore Genres: History, Form, and Performance*

type, with the fancy cowboy suit, the pearl-handled revolver, and the enormous spectacles of the myopic scholar. Close after him comes the cowboy of the cities, the "professional Texan" with his white Stetson, his embroidered boots, and his Cadillac. The sense of manliness passes from folklore to the movies and popular literature, where we have the scorned woman abused by the man, at times physically tortured by the *macho* in forms of undoubtedly sexual symbolism. North American *machismo* in this late and exaggerated form goes even further than does Mexican *machismo*, since the North American type is dignified in serious literature, in the novels of Frank Norris, Jack London, Ernest Hemingway, and many other lesser writers. In Mexico, too, the sense of manliness typical of the Revolution is converted into exaggerated *machismo* once the period of armed conflict has ended, more or less by 1930. This is also the date, by the way, that Vicente Mendoza singles out as marking the end of the truly folk *corrido*.[27] The *corrido* after 1930, according to Mendoza, passes from folklore to the movies and other mass media.

Both in Mexico and in the United States, *machismo* betrays a certain element of nostalgia; it is cultivated by those who feel they have been born too late. The North American *macho* acts as if the Wild West had never come to an end; the Mexican *macho* behaves as if he is still living in the times of Pancho Villa. But we must make an important distinction. The United States began with feelings of inferiority toward England; today it is perhaps England that may feel inferior in respect to its former colony. Such is not the case with Mexico, since despite its undeniable progress it still lives under the shadow of the old Colossus of the North, today more colossal than ever. And here, at least, Samuel Ramos may have been right. But he also remarked that to feel inferior is not the same as being so.[28] We might add that to feel poor and to be poor are not exactly the same thing; and even more, that often the first is a necessary condition in doing away with the second. Upward-moving groups and peoples on the go are among those most disposed to feelings of inferiority. Both in the United States and in Mexico, *machismo*, despite all its faults, has been part of a whole complex of impulses leading toward a more perfect realization of the potentialities of man.

- 10 -

The *Décima* on the Texas-Mexican Border: Folksong as an Adjunct to Legend

THE *DÉCIMA* IS A STANZA of ten octosyllables with a rhyme scheme presenting almost as many difficulties as the sonnet. Vicente T. Mendoza identifies more than twenty different rhyme patterns, though the most widely used is the "mirror" *décima,* or *espinela* (*a b b a a c c d d c*), named after the Spanish Golden Age poet Vicente Espinel, who is supposed to have invented it.[1] *Décimas* may be individual compositions, or they may be one of a series or sequence. It was during the Spanish Golden Age, however, with its fondness for poetic glosses, that the *décima* took its most characteristic form: four *décima* stanzas, usually *espinelas,* glossing a quatrain which almost invariably is a *redondilla,* four octosyllables rhyming *a b b a.*

This is scarcely a form one would expect to find among the folk; yet the *décima* for centuries has been an important folksong type among all peoples of Spanish culture. It acquired both secular and religious functions, serving as vehicle for ballad, lyric, and flyting. It was popular in contests between celebrated songmakers, who improvised in this difficult form if given a *planta,* or quatrain, to be glossed. Though the *décima* tradition has lost a great deal of its vigor, there are places where it still flourishes, retaining the old forms and functions. A notable example is given by Juan Uribe Echevarría, who describes ritual contests in *décima* improvisation among Chilean folk groups taking place as late as 1961.[2]

How a form as sophisticated as the *décima* became traditional is a question that cannot be discussed here at length. There are those who think the *décima* was cultivated by traditional singers before Vicente Espinel. It is more likely that it was developed by court poets and later taken up by the folk. Whatever the origins of the *décima* in Spain, it is clear that its diffusion in Spanish America came about through cultivated sources and that this occurred principally in three ways: through the popularization of Spanish Golden Age literature in the colonies; as a result of poetry-writing contests in schools, universities, and viceregal courts in which contestants were required to gloss a given stanza; and through the use of the *décima* by the Church in its missionary activities among the Indians. The influence of the clergy was especially important, as can be seen from the high proportion of religious *décimas* (*décimas a lo divino*) in most Spanish-American collections.

Secular *décimas* (*décimas a lo humano*) can treat almost any theme imaginable, but the custom of glossing or commenting on a text favors certain kinds of subjects. The *décima* rarely serves as a vehicle for straightforward narrative, though it often is used in the broadside kind of ballad that is a commentary on events, especially on miraculous or sensational happenings. Though it has been used for everything from riddles to love songs, the types that have had the greatest currency are those on satirical or humorous subjects. The secular *décima* reaches its zenith during the first half of the nineteenth century. Long cultivated for religious themes and for local subjects of importance to isolated groups, the *decima*'s uses for satire were expanded during the struggles for independence in Latin America at the beginnings of the nineteenth century and during the civil wars which followed independence. Thus in Mexico, according to Mendoza, it reached its apogee from the 1830s to the 1860s, a period of bloody civil wars and foreign invasions.[3] Eugenio Pereira Salas is of the opinion that the secular *décima* achieved greatest popularity in broadside form in cities throughout Latin America during the period of independence and civil war which occupied a good part of the early nineteenth century.[4] That, in brief, is the *décima* in Spanish America, but the immediate concern of this paper is one small segment of the whole tradition.

The region of the Lower Rio Grande, now the border area between South Texas and Mexico, was settled in 1749, by which time the *décima* was well established throughout Spanish America. By mid-nineteenth century one begins to hear of celebrated *decimeros* along the border, especially in the area downriver from Brownsville, Texas, and Matamoros, Tamaulipas. *Décima*-making seems to have been a general activity, but some families were especially known for the *decimeros* they produced. Two of these families illustrate the range of the tradition on the Lower Rio Grande. One was the Verduzco family, widely known folksingers and composers. The Verduzcos were traveling musicians who circulated through town and *rancho* on both the Mexican and the Texas sides of the river. They played at dances, sang ballads, and furnished music and poetic talent at wakes, novenas, and children's funerals. Because of a congenital weakness of the eyes general in the family, there were several blind singers among them. The last of the folksinging Verduzcos, a blind minstrel, still was composing and singing *decimas* and selling them as broadsides in the 1940s. The other family was the Cisneros, a numerous and influential clan of landowners who claimed descent from the original settlers of the region. Most celebrated of the Cisneros *décima*-makers was Don Santiago María, the patriarch of the family around the 1860s and 1870s. Some of the *décimas* attributed to him still are current. In 1951, I collected a *décima* composition from one of Don Santiago María's descendants, Fulgencio Cisneros. Fulgencio's *décimas* were about the collision of two U.S. Air Force planes which fell on the Mexican side of the border. Most *décimas* still current, though, are from seventy-five to one hundred years old. There is no difference apparent in style or subject matter between the compositions of the Cisneros and the Verduzcos. Nor is there any indication in the attitude of the people who preserved the *décimas* that either family—blind singers or landowners— was considered as producing a different type of poet. All belong to the same local tradition to which wandering musician, landowner, *vaquero,* and townsman contributed according to his talents.

Border *décimas* were of all sorts, but religious themes were in the minority, if what can be collected now is a good example of the tradition at its fullest. Nowhere in talking with informants have I discovered traces of the elaborate use of flyting contests for ritual purposes such as reported by Uribe Echevarría for Chile, though songs in *décima* form were composed and sung during religious festivals.[5] Few religious *décimas* survive, with the exception of those found in the texts of *pastorelas,* or shepherds' plays; so there may be some justice in the comments by early missionaries that the border people were a godless lot. But the *décima* was used to narrate events dealing with the life and workaday problems of *vaqueros* and farmers. Other compositions dealt with horse racing, one of the important amusements of the border people. Still others were little treatises in folk philosophy, proverbial in style, commenting on the impermanence of life and of good fortune and the certainty of death. Closely related to these last were memorializing *décimas* to the dead. Weddings or christenings might also be commemorated by *decimeros*. The majority of the Border *décimas,* however, were humorous or satirical. Almost absent was the political *décima;* the satires were purely local and most often personal, directed at the human weaknesses of some well-known member of the community or at some general quality or condition of the community as a whole. When directed at an individual, the satirical *décima* was not so much a jibe as a song-making challenge. The victim was supposed to answer, and he would acquit himself very well indeed if he was able to reply in a gloss of four *décimas* based on the same *planta* used by his challenger. This was the form the *contrapunto,* or flyting, took on the Lower Rio Grande Border. In contrast to such traditions as the Chilean, where it was highly formal and fulfilled religious functions, the Border *contrapunto* was informal and secular.

The challenge to a known *decimero* was not always made in a complete *décima* composition. An invitation to compose could be made by the presentation of a four-line *planta.* A favorite practice was to spring a *planta* on a folk poet, reciting it to him in the midst of a gathering. The *decimero* was then obliged to gloss the *planta,* turning the satire in the quatrain away from himself and toward the man who had offered the *planta.* Not always were *plantas* offered in this manner. It became the practice in the latter part of the nineteenth century, especially among the Cisneros clan, to send *plantas* or fully glossed compositions by messenger from one ranch to another, much in the spirit that comic valentines are sent in the United States. Instances are related in which satirical *décimas* in manuscript were nailed to trees at important crossroads, a rural counterpart of the city practice of writing *pasquines,* or satirical verses, on walls of buildings. At times the rhymed challenge would be circulated by word of mouth until it reached the intended person's ears. Still another practice was to issue a general call to composition by circulating a *planta* commenting on some well-known local event. I personally remember that in the 1920s a *planta* was circulated in the area concerning a noisy but bloodless altercation which had occurred at a rural dance nearby.

En el rancho de El Ranchito	At the ranch of El Ranchito
hubo un gran combate,	there was a great battle,
la Chicharra y el Mayate	the Cicada and the Beetle
contra un pobre Tacuachito.	against a poor little Possum.

In 1962, I questioned what few survivors of the old Cisneros family were left in the area, and as far as they knew no one had ever glossed the *planta* about the possum, the cicada, and the beetle. The custom of informal flytings had died out, though *décimas* still were being composed now and then. Sometimes people will send each other *décimas* in the folk style, no longer by messenger but by mail.

This *décima* tradition has scarcely been collected, much less studied. From what has been published on Texas-Mexican folksong, one could easily get the impression that most collectors have not even been aware of the *décima*'s existence on the border, though plenty of *décimas* have been collected in New Mexico. One reason is the impact of the *corrido* of border conflict on Texas-Mexican oral tradition after the 1860s, after border warfare between Americans and Mexicans developed. Border conflict became the main theme of the Texas-Mexican *corrido* and imposed itself on the consciousness of the border people. Most younger singers were turning from the *décima* to the *corrido* before the end of the century. Since border people composed little on sacred subjects, the *décima* did not have this final redoubt to fall back to. Because of this, collectors on the border, beginning their work in the 1930s, have found the situation different from that of New Mexico, where the *corrido* came late and where there exists a corpus of religious *décimas*. On the border, collectors have found mostly *corridos,* and if they scratch hard and deep they come up with a few sung *décimas.* The bulk of the *décima* tradition, based on the custom of the flyting and of personal satire, has sunk from view. It is not likely to be found at *cantinas* or large public gatherings, where the *corrido* has been common, but it still is alive on a more local and less public level. For while a few *décimas* changed their form and became *corridos,* many others retained their form but changed their function. They became endings to prose narrative, components of a local type of legend.

One must look for the legendary anecdote in order to find them. An incident is related, usually humorous, about some supposedly historical personage. Then some *décimas* are recited or sung, capping the narrative. The story is always that the main character in the anecdote composed the *décimas* as a result of the experiences just related. The *décima,* for so long a gloss to a quatrain, thus becomes a gloss or commentary in another sense.

It is the lyrical or the satirical *décima* that most often accompanies the anecdote, and usually the author and main actor in the narrative is identified as a celebrated *decimero* of the nineteenth century. Sometimes such narratives have a pretty definite historical basis, not only the existence of the *decimero* but the main outlines of the story being capable of verification. Such is the case with the story about the best known of the Border *contrapuntos,* said to have occurred in the late 1860s and involving Don Santiago María Cisneros. His opponent, known in tradition only as "El Indio" Córdova, is said to have belonged to Benito Juárez's staff, being like Juárez a full-blooded Indian from the interior of Mexico. Some accounts make him Juárez's minister of war. According to the story, Córdova came to the border during the dark days of Mexican resistance against Maximilian's empire. He fell in love with Don Santiago María's beautiful daughter at a dance in El Ranchito, the same place which would serve as battleground for the beetle, the cicada, and the possum half a century later. A *decimero* himself, El Indio Córdova asked for the girl's hand in glossed *décimas* and was curtly rejected by Don Santiago María, who answered by glossing Córdova's own *planta:*

Oye Santiago María	Hear me, Santiago María
Cisneros de apelativo,	Cisneros by appellation,
te ruego no seas esquivo	I beg you not be evasive
con esta consulta mía.	with this consultation of mine.

The existence of Don Santiago María and his daughter is vouched for by their descendants, as are the main outlines of the story about Córdova's unsuccessful suit. But enough has been added to the story to make it legendary. Other *décima* legends are made of much more fanciful materials. In some stories about horse racing which are capped with *décimas,* it is the horse which is the composer, or at least the speaker, so one may be justified in doubting their historical basis.

Though not all these *décimas* are humorous or satirical, the anecdote leading up to them usually is, and they depend for their effect on the story which precedes them. Take the *décimas* which are known as "Las décimas de don Mateo."* They gloss a *planta* that derives from the ornate style of the seventeenth century, being in fact an echo of some lines of Luis de Góngora.† The *planta* is as follows:

Llora el mar y sus arenas	The sea and its sands weep
lo que yo estoy padeciendo,	what I suffer;
llora la pluma escribiendo	the pen weeps as it writes
negras lágrimas de penas.	black tears of sorrow.

The four *décimas* glossing this quatrain are a complaint in which the lover claims that all nature weeps with him because he can no longer see his beloved. According to the story that goes with the *décimas,* Don Mateo's suffering was more physical than spiritual when he is said to have composed the lines. Don Mateo had been attracted by the young and pretty wife of one of his father's peons. It became his habit to visit her when the husband was not home, and as the master's son he was able to arrange for the husband to be away often. But one night, when Mateo was on his way from the woman's hut along a dark and lonely trail in the chaparral, he was set upon by several men with cudgels, who beat him until they had left him very much like Don Quijote after his encounter with the drovers. Don Mateo took to his bed while the whole countryside laughed. At first he vowed vengeance on the husband, but his father took the part of his peons and threatened to send Mateo off to be a soldier if he did not forget the whole thing. What was worse, the father forbade him to see the woman again. To soothe his wounded feelings as well as his bruised flesh, the story goes, Don Mateo composed the *décimas* which have been handed down along with the story. The whole thing is told with a tongue-in-cheek air so that the perceptive listener understands that Don Mateo is no more the true author of the *décimas* attributed to him than are horses the authors of the horse-racing *décimas.* It is obvious that one of the *decimeros* of the period made up the whole thing as a sort of insult-after-injury joke on the suffering Mateo. This is always implied, but never stated, except on direct questioning, and such questioning is looked upon by informants as a mark of

---

* *Décima* legends always mention family names, but most of them are left out here to avoid embarrassing families still well known in the region.
† Por una negra señora / un negro galán doliente / negras lágrimas derrama / de un negro pecho que tiene.

extreme density on the part of the collector, as if he had missed the point of the simplest kind of joke.

It is worth repeating that *décimas* of this type would have little interest for the average listener if he were not familiar with their stories. He is not concerned with Don Mateo's love complaint because he thinks it is fine poetry; it is because he can imagine Mateo's condition when he is supposed to have written the *décimas,* that the contrast between the fine words and Mateo's bruised state seems extremely funny to him. Similarly, the *décimas* exchanged between Don Santiago María Cisneros and El Indio Córdova would be much less interesting to the border narrator if he did not relish the situation in which old Don Santiago takes the measure of the *fuereño,* or outsider.

It is the story that makes the *décimas* interesting, but in contrast to the *corrido* it is the story before them, not the story behind them. The process usually associated with the *corrido* is the reverse. A singer will perform a *corrido* about Jacinto Treviño, let us say. After the singing there will be a pause and someone may remark, "He was a real man, that Jacinto Treviño." Then someone else will say, "Yes, but was it in a *cantina* where all the shooting took place?" There will follow a discussion of the background of the *corrido* and finally the narration of some parts of the legend associated with the song and its hero. In the *décima* it is the story which brings forth the recitation or song. Someone will say something about burros, or about peddlers, or about a peddler driving a burro. And another will add, "Like Luis S——, who ended up driving an ass loaded with coffee. He was given a good education and was engaged to marry a fine lady, but then things went bad for him." And the story follows, how Luis was forced to become a coffee peddler, and how once he came down the street driving an ass loaded with coffee before him when he met some of his former friends. Don Rafael María Cisneros was among them, and he hailed Luis with a *planta:*

Aquél que amaba a una curra	He who loved a female fop
en aquella edad florida	in his salad days
hoy se conserva en la vida	now barely gets along in life
con calma arreando una burra.	by calmly driving an ass.

Luis accepted the challenge and improvised the *décimas* that have been preserved to this day, in which Don Rafael María's quatrain is glossed with commentaries on the ups and downs of fortune and the joys of a simple life.

Or the talk may turn to horse racing, and the old-time cow ponies are extolled as the fleetest things that ever ran on four legs. Then someone is sure to tell the story of the fine-blooded horse brought to the border by some general or other, and how he was outrun by a riverbank *tordillo,* a hammerheaded, potbellied, hairy nag belonging to a sheepherder. This of course is the same story retold by J. Frank Dobie in *The Mustangs,* except that his characters are American army officers and Comanches.[6] After the race the sheepherder's horse taunts the fine stallion in *décimas,* telling the thoroughbred that perhaps he might do better as a sheepherder's mount than as a racer.

The resolution of each anecdote with *décimas* depends on the convention that the chief character in the story is the author of the *décimas,* which he either improvises on the spot or composes afterwards. The intrusion of the author is also found in some *corridos,* but this occurs within the ballad itself, usually in the conventional ending, or *despedida.* In such a case an actual ballad author is trying to have posterity remember him as a poet. In the *décima* legend the reputed author is remembered not as author but as an actor in the story, and his role rarely sheds glory on his name. The degree to which this is purely a convention varies with the story. Obviously no one takes the *tordillo* horse as the author of the *décimas* attributed to him. In some versions the story ends more realistically and more prosaically; we are told that after the race so-and-so composed the following *décimas* in which the *tordillo* speaks. Still, there is the same emphasis on the authorship of the composition. With the lovelorn "Décimas de don Mateo" it is more difficult to tell where remembered fact leaves off and legend and convention begin. It is not likely that Don Mateo would compose a love poem as a result of a beating given him for courting another man's wife, but the thing is not completely impossible. Even more probably, he could have composed the *décimas* for some other woman, under other circumstances, and the whole story of the peon's wife and the beating could have been invention. The story about Luis and how he came to drive a burro in his unfortunate days is at least plausible. Finally, stories such as the one about Don Santiago María and Córdova are mainly factual, with the addition of some legendary details.

The tale of Córdova's hopeless love for Don Santiago María's daughter is the patrimony of all border people who claim kinship with the numerous Cisneros group. In this sense one could call it part of a Cisneros saga. It is also well known among other old border families not directly related to the Cisneros because of the wide influence of this family in former times. In greater or lesser degree the same is true of other *décima* stories, so that here is at least one explanation of how the Texas-Mexican *décima* changed from folksong into an adjunct to legend. At its peak of influence it was associated with well-known *decimeros* in whom the community as a whole felt a kind of proprietary interest. As the *décima* declined with the rise of the *corrido,* the old *decimeros* came to be part of the community's semilegendary past, becoming more important than their compositions. The *décimas* were remembered in relation to the men who created them. This grew into an established custom, with anecdotes consciously invented to explain other *décimas* which had no histories of their own. It was at this point that the talents of the humorist would come fully into play, though even in such compositions where the poet-hero is said to be a horse, it is the mount of some *décima*-making ancestor who is thus endowed, or the ancestor somehow plays a part in the story.

The influence of the *contrapunto,* or flyting, was also important. It was the custom of the challenge to *décima* composition that often created in real life dramatic or humorous situations later preserved in legendary narratives. The particularly skillful *contrapuntista* would be remembered and made the hero of other anecdotes. We have a parallel from Chile, where a highly formal *contrapunto* tradition has flourished for over a century, and where a legendary encounter is recorded from the early nineteenth century between the mulatto singer Taguada and Don Javier de la Rosa.[7] The educated Don Javier defeated Taguada, who was more truly a folk composer, and legend has it that Taguada committed suicide after his defeat. Walter Rela prints two variants of the songs used in the contest, one from an 1890 manuscript and one from oral tradition of 1933. He theorizes that the defeat of Taguada symbolizes the triumph of city culture over rural folk tradition. Perhaps the people who sang the *décimas* and told the legend did not see the matter in such a sophisticated and historical way, but there is more than a hint of bias in the defeat of the uncultured mulatto by the educated *criollo,* or native of Spanish descent. The parallel with the legend of Córdova and Don Santiago María is close, since in both we have the *criollo* defeating Negro and Indian and putting them to shame. But there is an important difference: in the Border legend Córdova is an Indian but he represents the sophisticated side of the contest. He is a government official, the educated man from the great outside world. Don Santiago María, though a *criollo,* is representative of the rural and local culture. The legend's identification of Córdova as "the Indian" shows racial or social bias, it is true, though his supposed connection with Juárez may have something to do with this, in which case his designation as "el Indio" is a flattering rather than a derogatory one. The tone of condescension taken toward Córdova by Don Santiago María arises principally from the fact that Córdova— besides being younger and a suitor—is an outsider, a *fuereño.* There are other legends telling of the deadly hostility of the Cisneros clan toward newly arrived Spaniards who attempted to court their women. In this legend, furthermore, Córdova is a romantic though defeated figure. At all events, if the Taguada–De la Rosa *contrapunto* symbolizes the triumph of the city over the country, as Rela believes, then the Córdova-Cisneros contest shows the defeat of city culture by the *ranchero.*

The resemblance of the legend capped with *décimas* to the cante-fable is an obvious one, bringing up questions as to the true origins of the *décima* legend and the relationship of the cante-fable to genres like the folk ballad. The theory that ballads and other types of folksong may have arisen from the decay of the cante-fable was first stated in the nineteenth century. The question has been pursued much more recently by Herbert Halpert.[8] There is no evidence that the *décima* is the result of a decayed cante-fable of which our legends would be survivals. There is pretty strong evidence to the contrary, that the process has gone from the song to the legend or anecdote. This parallels what we know of the Border *corrido* tradition, in which long, circumstantial ballads are sung while the events are still fresh in the minds of singer and audience. As the events recede into the past, a legend develops about the *corrido* hero, with the legend growing as the *corrido* diminishes. The history of "El corrido de Gregorio Cortez" is a good example of this process.[9] At times the *corrido* is forgotten, or only fragments of it may remain. Still the legend about the hero will persist in prose form, taking on supernatural or magical qualities alien to the heroic *corrido* tradition. Such has been the case with the "Corrido de José Mosqueda," which has been forgotten by most border people while Mosqueda lives on in legends.[10]

This does not prove or disprove anything about the cante-fable. While there is a formal resemblance, the cante-fable deals with the wonderworld of the *Märchen,* while *corrido* and *décima* concern themselves with historical events that have become legendary. We cannot say that the *décima* legends throw any light on the cante-fable question except that they show it is possible for prose narratives to develop out of folksongs. This adaptation of a folk form to new functions preserved many *décimas* that otherwise would have been forgotten. It is a use of the *décima* that to my knowledge has not been previously reported in Spanish America or the southwestern United States. A pattern well known in folklore—that of the cante-fable—is repeated in recent times with the use of relatively sophisticated materials, the comic anecdote and the *décima.*

~ 11 ~

The Undying Love of "El Indio" Córdova: *Décimas* and Oral History in a Border Family

W HEN I WAS INVITED to talk before you this afternoon, I was faced with a particular problem. I did not know how many of you might be familiar with the *décima* or *espinela*, the *glosa*, the *redondilla*, the *contrapunto* or *canto a desafío*. So, just in case, I have asked my hosts to distribute the handouts that are before you.*

At the top is the *planta*, as many *decimeros* call a stanza to be glossed. Most often, as in our handout, it is a *redondilla*, an octosyllabic quatrain rhyming *a b b a*. It is glossed (explained or expanded upon) by two sets of *décimas espinelas:* octosyllabic ten-line stanzas rhyming *a b b a a c c d d c*. You may notice that the rhyme scheme forms a mirror, sometimes called the *décima* mirror. The first set of *décimas* in our handout was composed by a man known in Lower Rio Grande Border tradition as "El Indio" Córdova, who sent them to Don Santiago María Cisneros, a member of one of the large extended families in the area downriver from Brownsville, Texas, and Matamoros, Tamaulipas. Don Santiago María regarded Córdova's *décimas* as a *desafío*, or challenge, and he answered them using Córdova's own *redondilla* as his *planta*.

But the *décimas* also are a pair of messages. Córdova asks for Don Santiago María's daughter in marriage, and Don Santiago María refuses in no uncertain terms. And thereby hangs a tale, which is the true subject of my talk. But first it is necessary to say a few words about the

---

* This chapter is the text of the inaugural Ernesto Galarza Lecture, delivered at Stanford University in 1986. The handout referred to herein contained the *décimas de pedimento* that appear at the end of the chapter. —ED.

origins of the *décima* and its universality in Hispanic oral tradition. I will be very brief, at risk of oversimplification.

The *décima*, or *espinela*—or sometimes *décima espinela*—dates from the Spanish Golden Age and supposedly was invented by the poet and musician Vicente Espinel in 1591, although this supposition has been challenged. In passing, it is worth mentioning that the *décima* often is sung, but we do not have time to go into its music and performance on this occasion.

The *décima* quickly spread to the Spanish colonies in America. It was cultivated in the viceregal courts of Lima and Mexico City, and it was also used by the friars in their evangelical labors. The *redondilla* glossed in *décimas* is common in the shepherds' plays that have survived in some parts of Greater Mexico. From the Church and the colonial aristocracy, *décimas* soon passed to the people. In Mexico, it was the *décima* and not the *romance* that along with the *copla* became the dominant form of folk poetry until it was overwhelmed by the impact of the *corrido* at the beginning of the twentieth century. In some other parts of Hispanic America, the *décima* has continued to flourish.

Cantos a desafío have also been popular both in Spain and in America, in ritual and on festive occasions, though the verse forms used have more often been four-line *coplas* rather than *décimas*. Some of these poetic encounters have become legendary, such as the contest between El Mulato Taguada and Don Javier de la Rosa in Chile.

The *décima* on the Lower Texas-Mexican Border has been part of the Greater Mexican tradition, of course, but in the area downriver from Brownsville and Matamoros it took on special characteristics, to a great extent because of the *décima* text that is before you, the locally celebrated *décimas de pedimento* between El Indio Córdova and Don Santiago María Cisneros. In its initial stages, the tradition of Córdova and Don Santiago María resembles the also semilegendary encounter between Taguada and Don Javier de la Rosa in Chile. Taguada is supposed to have committed suicide because he lost to Don Javier de la Rosa. There is a hint of racism in that Don Javier was white-skinned and Taguada was black. The way Chilean scholars have seen it is as a triumph of the city over the country. Don Javier was a city man and Taguada was a man from the country. But the encounter between Córdova and Don Santiago María did not become a closed chapter in oral history. Other family traditions developed around it, leading to an extended family preference for the *décima* in certain social situations, a preference that kept the *décima* alive even during the heyday of the revolutionary *corrido*, not only encouraging further composition in the genre but setting it in a series of anecdotes about members of the family, so that individual *décima* compositions survive as poetic endings to passages of oral history. And the root from which these later narrative-poetic phenomena grow is the story about El Indio Córdova, Don Santiago María Cisneros, and his daughter, Francisca Cisneros Gómez, best remembered as "Panchita" Cisneros.

I heard the story as a child during my summers on the ranches downriver from Matamoros—in hundreds of evening gatherings in darkened patios where the old men of the Cisnerada clan gathered to talk about the past and of what the future would be like, now that Villa had made his peace with the government and the Great War was over; and on sleepy afternoons when the women of the ranches passed the time sewing and embroidering (and talking) until it was time to start supper for the men, who would be coming home from the *campo* at nightfall. And so I learned it, in tantalizing fragments. But like some work of embroidery wrought into shape over weeks and months, it was all of one piece when it was finished. At times *décimas* were recited with the stories, at times they were sung. But the narrative, which the *décimas* adorned like colorful motifs on a larger design—the narrative was the important thing, because it bound the *décimas* together, and all of us as well.

It was 1865, during the darkest days of the resistance against French occupation of Mexico. Benito Juárez, symbol of that resistance, had been pushed farther and farther north toward the border with Texas. Texas was one of the Confederate States, in sympathy with the emperor Maximilian, who had arrived in Mexico in May of 1864. But the Civil War in the United States was coming to an end, and Juárez had good reason to expect aid in arms and ammunition from the victorious Union. So it was not surprising that *juarista* officials should be frequent visitors to the Mexican cities bordering Texas, from Matamoros to El Paso del Norte, later to be known as Ciudad Juárez.

It was about this time, in 1865 or 1866, that Juárez's minister of war visited Matamoros on some affair of state. His last name was Córdova, but oral tradition has not preoccupied itself with his first name. It is affirmed that he was an *indio puro,* a genuine Indian like Juárez himself; so that he came to be known simply as "El Indio" Córdova.

There was no one alive who remembered what Córdova's business was as a Juárez agent in Matamoros. He disguised his mission by passing as a civilian and engaged in the social activities of the *municipio.* Córdova attended a dance at the village of El Ranchito, downriver from Matamoros. And it was there that he met the beautiful Panchita Cisneros and promptly fell in love with her. Francisca Cisneros Gómez was about sixteen at the time, a rosy-faced beauty with green eyes and light-brown hair. She was the daughter of Santiago María Cisneros and Isabel Gómez, both members of the area's large landowning families, the "Thirteen Families" that had founded Matamoros and held extensive tracts of land between that city and the Gulf. If there was anything resembling a gentry among the *rancheros* of the Rio Grande country, it was families such as these.

At that time they had a reputation for clannishness. They could be gracious enough with outsiders who visited their domains, but they steadfastly and sometimes fiercely opposed having their daughters marry *fuereños,* or outsiders, whatever their origins or rank might be.

So it was no surprise to anyone that Panchita's father looked on Córdova's suit with disfavor, despite his high rank in the Juárez government. He was a *fuereño* and, like Juárez himself, an *indio* from southern Mexico as well. Don Santiago María did not even give Córdova's marriage proposal the dignity of a formal refusal, as custom demanded. But Córdova was not easily put off. He changed his tactics and sent Don Santiago María a written petition for Panchita's hand in the form of a set of *décimas con planta.* The Cisneros family had a local reputation as oral poets and improvisers, and among them Don Santiago María was considered one of the best. Coming from a similar *décima* tradition, and a skilled *decimero* himself, Córdova knew that Don Santiago María would have to answer or lose prestige in his own community, because Córdova's *décimas* were at the same time a plea for Panchita's hand and a poetic challenge. Don Santiago María's answer was not long in coming, in *décimas* glossing Córdova's *planta,* and the answer again was no. Copies of the exchange between Córdova and Don Santiago María were circulated beyond the confines of the Matamoros downriver area, usually with the glosses paired in parallel columns and the *planta* at the head. They came to be known as the *décimas del pedimento,* and it was generally conceded—among the Cisnerada, at least—that Don Santiago María had vanquished Córdova in their poetic contest.

Córdova apparently did not see it that way, for he persisted in his suit, vowing that his love for Panchita Cisneros was eternal, and that he had enshrined her in his heart as his patron saint. Meanwhile, the war continued to go badly for the Republican forces. Matamoros fell to the Imperialists, and Córdova joined *juarista* forces farther west. But the Civil War in the United States ended, and North American arms and ammunition poured across the border to the Juárez forces. Napoleon III, threatened at home by the growing power of Prussia, decided it was time to withdraw his troops from Mexico. Maximilian was captured, tried, and executed—the first "war criminal" of modern times*—and Juárez entered Mexico City in triumph.

Somewhere in all of this, El Indio Córdova was doing his part for the Republic, his heart still full of love for Don Santiago María's daughter, and still writing *décimas* to Don Santiago María. One of these compositions, supposedly Córdova's last, has been preserved. It is not a *décimas con planta* poem, being merely two *décimas* long. In it Córdova again expresses his eternal love for Don Santiago María's daughter and asks (not for the first time it is certain) why his suit was rejected by her father. Córdova also mentions that he has been wounded in battle at a place called Santa Clara. Don Santiago María dismisses Córdova with a quatrain, accusing him of having been afraid during the battle. After that Córdova drops out of sight. According to family tradition, he died of his wounds, his heart still full of love for Panchita Cisneros. Panchita, meanwhile, had married a member of another of the Thirteen Families, Prudencio Hinojosa Salinas, to whom she bore twelve children.

But the romantic story lived on: of the urbane, cultured Indian, lovesick for a beautiful country girl who was denied to him in marriage even though he was the nation's minister of war, and of his heroic death fighting the invaders of his homeland. And the *décimas de pedimento* were recited over and over in countless gatherings of the Cisneros

---

* He had signed decrees that any Mexican caught with arms in his hands was to be summarily shot; his troops often burned villages in which they had been sniped at; in others they did not burn, but executed the *presidente municipal* and the city council.

extended family, as part of that story of love unfulfilled or unrequited, until most members knew them by heart. The *décimas* became a kind of substitute for an ID card among members of the widespread Cisnerada and their allied families. Knowing the *décimas,* or at the very least parts of them, established you as someone who belonged in a special poetic and familial circle.*

So did I hear the story told. Tracing it in detail and collecting all known *décimas* composed by members of the Cisnerada became one of my dream projects by the time I was in high school, around 1933. But life leads us where it will, and though I picked up *décimas* and bits of information in the intervening years, it was not until half a century later, in 1983, that I was able to attempt some serious work on the subject. By that time, much of the information I had counted on was lost. I had expected to get reliable oral accounts from the old people I had known in my childhood, who had personally known some of the principals in the story. But by 1983, I was a *viejo* myself, and all the *viejos* of my youth were gone. Still, the family history had been passed on to those members of the extended family who had remained on the Lower Rio Grande Border, especially among those who had retained much of the old way of life. Besides, there would be some documentary materials I could draw upon to fill out what I knew from oral accounts.

My first preoccupation was to learn more about the mysterious Córdova, Juárez's minister of war. I had been told by reliable informants that his name probably was Antonio. This was a good beginning; even secondary sources could tell me something about an Antonio Córdova who was Juárez's minister of war during the 1860s. Printed sources, however, gave me nothing at all. President Benito Juárez, I discovered, had several ministers of war in the ten years of virtually continuous warfare the Mexican Liberals endured in defense of constitutional reform. But none of them was named Córdova. I knew that in oral transmission names may be distorted or replaced by others that resemble them. But the names recorded for Juárez's ministers of war did not bear the remotest resemblance to the name of Panchita Cisneros's poetical admirer. Score one against oral history.

* I had the experience of meeting on a street in Brownsville a lady that I always considered an Anglo (she had an Anglo name) and she said, "Yo soy Cisneros. . . 'Oye, Santiago María, / Cisneros de apelativo. . .'"

So Córdova did not hold the exalted position attributed to him by oral tradition. Still, he could have been an aide to one of Juárez's ministers, stationed in Matamoros during 1865 and 1866 on some special assignment. Again, documentary evidence contradicted oral tradition. In August 1864 French naval forces occupied the Mexican port of Bagdad at the mouth of the Rio Grande. A month later, Mexican Imperialist forces under General Tomás Mejía marched into Matamoros. Mejía occupied the city until June 1866, when he surrendered it to General José María Carvajal. Mejía, by the way, was said to be of Indian origins and also was known, at least on the border, as "El Indio" Mejía.

Four days after Mejía evacuated Matamoros a Liberal city government was established, but Antonio Córdova's name does not appear among its constituents. At all events, if Córdova met and courted Panchita Cisneros "about 1865 or 1866" it could not have been until after June 1866, when the Liberals were again in control of the city.

The genealogical charts available to me in 1983 are really records of land ownership and inheritance among the old downriver families. Though they clearly show lines of descent, they do not give dates of birth, death, or marriage. The clergy in Matamoros is notoriously uncooperative with descendants of anticlerical Freemasons, while the municipal archives are so organized that I would have had to reside in Matamoros for a goodly length of time (more than I can spare at this stage of my life) to unearth the few bits of information I desired. For having, very tentatively, established the date of the *décimas de pedimento,* I now wanted to make the date less tentative by discovering the approximate birth and death dates of the principals in this piece of oral history. There still were a few family members in Brownsville who had been born at the end of the nineteenth century, and they had some idea about the date of Doña Francisca's death. "She was an old lady in her seventies when she died at the beginning of this century," I was told. And that was the sum of information I could get until one of them mentioned, quite casually, that the old family cemetery of the Hinojosas at La Burrita probably still existed. "You will have to hunt for it in the underbrush," I was told, "because it has been abandoned for many years."

On June 17, 1983, I made the trip to the Hinojosa cemetery at the site where La Burrita once had been. I was in for some surprises. Though it stood isolated, with no houses anywhere in sight, the cemetery was clear

254 ~ The Folklore Genres: History, Form, and Performance

of brush and well tended. A notable thing about the tombstones in the Hinojosa family cemetery, as well as in that of the Cisneros in La Carrera, is the simplicity of the inscriptions carved upon them. There are no religious or philosophical phrases, either in verse or prose. On most there is only the name of the deceased, followed by the dates of birth and death, sometimes only the date of decease. The initials "Q.E.P.D." (*Que En Paz Descanse*) or a simple "Un Recuerdo" are the only comments inscribed. Considering the reputation as poets enjoyed by the Cisneros and Hinojosa families, it is remarkable that they did not exercise their talents on the graven stones placed over their dead. They did memorialize their deceased relatives, but they did so in *décimas*, some of which have remained in oral tradition for several generations.

My most interesting find, of course, was the grave of the muse of El Indio Córdova. Her name was on a large, stela-like marble slab, below her husband's and above three other names. The stone read, "Francisca C. Vda. de Hinojosa, born 1836, died May 25, 1902."

This was a second and a more serious blow to the traditional dating of the *décimas de pedimento* in 1865 or 1866. True, the *juaristas* had retaken Matamoros in June 1866. And, war minister or not, a man named Antonio Córdova could very well have met and fallen in love with a young country beauty named Francisca Cisneros after the Imperialists evacuated the city. But by 1866 Francisca Cisneros, though probably still a beautiful woman, would have been thirty years old. And according to the standards of the time, an unmarried woman of thirty was an old maid and not a "young virgin" as she is called in some of the *décimas*.

Then my research assistant in Brownsville, Humberto Cisneros Hinojosa, came up with an *hoja suelta*, or broadside, that reprinted the *décimas de pedimento*, with the title "Décimas cambiadas el año de 1848 entre los Señores Antonio Córdova y Santiago María Cisneros." If one was to believe the broadside, Córdova had asked to marry Panchita Cisneros in 1848, when she was twelve years old. There is no date given for the broadside, but the printer is identified as the "Preciado Pub. Co.— Brownsville." La Imprenta Preciado (not the "Preciado Publishing Company") was an old institution in Brownsville by the time I became aware of it on my way to and from grammar school. Its printing was done with handset type on a flatbed press. Among its publications were a small newspaper, *El Porvenir,* and the usual output from the typical "folk" press: broadsides of different kinds, *novenas,* and such. But the Preciados also published occasional documents of historical interest. At one time they had reprinted the *Informe de la Comisión Pesquisidora de la Frontera del Norte* (1877), a book that had become a rarity in Texas because some wealthy South Texas ranchers bought and destroyed most of the copies in circulation. But as far as the *décimas de pedimento* were concerned, the Preciados seemed to be in error. It was not uncommon in mid-nineteenth-century times for girls to marry at fifteen, but it seemed inconceivable that Córdova would want a twelve-year-old girl for his bride.

I then made my way to the Barker Texas History Center of the University of Texas, Austin, which possesses photostatic copies of parts of the Matamoros archives. They are not in chronological order, and the quality of reproduction is uneven. But it was here that I found traces of that elusive character Antonio ("El Indio") Córdova.

The signature of an "A. Córdova, Secretario" appears in entries dating from 1844 to 1849, in association with the names of Colonels Leonardo Manso and Francisco Lojero. Manso and Lojero had served in their country's armed forces since the beginning of Mexico's war of independence; and more than forty years later, in an army noted for an abundance of generals, they had not risen above the rank of colonel. The reason may have been that they were among the few survivors of the original officers who had fought for independence. Most of the others were captured and executed by royalist forces led by Mexican *criollo* aristocrats. With the notable exception of Nicolás Bravo, the Mexican generals of the period from 1821 to the 1850s were former royalist officers, who had worked assiduously to exterminate the insurgents but who switched sides and became "insurgents" in 1821, when Spain adopted a liberal constitution that threatened the privileges of the Mexican *criollos.*

Nevertheless, in the 1840s Manso and Lojero were still giving faithful service to their country. The 1830s and 1840s were turbulent years for the Lower Rio Grande area of Tamaulipas—with revolt in Texas, intensified Indian raids, attacks by Texan filibusters, and finally the U.S. invasion of Mexico by troops under Zachary Taylor. To all this was added the quarrelsome character of the local chieftains, who very often fought among themselves. It is not strange, then, to find military men serving in high civilian posts along the Rio Grande.

Lojero served as *alcalde,* or mayor, of Matamoros during this period, while Manso, apparently headquartered in Ciudad Victoria, at times was sent to the Rio Grande to serve as arbitrator between feuding Mexican factions. Later he became *jefe político* for northern Tamaulipas, a kind of military supervisor for the area. It is in connection with these events that we find A. Córdova's signature in the Matamoros archives, as secretary or representative of Colonel Manso. From June 19, 1844, until November 6, 1849, the Matamoros archives record communications to Manso and Lojero from A. Córdova, who reported on civilian and military matters from Mier, Matamoros, and Ciudad Victoria.

A letter of November 6, 1849, is the last reference to A. Córdova that I have been able to find. In his last verse communication with Don Santiago María Cisneros, El Indio Córdova says that after being denied Francisca Cisneros's hand he became a soldier, "accompanied by others," and that he was wounded in battle. Oral tradition has him dying of his wounds, and assumes that Córdova took part in one of the last battles against the Imperialist forces seeking to perpetuate Maximilian's rule, perhaps in 1866 or 1867. This assumption is put in great doubt if the A. Córdova whose name appears in the Matamoros archives is the same man as the Antonio ("El Indio") Córdova who loved Panchita Cisneros. And there is no other Córdova whose existence I have been able to document, either in the 1840s or the 1860s. So if Antonio Córdova did participate in combat it must have been soon after 1849, and not against Maximilian's forces but in the fratricidal conflicts that continued to rack Mexico between the North American invasion and the French invasion in 1861.

All this left me with three pieces of "hard" documentary evidence that, put together, did not seem to make sense: a broadside stating that the *décimas de pedimento* were composed in 1848; parts of the Matamoros archives showing that a *fuereño* named A. Córdova, a man of some consequence at the time, had been in Matamoros during the period from 1844 to 1849; and a tombstone showing the birth date of Francisca Cisneros de Hinojosa as 1836. So Córdova must have courted Panchita

Cisneros in 1848. Yet, it seemed highly improbable that a man would court a child of twelve, especially a cultured man such as Córdova seems to have been. Furthermore, in his answer to Córdova's plea, Don Santiago María refers to the object of Córdova's love as a woman: "la mujer de tu conquista / creo será bella dama." This time "solid" documentary evidence seemed to be in conflict.

This invited another, more critical look at what literally was the most solid piece of evidence, the stone over Francisca Cisneros's grave at La Burrita. It is a rectangular marble slab, arched at the top and bearing five names. Immediately below the arch that tops the slab is the legend "Familia Hinojosa," followed by a semirecumbent Latin cross with the initials "Q.E.P.D." (*Que En Paz Descansen*), each letter occupying one of the four angles made by the cross. At the bottom of the slab is a single word, "Recuerdo." There is no other decoration or inscription except for the names of those buried there. The fifth and last name is that of Emilio Hinojosa, born September 14, 1882, and died October 26, 1948. The stone shows little wear by the elements, and the names incised upon it evince an equal degree of weathering; so it seems clear that the stone was cut and placed over the grave as it now stands some time after October 26, 1948, the date of Emilio Hinojosa's death.

Above Emilio's name is that of Celedina C. de Hinojosa, born February 3, 1857, and died February 17, 1926. A daughter-in-law rather than a daughter, she probably came from one of the branches of the Cisneros family. Her husband, a son of Prudencio Hinojosa and Francisca Cisneros, must have been born in the 1850s as well, evidence that Prudencio Hinojosa and Francisca Cisneros were married and having children by the 1850s, and further proof that Córdova did not court Panchita Cisneros in the mid-1860s. This also supports the Preciado broadside's assertion that the *décima* exchange between Córdova and Don Santiago María occurred in 1848.

Yet, the gravestone also tells us that Panchita Cisneros was twelve years old in 1848. But even messages inscribed in stone may bear some scrutiny, and looking at the three names above Celedina's gives us a clue. Just above her name is that of Quintín Hinojosa, born October 31, 1878, and died February 4, 1898. Above his name is that of his mother: Francisca C. Vda. de Hinojosa, born in 1836 and died May 25, 1902.

Above hers, at the very top of the list, is her husband's name: Prudencio Hinojosa, died January 25, 1893.

Evidently, the members of the Hinojosa family who put up the stone after Emilio's death in 1948 did not have verifiable records of family births and deaths prior to the 1850s. Complete dates are given for the three children. But for Francisca Cisneros Vda. de Hinojosa, only the date of her death is fully recorded. For her birth date the year alone is given. And for her husband even less information is recorded. Only the date of his death appears on the stone. Apparently even the year of his birth was unknown to his descendants, at least to the ones concerned with the erection of the stone.

With that in mind, it seems highly probable that the year of Doña Francisca's birth was handed down orally rather than preserved in some family document. And that, of course, allows for a significant margin of error. Oral transmission of dates sometimes can be quite precise, especially if the date records an event within living memory or one of great historical import. The Border *corrido* "La toma de Matamoros," for example, records the precise date, day of the week, and time of day when revolutionary chief Lucio Blanco's forces began their attack on the city. The *corrido* begins, "Día martes tres de junio de mil novecientos trece a las diez de la mañana Lucio Blanco se aparece." And you go to the records and it was a Tuesday, June 3, 1913, that Blanco attacked Matamoros, and at ten in the morning. The only difference is that he did not appear before Matamoros at ten. The assault of Matamoros began at ten that morning. There oral tradition gives you historical fidelity. But some versions of the *corrido* about the capture and death of the celebrated smuggler Mariano Reséndez set the events in 1900, when they did happen, while others locate them in 1800. In oral transmission, "año de mil novecientos" can easily become "año de mil ochocientos." I think that the key there is that "ochocientos" and "novecientos" sound alike enough so that in oral tradition they could be changed. It is even easier for such a thing to happen in the transmission of prose oral narratives, which are not as tightly structured as is folksong. It is much more likely that Panchita Cisneros was born in 1833, and that "el año de treinta y tres" became "el año de treinta y seis" in oral transmission. She would then have been fifteen in 1848 when Antonio Córdova fell in love with her, and sixty-nine when she died in 1902. Her descendants who were living when she passed away would later describe her as "an old lady about seventy years old." The preference for the year 1836 in oral tradition is understandable, considering the devastating events visited on the border people for a long period of time beginning in 1836—Indian raids, Anglo-Texan raids, followed later by Zachary Taylor's invasion, and so on.

The story of Panchita Cisneros and El Indio Córdova as it has survived for almost 140 years is fundamentally true, though a couple of key facts have been rearranged to make it a more satisfying whole in the minds of Panchita's descendants. The most important is the changing of the date of Córdova's courtship from 1848 to 1866. The change has served the function of identifying Antonio ("El Indio") Córdova with Mexico's greatest "Indio," Don Benito Juárez. But there is more to the legendary aspects of this family tradition than the switching of a couple of dates. In the development of a historical occurrence into a romantic story, some important parts of family history have been forgotten or simply ignored.

Though he did occupy an important post as Colonel Leonardo Manso's secretary in the 1840s, Antonio Córdova never was Juárez's minister of war. But a relative of Prudencio Hinojosa, Panchita's husband, did occupy that post. Don Pedro Hinojosa (1822–1903) was Juárez's minister of war in 1861. During the Porfirio Díaz regime, General Hinojosa again was minister of war, from 1884 to 1896. All this I have learned from documentary sources, not from family oral tradition. Tradition has suppressed all of this, and given Córdova the honor of being minister of war—an interesting vagary of oral history that could only be explained by a detailed study of national and family attitudes, if such were available.

Both the Cisneros and the Hinojosas were active in political and military affairs during the 1850s and 1860s. In 1855, under the leadership of Liberal officers like General Ignacio Zaragoza and Colonel Leonardo Manso, the state of Tamaulipas declared its support for the Plan de Ayutla, which permanently expelled Santa Anna from Mexican politics and initiated the Liberal reforms that Juárez would soon implement. The Matamoros archives for 1858 include a list of persons from the

Matamoros area who had supported the "liberation of the State in 1855."
Among those listed is Prudencio Hinojosa, who must have been a married man by that time, since Panchita Cisneros would have been about twenty-two by then.

In 1861, with French ships already before Veracruz, a dispute over a gubernatorial election led to bloody warfare in Matamoros between adherents of the two Liberal candidates. Other Liberal leaders mediated the dispute, and both factions became part of a "División del Norte"— antedating Francisco Villa's better-known División del Norte by half a century—which marched south in 1862, to take part in the Cinco de Mayo victory over the French at Puebla. Among those participants in the bitter fratricidal struggle in Matamoros who did not march to Puebla was Prudencio Hinojosa. He was seriously wounded in 1861 and apparently survived because of the care given him by his brother-in-law, José María Cisneros. In June 1866, after the Imperialist general Tomás Mejía evacuated Matamoros, a Liberal city government was established with men of the *juarista* forces as its members. The chief of police was José María Cisneros.

The wound he received in 1861 apparently did not dull Prudencio's appetite for feats of arms. In a set of *décimas,* undated but obviously composed some time after 1867, José María takes his brother-in-law to task for wanting to join in another revolution:

Prudencio, ¿qué te motiva	Prudencio, what motivates you
meterte en revolución?	to get mixed up in a revolution?
¿Qué te queda o con qué acción	What will you gain, or for what reason
mueres tú por que otro viva?	are you willing to die so that someone
	else may "live"? [so that someone
	else may be acclaimed with shouts
	of "¡viva!"]

None of these details, which I have gleaned from scattered documentary sources, was part of the stories I used to hear in the downriver ranches when I was a boy. As with Pedro Hinojosa, who in fact was one of Juárez's ministers of war, Cisneros family traditions have ignored the deeds of their own members and even attributed some of them to the romantic (and distant) figure of the legendary Indio Córdova.

Perhaps Antonio Córdova died as a result of wounds suffered in a skirmish at a place called Santa Clara, though his final *décimas* to Don Santiago María do not sound like the work of a dying man. More than likely he survived, got over his infatuation for Panchita Cisneros, and married someone else. But in Border tradition he remains the image of the steadfast lover who dies with the name of his beloved on his lips, a sacrifice to his country's independence from foreign domination.

Córdova swore undying love for the woman who "imprisoned" him when he danced with her in El Ranchito. Millions of other lovers have done the same. But El Indio Córdova has been fortunate in having others see to it that his love be an undying one. It still lives to this day, 138 years after he wrote his *décimas* to Don Santiago María Cisneros and was put down by the old *decimero*. The irony is that it has been the extended family of the woman he loved, the family who considered him an unfit husband for one of their own, who have seen to it that Córdova and his love for Panchita Cisneros continue to live for almost a century and a half.

History (oral and written) is a dynamic process that is always open to change; and like the Martian in Ray Bradbury's story, it tends to reshape itself according to the half-conscious desires and yearnings of those who behold it, changing a detail here, a name there, making itself less what probably was and more what it should have been. Our crucial question is why. What particular emotional needs of the Cisneros extended family are fulfilled by the story of El Indio Córdova's deathless love for Panchita Cisneros? It is a question I am not prepared to explore today.

On the other hand, I think again of Ernesto Galarza, whom we are honoring today. He told a richer and fuller family history in *Barrio Boy*. And for his epigraph he chose a passage from Henry Adams about the past remembered. Memories are like that; with the passing of the years they change a bit. But the memory is all that matters.

Del Indio Córdova y don Santiago María

El Indio Córdova:

Oye, Santiago María,
Cisneros de apelativo,
te ruego no seas esquivo
con esta consulta mía.

Hear me, Santiago María,
Cisneros by appellation,
I beg you not be evasive
with this consultation of mine.

1

No te juzgo hombre de ciencia
como el mejor sin segundo,
tienes algo y mucho mundo
y más que yo de experiencia;
quiero que esa tu indulgencia
me saque de esta porfía
que me tiene en agonía
como hombre y apasionado,
y tú serás mi abogado,
oye, Santiago María.

I do not judge you a man of learning
of the best and without peer,
but you have somewhat greater wisdom
and more experience than I;
I appeal to your forbearance
to give relief to this obsession
that has me in anguish
as a man and as a lover,
and you shall be my advocate,
hear me, Santiago María.

2

Amo a una bella criatura
cuya vista al sol sujeta,
de aquélla que el Sabio Poeta
hizo una fina pintura;
no la iguala en hermosura
la luna en el cielo vivo
y si sus gracias describo
por Dios que me fatalizo,
imagen que divinizo,
Cisneros de apelativo.

I love a beautiful creature
whose gaze can control the sun,
she whom the Wise Poet
made into a wonderful picture;
she is not equaled in beauty
by the moon in a brilliant sky,
and if I describe her charms
I swear I shall be undone,
image that I deify,
Cisneros by appellation.

3

La amo, y malhaya mi vida
cuando la imagen que adoro
vio pasarme, triste lloro,
sin darse por entendida;
ésta es causa que te pida
consejo por tal motivo,
dame un voto decisivo

I love her, accursed be my life
when the vision I adore
saw me pass by, sad I lament,
and took no notice of me;
that is why I ask of you
your counsel, for such a reason,
give me a final decision

en tal batalla de amor
y al pedirte este favor
te ruego no seas esquivo.

in this battle of love,
and in asking you this favor
I beg you not be evasive.

4

Para lograr lo que quiero
a tu consejo me atengo,
seguro que ya prevengo
valor, constancia y dinero;
estudia de cuero a cuero
tu historia de vida impía
por si te occurió algún día
cuando joven arrogante
algún caso semejante
con esta consulta mía.

To attain what I desire
I rely upon your counsel,
certain that I'm well possessed
of courage, perseverance, and money;
read over from cover to cover
the story of your godless life,
perhaps you once had
when you were an arrogant youth
a comparable experience
with this consultation of mine.

Don Santiago María:

1

Recibí las expresiones
que le fiastes al papel,
donde me dices en él
te dé algunas instrucciones;
no te ciegues de pasiones
por seguir en tu porfía,
yo no sé cual sea la guía
de tu amor, que a mí me avise,
pues sólo en el papel dice:
oye, Santiago María.

I have received the phrases
you entrusted to the paper,
in which you ask me
to give you some advice;
do not let your passion blind you
to persist in your obsession,
I don't know what may be the lodestar
of your love, that it should concern me,
since all that the paper says is:
hear me, Santiago María.

2

La mujer de tu conquista
creo será bella dama,
mas siempre el que feo ama
se le hace la nuncavista;
entre tu pecho registra
si encuentras un atractivo
que te sirva de motivo
de donde tu amor proviene,
pues sólo advierto que tiene
Cisneros de apelativo.

The woman who has won your love
must be a beautiful damsel,
but he who loves an ugly woman
considers her a rare beauty;
search within your breast
to find in her something attractive
that may serve you as the source
from which your love arises,
for all I know is that she is
Cisneros by appellation.

3

La vida nunca renace,	Life never comes to us twice,
tú la maltratas hablando,	you abuse it with your talking,
siempre vivirás penando	you will live longing for her
y a ella que ni fuerza le hace;	and she will not care at all;
es muy justo que te pase	it's very just that I give you
un golpe bien decisivo	a very decisive blow,
y si pierdes el sentido	and if you lose your wits
voy a pedirte un favor,	I will ask you a favor,
que al sufrir este rigor	in facing up to this rigor
te ruego no seas esquivo.	*I beg you not be evasive.*

4

Todo hombre que por mujer	Any man who for a woman
arriesga plata y firmeza,	risks his wealth and his integrity,
cuando no cae de cabeza	if he doesn't fall on his head
de narices suele caer;	he's likely to fall on his face;
es cosa que vas a ver	that's something that you will see
si sigues en tu porfía,	if you persist in your obsession,
gastas la última cuartilla	you will spend your last penny
y entonces será el atraso,	and then things will catch up with you,
quedarás como un bagazo	you will end up like a piece of trash
con esta consulta mía.	*with this consultation of mine.*

LAST KNOWN EXCHANGE BETWEEN "EL INDIO" CÓRDOVA
AND DON SANTIAGO MARÍA

El Indio Córdova:

Andando yo desterrado,	Being in exile,
andando en ajena tierra	being in an alien land,
me marché para la guerra	I went away to war
con otros acompañado;	in the company of others;
quise ver si de soldado	I wanted to see whether as a soldier
me hacía de fama un día	I could attain fame some day,
pero por Dios no podía,	but by the Lord I could not;
era mi suerte tan rara	my destiny was so strange
que gritaba en Santa Clara:	that my war cry at Santa Clara was,
—¡Oye, Santiago María!—	"Hear me, Santiago María!"
Vida y sangre derramé	Of my life's blood I have spilled
en la lid más que una gota,	in combat more than a drop;
que si no es por mi devota,	had it not been for my patron saint,
aquella virgen que amé—	that maiden that I have loved—
Dime, Cisneros, por qué	Tell me, Cisneros, why
esa virgen me has negado;	have you denied me that maiden;
me tiene a sus pies postrado,	she has me prostrate at her feet,
triste de mí, pobrecito.	sad is my lot, woe is me.
Le dije allá en El Ranchito:	I told her there at El Ranchito,
—Me tienes apasionado.—	"I love you passionately."

Don Santiago María:

Si en la lid te entraron corvas,	If being in combat scared you,
viéndote en lance profundo,	finding yourself in grave predicament,
por Dios estás en el mundo,	you're still in this world because God
no por la virgen que nombras.	willed it,
	not because of the maiden you mention.

Notes

Introduction (by Richard Bauman)

I have benefited in the writing of this introductory essay from the critical comments and suggestions of Linda Kinsey Adams, John H. McDowell, Ramón Saldívar, and Beverly J. Stoeltje.

1. Américo Paredes, *Between Two Worlds* (Houston: Arte Público Press, 1991); Américo Paredes, *George Washington Gómez* (Houston: Arte Público Press, 1990).

2. Tomás Rivera, "Interview," in *Chicano Authors: Inquiry by Interview,* ed. Bruce-Novoa (Austin: University of Texas Press, 1980), 137–161; and Ramón Saldívar, *Chicano Narrative: The Dialectics of Difference* (Madison: University of Wisconsin Press, 1990).

3. José E. Limón, *The Return of the Mexican Ballad: Américo Paredes and His Anthropological Text as Persuasive Political Performance,* SCCR Working Paper no. 16 (Stanford: Stanford Center for Chicano Research, Stanford University, 1986).

4. Américo Paredes, *"With His Pistol in His Hand": A Border Ballad and Its Hero* (Austin: University of Texas Press, 1958), 164–165.

5. Américo Paredes, "The Ancestry of Mexico's *Corridos:* A Matter of Definitions," *Journal of American Folklore* 76 (1963): 233.

6. Joe Graham, "The *Caso:* An Emic Genre of Folk Narrative," in *"And Other Neighborly Names": Social Process and Cultural Image in Texas Folklore,* ed. Richard Bauman and Roger D. Abrahams (Austin: University of Texas Press, 1981), 11–43.

7. Peter Monahan, "Anthropologist Who Sparked Dispute by Criticizing Margaret Mead's Research on Samoan Life Finds New Backing for His Claims," *Chronicle of Higher Education* 35, no. 47 (2 August 1989): A4–A6; compare

Beverly J. Stoeltje, "The Performance of the Exotic: Rodeo Made Strange," *Semiotica* 44 (1983): 137–147.

1. The Folklore of Groups of Mexican Origin in the United States [1979]

This essay appeared in more extensive form as "El folklore de los grupos de origen mexicano en Estados Unidos" in *Folklore Americano* 14 (1966): 146–163. The present English translation was originally published under the title "The Folk Base of Chicano Literature" in *Modern Chicano Writers: A Collection of Critical Essays*, ed. Joseph Sommers and Tomás Ybarra-Frausto (Englewood Cliffs, N.J.: Prentice-Hall, 1979), 4–17. The translation is by Kathleen Lamb.

1. Cecil Robinson, *With the Ears of Strangers: The Mexican in American Literature* (Tucson: University of Arizona Press, 1963).

2. Arthur L. Campa, "The Spanish Folksong in the Southwest," *University of New Mexico Bulletin*, Modern Language Series, no. 4.1 (1933): 7–8, 13, 32–33, 54–56, 66.

3. Richard M. Dorson, *American Folklore* (Chicago: University of Chicago Press, 1959), 75.

4. Richard M. Dorson, *Buying the Wind: Regional Folklore in the United States* (Chicago: University of Chicago Press, 1964), 415–495.

5. Aurelio M. Espinosa, "Comparative Notes on New Mexican and Mexican Spanish Folktales," *Journal of American Folklore* 27 (1914): 211–231; José Manuel Espinosa, *Spanish Folktales from New Mexico* (New York: American Folklore Society, 1937); Campa, "Spanish Folksong," 16, 23–33; and M. R. Cole, *Los Pastores: A Mexican Play of the Nativity* (Boston: Houghton Mifflin, 1907).

6. Vicente T. Mendoza, *El corrido mexicano* (Mexico City: Fondo de Cultura Económica, 1954), xv; and Vicente T. Mendoza, *Lírica narrativa de México: El corrido*, Estudios de Folklore, no. 2 (Mexico City: Instituto de Investigaciones Estéticas, Universidad Nacional Autónoma de México, 1964), 14.

7. Mendoza, *Lírica narrativa*, 35, 204.

8. Manuel Gamio, *Mexican Immigration to the United States* (Chicago: University of Chicago Press, 1930), 96.

9. Paul S. Taylor, *Mexican Labor in the United States*, vol. 2, University of California Publications in Economics Series, no. 7.1 (Berkeley: University of California Press, 1932), vii–ix.

10. Charles E. Kany, *American-Spanish Semantics* (Berkeley: University of California Press, 1960); Charles E. Kany, *American-Spanish Euphemisms* (Berkeley: University of California Press, 1960); and Munro S. Edmonson, *Los Manitos* (New Orleans: Middle American Research Institute, Tulane University, 1957).

2. The Problem of Identity in a Changing Culture: Popular Expressions of Culture Conflict along the Lower Rio Grande Border [1978]

Originally published in *Views across the Border: The United States and Mexico,* ed. Stanley Ross (Albuquerque: University of New Mexico Press, 1978), 68–94. Reprinted by permission.

1. Howard F. Cline, ed., *Guide to Ethnohistorical Sources* (pt. 1), vol. 12 of *Handbook of Middle American Indians,* ed. Robert Wauchope (Austin: University of Texas Press, 1972), 167. Adapted from R. C. West and J. P. Angelli, *Middle America: Its Lands and Peoples* (Englewood Cliffs, N.J.: Prentice-Hall, 1966).

2. Walter Prescott Webb, *The Great Plains* (Boston: Ginn, 1931), 205–269.

3. O. Henry, *Rolling Stones* (New York: Doubleday, Page, 1912), 258.

4. N. Howard ("Jack") Thorp, *Songs of the Cowboys* (1908; facsimile ed. with variants, commentary, notes, and lexicon by Austin E. Fife and Alta S. Fife [New York: Clarkson N. Potter, 1966]), 87–90.

5. John C. Duval, *The Adventures of Big-Foot Wallace* (Macon, Ga.: J. W. Burke, 1871; facsimile ed. [Austin: University of Texas Press, 1947]), 171–172, 180, 197, et passim.

6. Américo Paredes, "Estados Unidos, México y el machismo," *Journal of Inter-American Studies* 9 (1967): 65–84.

7. Lester V. Berrey and Melvin Van den Bark, *The American Thesaurus of Slang,* 2d ed. (New York: Thomas Y. Crowell, 1956).

8. H. L. Mencken, *The American Language,* suppl. 1 (New York: Alfred A. Knopf, 1948), 609–610.

9. Duval, *Big-Foot Wallace,* 225.

10. Duval, *Big-Foot Wallace,* 216.

11. Ed Cray, "Ethnic and Place Names as Derisive Adjectives," *Western Folklore* 21 (1962): 27–34.

12. Cray, "Ethnic and Place Names," 28.

13. Mencken, *American Language,* 595.

14. Mencken, *American Language,* 638.

15. Francisco J. Santamaría, *Diccionario de mejicanismos* (Mexico City: Editorial Porrúa, 1959), 697.

16. Angel Bassols Batalla et al., *Temas y figuras de la intervención* (Mexico City: Primer Congreso Nacional de Historia para el Estudio de la Guerra de Intervención, 1963), 71.

17. Bassols Batalla et al., *Temas y figuras,* 30.

18. Américo Paredes, "The Mexican *Corrido:* Its Rise and Fall," in *Madstones and Twisters,* ed. Mody C. Boatright, Wilson M. Hudson, and Allen Maxwell,

Publications of the Texas Folklore Society, no. 28 (Dallas: Southern Methodist University Press, 1958), 91–105; and Américo Paredes, *"With His Pistol in His Hand": A Border Ballad and Its Hero* (Austin: University of Texas Press, 1958), 129–150.

19. William Hugh Jansen, "The Esoteric-Exoteric Factor in Folklore," *Fabula: Journal of Folktale Studies* 2 (1959): 205–211; reprinted in *The Study of Folklore*, ed. Alan Dundes (Englewood Cliffs, N.J.: Prentice-Hall, 1965), 43–51.

20. Carey McWilliams, *North from Mexico* (New York: J. B. Lippincott, 1949), 234.

21. Octavio Paz, *The Labyrinth of Solitude*, trans. Lysander Kemp (New York: Grove Press, 1961), 16.

22. Octavio Paz, *México: La última década* (Austin: University of Texas Press, 1969), 10–11.

3. Folk Medicine and the Intercultural Jest [1968]

Originally published in *Spanish-Speaking People in the United States*, ed. June Helm. Proceedings of the 1968 Annual Spring Meeting of the American Ethnological Society (Seattle: American Ethnological Society, 1968), 104–119. Reprinted by permission. The Spanish texts of the jests are published here for the first time. My fieldwork was made possible by a fellowship from the John Simon Guggenheim Foundation and a supplementary grant from the University of Texas, which I acknowledge with thanks.

1. Francisco J. Santamaría, *Diccionario de mejicanismos* (Mexico City: Editorial Porrúa, 1959).

2. Ruth Dodson, *Don Pedrito Jaramillo: Curandero* (San Antonio: Casa Editorial Lozano, 1934); and Ruth Dodson, "Don Pedrito Jaramillo: The Curandero of Los Olmos," in *The Healer of Los Olmos and Other Mexican Lore*, ed. Wilson M. Hudson, Publications of the Texas Folklore Society, no. 24 (Dallas: Southern Methodist University Press, 1951), 9–70.

3. Octavio Ignacio Romano, "Charismatic Medicine, Folk-Healing, and Folk-Sainthood," *American Anthropologist* 67 (1965): 1151–1173.

4. William Madsen, *The Mexican-Americans of South Texas* (New York: Holt, Rinehart and Winston, 1964), 43.

5. Aurelio M. Espinosa, "New Mexican Spanish Folklore," *Journal of American Folklore* 27 (1914): 105–147, text 48.

6. Stith Thompson, *Motif-Index of Folk Literature*, 6 vols. (Bloomington: Indiana University Press, 1955–1958).

7. Madsen, *Mexican-Americans*, 93–94.

8. Dodson, *Don Pedrito Jaramillo*, 129–146.

9. Madsen, *Mexican-Americans*, 41–43.

4. On Ethnographic Work among Minority Groups: A Folklorist's Perspective [1977]

Originally published in *New Scholar* 6 (1977): 1–32. Reprinted by permission. I am grateful to Solveig Astrid Turpin for allowing me to quote from her paper and field notes done for a class in Greater Mexican folklore in 1974. My thanks also to Richard Bauman, for his valuable comments on an earlier version of this essay.

1. William Madsen, *The Mexican-Americans of South Texas* (New York: Holt, Rinehart and Winston, 1964).

2. Thomas Weaver, "Sampling and Generalization in Anthropological Research on Spanish-Speaking Groups," in *Spanish-Speaking People in the United States,* ed. June Helm (Seattle: American Ethnological Society, 1968), 1–18.

3. Arthur J. Rubel, *Across the Tracks: Mexican-Americans in a Texas City* (Austin: University of Texas Press, 1966), 126.

4. Madsen, *Mexican-Americans,* 72.

5. Madsen, *Mexican-Americans,* 72.

6. Madsen, *Mexican-Americans,* 73.

7. Michael Kearney, *The Winds of Ixtepeji: World View and Society in a Mexican Town* (New York: Holt, Rinehart and Winston, 1972), 88.

8. Munro S. Edmonson, "Narrative Folklore," in *Social Anthropology,* ed. Manning Nash, vol. 6 of *Handbook of Middle American Indians,* ed. Robert Wauchope (Austin: University of Texas Press, 1967), 359.

9. William Shakespeare, *The Complete Works of Shakespeare,* ed. Hardin Craig (Chicago: Scott, Foresman, 1951).

10. Munro S. Edmonson, "Play: Games, Gossip, and Humor," in *Social Anthropology,* ed. Manning Nash, vol. 6 of *Handbook of Middle American Indians,* ed. Robert Wauchope (Austin: University of Texas Press, 1967), 191.

11. Kearney, *Winds of Ixtepeji,* 110.

12. Roger D. Abrahams, "Introductory Remarks toward a Rhetorical Theory of Folklore," *Journal of American Folklore* 81 (1968): 143–158.

13. Daniel J. Crowley, *I Could Talk Old Story Good: Creativity in Bahamian Folklore* (Berkeley: University of California Press, 1966).

14. William R. Bascom, "Verbal Art," *Journal of American Folklore* 68 (1955): 245–252.

15. William Hugh Jansen, "The Esoteric-Exoteric Factor in Folklore," *Fabula: Journal of Folktale Studies* 2 (1959): 205–211.

16. Madsen, *Mexican-Americans,* 19.

17. Gene Bluestein, "'The Arkansas Traveler' and the Strategy of American Humor," *Western Folklore* 20 (1962): 153–160.

18. Bluestein, "'Arkansas Traveler,'" 157.

19. Bluestein, "'Arkansas Traveler,'" 156.

20. Rubel, *Across the Tracks*, 156.

21. Américo Paredes, "Folk Medicine and the Intercultural Jest," in *Spanish-Speaking People in the United States*, ed. June Helm (Seattle: American Ethnological Society, 1968), 107–109, 115.

22. Rubel, *Across the Tracks*, 155–156.

23. Madsen, *Mexican-Americans*, 26.

24. Rubel, *Across the Tracks*, 107.

25. Rubel, *Across the Tracks*, 108–110.

26. Rubel, *Across the Tracks*, 114.

27. Rubel, *Across the Tracks*, 108.

28. Richard M. Dorson, *American Folklore* (Chicago: University of Chicago Press, 1959), 258–259.

29. Ruth Dodson, "The Ghost Nun," in *Backwoods to Border*, ed. Mody C. Boatright and Donald Day, Publications of the Texas Folklore Society, no. 18 (Dallas: Southern Methodist University Press, 1943), 137–139.

30. Virginia Rodríguez Rivera (Mexican folklorist), personal communication, 1962.

31. Rubel, *Across the Tracks*, 80.

32. Sidney W. Mintz and Eric R. Wolf, "An Analysis of Ritual Co-Parenthood (*Compadrazgo*)," *Southwestern Journal of Anthropology* 6 (1950): 356.

33. Lee Haring, "Performing for the Interviewer: A Study in the Structure of Context," *Southern Folklore Quarterly* 36 (1972): 383–398.

34. Harald Eidheim, "When Ethnic Identity Is a Social Stigma," in *Ethnic Groups and Boundaries*, ed. Fredrik Barth (London: George Allen and Unwin, 1969), 44.

35. Rubel, *Across the Tracks*, 122.

36. Rubel, *Across the Tracks*, 123.

37. Madsen, *Mexican-Americans*, 15.

38. Rubel, *Across the Tracks*, 86.

39. Rubel, *Across the Tracks*, 38.

40. Rubel, *Across the Tracks*, 66.

41. Paredes, "Folk Medicine," 106–107.

42. Madsen, *Mexican-Americans*, 100–104.

43. Madsen, *Mexican-Americans*, 33.

44. Madsen, *Mexican-Americans*, 33.

45. Madsen, *Mexican-Americans*, 23.

46. Madsen, *Mexican-Americans*, 108.

47. Richard Bauman, "Verbal Art as Performance," *American Anthropologist* 77 (1975): 295.

48. C. Hugh Holman, *A Handbook to Literature,* 3d ed. (New York: Odyssey Press, 1972), 259.

49. Jansen, "Esoteric-Exoteric Factor," 205–211.

5. Some Aspects of Folk Poetry [1964]

Originally published in *Texas Studies in Literature and Language* 6 (1964): 213–225. Reprinted by permission.

1. MacEdward Leach, "The Singer or the Song," in *Singers and Storytellers,* ed. Mody C. Boatright, Wilson M. Hudson, and Allen Maxwell, Publications of the Texas Folklore Society, no. 30 (Dallas: Southern Methodist University Press, 1961), 30–45.

2. Leach, "The Singer or the Song," 40.

3. S. J. Sackett, "Simile in Folksong," *Midwest Folklore* 13 (1963): 5–12.

4. Sackett, "Simile in Folksong," 11.

5. Sackett, "Simile in Folksong," 12.

6. Albert B. Friedman, *The Ballad Revival* (Chicago: University of Chicago Press, 1961), 21.

7. Américo Paredes, "'El corrido de José Mosqueda' as an Example of Pattern in the Ballad," *Western Folklore* 17 (1958): 154–162.

8. Claude Lévi-Strauss, "The Structural Study of Myth," *Journal of American Folklore* 68 (1955): 428–444; and Elli-Kaija Köngäs and Pierre Maranda, "Structural Models in Folklore," *Midwest Folklore* 12 (1962): 133–192.

9. Alan Dundes, "Trends in Content Analysis: A Review Article," *Midwest Folklore* 12 (1962): 31–38.

10. Helen Child Sargent and George Lyman Kittredge, *English and Scottish Popular Ballads,* Student's Edition (Boston: Houghton Mifflin, 1932), xxv–xxvi.

6. The Mexican *Corrido:* Its Rise and Fall [1958]

Originally published in *Madstones and Twisters,* ed. Mody C. Boatright, Wilson M. Hudson, and Allen Maxwell, Publications of the Texas Folklore Society, no. 28 (Dallas: Southern Methodist University Press, 1958), 91–105. Reprinted by permission.

1. Héctor Pérez Martínez, *Trayectoria del corrido* (Mexico City, 1935), 16.

2. Arthur L. Campa, *Spanish Folk-Poetry in New Mexico* (Albuquerque: University of New Mexico Press, 1946), 12–16.

3. Vicente T. Mendoza, *El romance español y el corrido mexicano* (Mexico City: Ediciones de la Universidad Nacional Autónoma, 1939).

4. Vicente T. Mendoza, *El corrido mexicano* (Mexico City: Fondo de Cultura Económica, 1954), xiii.

5. Mendoza, *El corrido mexicano,* xiv.

6. Julio Vicuña Cifuentes, *Romances populares y vulgares, recogidos de la tradición oral chilena* (Santiago, Chile: Imprenta Barcelona, 1912).

7. Higinio Vázquez Santa Ana, *Historia de la canción mexicana,* vol. 3 (Mexico City: Talleres Gráficos de la Nación, 1931), 24, 91.

8. Vicente T. Mendoza, *La décima en México* (Buenos Aires: Instituto Nacional de la Tradición, 1947), 228.

9. Vázquez Santa Ana, *Historia de la canción,* 45.

10. Manuel F. Zárate and Dora Pérez de Zárate, *La décima y la copla en Panamá* (Panama City: Talleres de "La Estrella de Panamá," 1953), 20–21.

11. Mendoza, *La décima,* passim.

12. Mendoza, *La décima,* 400.

13. Mendoza, *El corrido mexicano,* xxvii.

14. Higinio Vázquez Santa Ana, *Canciones, cantares y corridos mexicanos* (Mexico City: Imprenta M. León Sánchez, 1925), 225.

15. Vázquez Santa Ana, *Historia de la canción,* 250.

16. Vázquez Santa Ana, *Canciones,* 210.

17. Pérez Martínez, *Trayectoria del corrido,* 18.

7. The Concept of the Emotional Core Applied to the Mexican *Corrido* "Benjamín Argumedo" [1972]

This essay was first published as "El concepto de la 'médula emotiva' aplicado al corrido mexicano 'Benjamín Argumedo'" in *Folklore Americano* 17 (1971–72): 139–176. English translation, with additions, by the author. (The principal addition is the tune of the *corrido,* which was printed in Américo Paredes, *A Texas-Mexican Cancionero: Folksongs of the Lower Border* [Urbana: University of Illinois Press, 1976], 91.)

1. Francis James Child, *The English and Scottish Popular Ballads,* 5 vols. (Boston: Houghton Mifflin, 1882–1898).

2. Helen Child Sargent and George Lyman Kittredge, *English and Scottish Popular Ballads* (Boston: Houghton Mifflin, 1904), xxvi.

3. Francis B. Gummere, *The Popular Ballad* (Boston: Houghton Mifflin, 1907), 101.

4. Sargent and Kittredge, *English and Scottish Popular Ballads,* xxx.

5. G. B. Depping, *Romancero castellano,* vol. 1 (Leipzig: F. A. Brockhaus, 1844), xii.

6. William James Entwistle, *European Balladry* (Oxford: Clarendon Press, 1939), 180.

7. Ramón Menéndez Pidal, *Flor nueva de romances viejos* (Madrid: Espasa-Calpe, 1938), 27–28.

8. D. K. Wilgus, *Anglo-American Folksong Scholarship since 1898* (New Brunswick, N.J.: Rutgers University Press, 1959).

9. Tristram P. Coffin, "Mary Hamilton and the Anglo-American Ballad as an Art Form," *Journal of American Folklore* 70 (1957): 208–214.

10. Roger D. Abrahams and George Foss, *Anglo-American Folksong Style* (Englewood Cliffs, N.J.: Prentice-Hall, 1968), 49.

11. Daniel Moreno, *Los hombres de la Revolución: 40 estudios biográficos* (Mexico City: Libro Mex, 1960), 186.

12. Armando de María y Campos, *La Revolución Mexicana a través de los corridos populares,* vol. 2 (Mexico City: Biblioteca del Instituto Nacional de Estudios Históricos de la Revolución Mexicana, 1962), 156.

13. María y Campos, *Revolución Mexicana,* 156.

14. María y Campos, *Revolución Mexicana,* 141.

15. María y Campos, *Revolución Mexicana,* 179–180.

16. Marcela Ruiz de Velasco Padierna, "Estado actual del corrido en Monterrey, N.L." (Tesis profesional, Universidad Iberoamericana, 1965).

17. María y Campos, *Revolución Mexicana,* 141.

18. Moreno, *Hombres de la Revolución,* 185.

19. Coffin, "Anglo-American Ballad," 214.

20. Albert B. Lord, *The Singer of Tales* (Cambridge: Harvard University Press, 1960).

8. José Mosqueda and the Folklorization of Actual Events [1973]

A Spanish-language version of this paper was read before the Second Summer Institute of Latin American Folklore at the University of California, Los Angeles, in June 1967. Originally published in *Aztlán* 4 (1973): 1–30. The Spanish text of the José Mosqueda legend was previously published as an appendix to a reprint of the article in *Folklore Americano* 20 (1975): 55–82. An English translation of the José Mosqueda *corrido* has also been added (from Américo Paredes, *A Texas-Mexican Cancionero: Folksongs of the Lower Border* [Urbana: University of Illinois Press, 1976], 63–64).

1. Gustavo Durán, *14 Traditional Spanish Songs from Texas* (Washington, D.C.: Music Division, Pan American Union, 1942).

2. Durán, *14 Traditional Spanish Songs,* 2.

3. Américo Paredes, "'El corrido de José Mosqueda' as an Example of Pattern in the Ballad," *Western Folklore* 17 (1958): 154–162.

4. John C. Rayburn and Virginia Kemp Rayburn, eds., *Century of Conflict, 1821–1913: Incidents in the Lives of William Neale and William A. Neale, Early Settlers in South Texas* (Waco, Tex.: Texian Press, 1966), 125–134.

5. W. H. Chatfield, *The Twin Cities of the Border* (New Orleans, 1893).

6. Rayburn and Rayburn, *Century of Conflict*, 125–126.

7. Rayburn and Rayburn, *Century of Conflict*, 126.

8. Rayburn and Rayburn, *Century of Conflict*, 130.

9. Rayburn and Rayburn, *Century of Conflict*, 127.

10. Rayburn and Rayburn, *Century of Conflict*, 127.

11. Rayburn and Rayburn, *Century of Conflict*, 129.

12. Rayburn and Rayburn, *Century of Conflict*, 130–132.

13. Rayburn and Rayburn, *Century of Conflict*, 132.

14. Rayburn and Rayburn, *Century of Conflict*, 130.

15. Rayburn and Rayburn, *Century of Conflict*, 129.

16. Chatfield, *Twin Cities*, 27, column d.

17. Rayburn and Rayburn, *Century of Conflict*, 133.

18. Rayburn and Rayburn, *Century of Conflict*, 133.

19. Rayburn and Rayburn, *Century of Conflict*, 132.

20. Paredes, "'El corrido de José Mosqueda,'" 160–162.

21. Américo Paredes, *"With His Pistol in His Hand": A Border Ballad and Its Hero* (Austin: University of Texas Press, 1958), 108–125.

22. Elsie Clews Parsons, "Zapoteca and Spanish Tales of Mitla, Oaxaca," *Journal of American Folklore* 45 (1932): 310.

9. The United States, Mexico, and *Machismo* [1971]

This article is translated from Américo Paredes, "Estados Unidos, México y el machismo," *Journal of Inter-American Studies* 9 (1967): 65–84, by Marcy Steen. The current version was originally published in *Journal of the Folklore Institute* 8 (1971): 17–37. Reprinted by permission.

1. Vicente T. Mendoza, *Lírica narrativa de México: El corrido*, Estudios de Folklore, no. 2 (Mexico City: Instituto de Investigaciones Estéticas, Universidad Nacional Autónoma de México, 1964), 34; and Vicente T. Mendoza, "El machismo en México al través de las canciones, corridos y cantares," *Cuadernos del Instituto Nacional de Antropología* 3 (1962): 75.

2. Ezequiel Martínez Estrada, *Radiografía de la Pampa*, 2 vols. (Buenos Aires: Editorial Losada, 1942).

3. Santiago Ramírez, *El mexicano: Psicología de sus motivaciones* (Mexico City: Editorial Pax-México, 1959), 63.

4. Felipe Montemayor, "Postemio antropológico," in *Picardía mexicana,* ed. A. Jiménez (Mexico City: Libro Mex, 1960), 229–230.

5. Mendoza, "El machismo en México," 75–86.

6. Mendoza, "El machismo en México," 75–76.

7. Vicente T. Mendoza, *La décima en México* (Buenos Aires: Instituto Nacional de la Tradición, 1947), 611.

8. Mendoza, "El machismo en México," 82.

9. Mendoza, *Lírica narrativa,* 95.

10. Mendoza, *Lírica narrativa,* 82.

11. Mendoza, *Lírica narrativa,* 146.

12. C. M. Bowra, *Primitive Song* (New York: New American Library, 1962), 122.

13. William Morris, trans., *Volsunga Saga: The Story of the Volsungs and Niblungs,* with a new introduction by Robert W. Gutman (New York: Crowell-Collier, 1962), 113.

14. Roger D. Abrahams, *Deep Down in the Jungle: Negro Narrative Folklore from the Streets of Philadelphia* (Hatboro, Pa.: Folklore Associates, 1964), 147.

15. Walter Prescott Webb, *The Great Plains* (Boston: Ginn, 1931), 114–138, 509.

16. Webb, *The Great Plains,* 168.

17. Webb, *The Great Plains,* 169.

18. Webb, *The Great Plains,* 180–184.

19. Webb, *The Great Plains,* 167–179.

20. Webb, *The Great Plains,* 173–175.

21. Webb, *The Great Plains,* 168.

22. Martínez Estrada, *Radiografía de la Pampa,* vol. 1, 64.

23. Miguel de Cervantes Saavedra, *Don Quixote of the Mancha,* vol. 1, trans. John Ormsby (Barcelona: Limited Editions Club, 1933), 374.

24. José Hernández, *Martín Fierro* (Buenos Aires: Espasa-Calpe Argentina, 1938), 51, 54, 89.

25. Paul S. Taylor, "Songs of the Mexican Migration," in *Puro Mexicano,* ed. J. Frank Dobie, Publications of the Texas Folkore Society, no. 12 (Austin: Texas Folklore Society, 1935), 241–245.

26. Mody C. Boatright, "Theodore Roosevelt, Social Darwinism, and the Cowboy," *Texas Quarterly* 7.4 (1964): 17.

27. Mendoza, *Lírica narrativa,* 14.

28. Samuel Ramos, *El perfil del hombre y la cultura en México* (Mexico City: Espasa-Calpe Mexicana, 1951), 52.

10. The *Décima* on the Texas-Mexican Border: Folksong as an Adjunct to Legend [1966]

Originally published in *Journal of the Folklore Institute* 3 (1966): 154–167. Reprinted by permission. The original article included the text of the *décimas* of El Indio Córdova and Don Santiago María; in this volume, the *décimas* appear at the end of chapter 11.

1. Vicente T. Mendoza, *La décima en México* (Buenos Aires: Instituto Nacional de la Tradición, 1947), 46–47.
2. Juan Uribe Echevarría, *Cantos a lo divino y a lo humano en Aculeo: Folklore de la Provincia de Santiago* (Santiago, Chile: Editorial Universitaria, 1962), passim.
3. Mendoza, *La décima en México,* 646.
4. Eugenio Pereira Salas, "Nota sobre los orígenes del canto a lo divino en Chile," *Revista Musical Chilena* 16.79 (1962): 41–48.
5. Uribe Echevarría, *Cantos a lo divino y a lo humano.*
6. J. Frank Dobie, *The Mustangs* (New York: Bramhall House, 1952), 48.
7. Walter Rela, "Un documento poético-popular chileno del Siglo XIX," *Revista Nacional,* 2d ser., 4 (Montevideo, 1959): 391–405.
8. Herbert Halpert, "The Cante Fable in Decay," in *Folklore in Action: Essays for Discussion in Honor of MacEdward Leach,* ed. Horace Palmer Beck (Philadelphia: American Folklore Society, 1962), 139–150.
9. Américo Paredes, *"With His Pistol in His Hand": A Border Ballad and Its Hero* (Austin: University of Texas Press, 1958), 108–125.
10. Américo Paredes, "'El corrido de José Mosqueda' as an Example of Pattern in the Ballad," *Western Folkore* 17 (1958): 154–162.

11. The Undying Love of "El Indio" Córdova: *Décimas* and Oral History in a Border Family [1987]

Originally delivered as the inaugural Ernesto Galarza Lecture (1986) at Stanford University and published as the *Ernesto Galarza Commemorative Lecture: Inaugural Lecture 1986* (Stanford: Stanford Center for Chicano Research, Stanford University, 1987). Reprinted by permission. The author's English translation of the *décimas* of El Indio Córdova and Don Santiago María has been added for this volume, as has the text (with English translation) of their last known exchange.

Bibliography:
The Scholarly Writings of Américo Paredes

Compiled by Linda Kinsey Adams

Note: The bibliography is arranged chronologically, by year. Within a year, entries are listed in the following order: books, articles, prefaces and forewords, reviews, edited works, and translations. Within these categories, entries are listed alphabetically, by title of work.

1942

"The Mexico-Texan Corrido." *Southwest Review* 27: 470–481.

1953

"The Love Tragedy in Texas-Mexican Balladry." In *Folk Travelers: Ballads, Tales, and Talk,* edited by Mody C. Boatright, Wilson M. Hudson, and Allen Maxwell, 110–114. Publications of the Texas Folklore Society, no. 25. Dallas: Southern Methodist University Press.

1957

"The Legend of Gregorio Cortez." In *Mesquite and Willow,* edited by Mody C. Boatright, Wilson M. Hudson, and Allen Maxwell, 3–22. Publications of the Texas Folklore Society, no. 27. Dallas: Southern Methodist University Press.
•Reprinted in *"With His Pistol in His Hand": A Border Ballad and Its Hero,* by Américo Paredes, 34–54. Austin: University of Texas Press, 1958.

1958

"With His Pistol in His Hand": A Border Ballad and Its Hero. Austin: University of Texas Press.
•English translation of variant B of Gregorio Cortez *corrido* reprinted in *Buying the Wind: Regional Folklore in the United States,* edited by Richard M. Dorson, 480–483. Chicago: University of Chicago Press, 1964.

•Chapter 2 reprinted as "The Legend of Gregorio Cortez" in *Speaking for Ourselves: American Ethnic Writing,* edited by Lillian Faderman and Barbara Bradshaw, 265–279. Glenview, Ill.: Scott, Foresman, 1969. 2d ed., 1975 (328–341).

•Excerpt of Gregorio Cortez *corrido* reprinted in *Ómnibus de poesía mexicana,* edited by Gabriel Zaíd, 210–211. Mexico City: Siglo XXI, 1971.

•Excerpt of chapter 2 reprinted as "The Legend of Gregorio Cortez" in *Mexican-American Authors,* edited by Américo Paredes and Raymund Paredes, 35–49. Boston: Houghton Mifflin, 1972.

•Excerpt of chapter 1 reprinted as "The Simple Pastoral Life (Texas)" in *Aztlán: An Anthology of Mexican American Literature,* edited by Luis Valdez and Stan Steiner, 47–50. New York: Alfred A. Knopf, 1972.

•Excerpt of chapter 3 reprinted as "Gregorio Cortez" in *Furia y muerte: Los bandidos chicanos,* edited by Pedro Castillo and Albert Camarillo, 114–166. Los Angeles: Aztlán Publications, Chicano Studies Center, University of California, 1973.

•Excerpt of chapter 1 reprinted as "With His Pistol in His Hand" in *Chicano: The Evolution of a People,* edited by Renato Rosaldo, Robert A. Calvert, and Gustav L. Seligmann, 102–113. Minneapolis: Winston Press, 1973. 2d ed., Malabar, Fla.: Robert E. Krieger, 1982 (98–109).

"'El corrido de José Mosqueda' as an Example of Pattern in the Ballad." *Western Folklore* 17: 154–162.

"The Mexican *Corrido:* Its Rise and Fall." In *Madstones and Twisters,* edited by Mody C. Boatright, Wilson M. Hudson, and Allen Maxwell, 91–105. Publications of the Texas Folklore Society, no. 28. Dallas: Southern Methodist University Press.

•Chapter 6 in this volume.

Review of *American Murder Ballads,* by Olive Wooley Burt. *New Mexico Quarterly* 28: 204–205.

Review of *The Mexican Corrido as a Source for Interpretive Study of Modern Mexico (1870–1950),* by Merle E. Simmons. *Journal of American Folklore* 71: 582–583.

1959

"The Bury-Me-Not Theme in the Southwest." In *And Horns on the Toads,* edited by Mody C. Boatright, Wilson M. Hudson, and Allen Maxwell, 88–92. Publications of the Texas Folklore Society, no. 29. Dallas: Southern Methodist University Press.

"The University of Texas Folklore Archive." *Folklore and Folk Music Archivist* 2.3: 1, 4.

Review of *The Restlessness of Shanti Andia and Other Writings*, by Pío Baroja. *Houston Post*, 13 September.

1960

"Gringo." *Western Folklore* 19: 277.
"Luis Inclán: First of the Cowboy Writers." *American Quarterly* 12: 55–70.
"The Mexican Contribution to Our Culture." *Texas Observer*, 19 August, 6–7.
"Mexican Riddling Wellerisms." *Western Folklore* 19: 200.
"Tag, You're It." *Journal of American Folklore* 73: 157–158.
"Where Cultures Clashed and Merged." *Texas Observer*, 12 August, 7.
Review of *The True Story of Billy the Kid*, by William Lee Hamlin. *Midwest Folklore* 10: 111–112.

1961

"Folklore and History." In *Singers and Storytellers*, edited by Mody C. Boatright, Wilson M. Hudson, and Allen Maxwell, 56–68. Publications of the Texas Folklore Society, no. 30. Dallas: Southern Methodist University Press.
"Folklore Bibliography for 1960." *Southern Folklore Quarterly* 25: 1–89.
"On *Gringo, Greaser*, and Other Neighborly Names." In *Singers and Storytellers*, edited by Mody C. Boatright, Wilson M. Hudson, and Allen Maxwell, 285–290. Publications of the Texas Folklore Society, no. 30. Dallas: Southern Methodist University Press.
[Translator] Mendoza, Vicente T. "Some Forms of the Mexican *Canción*." In *Singers and Storytellers*, edited by Mody C. Boatright, Wilson M. Hudson, and Allen Maxwell, 46–55. Publications of the Texas Folklore Society, no. 30. Dallas: Southern Methodist University Press.
[Translator] "Translations of Corridos and Calaveras." In *Corridos and Calaveras*, by Edward Larocque Tinker, 41–58. Austin: University of Texas Press.

1962

"Folklore Bibliography for 1961." *Southern Folklore Quarterly* 26: 1–96.
"El folklore en los Estados Unidos durante la última década (1953–1962)." *Folklore Americano* 10 (1963): 256–262.
Review of *Cantares históricos de la tradición argentina*, edited by Olga Fernández Latour. *Journal of American Folklore* 75: 356.

1963

"The Ancestry of Mexico's *Corridos:* A Matter of Definitions." *Journal of American Folklore* 76: 231–235.

"El cowboy norteamericano en el folklore y la literatura." *Cuadernos del Instituto Nacional de Antropología* 4: 227–240.
•Reprinted as no. 22 in the Institute of Latin American Studies Offprint Series. Austin: Institute of Latin American Studies, University of Texas, n.d.
"Folklore Bibliography for 1962." *Southern Folklore Quarterly* 27: 1–111.
"Texas' Third Man: The Texas-Mexican." *Race: The Journal of the Institute of Race Relations* 4.2: 49–58.
Review of *Las "pintaderas" mejicanas y sus relaciones,* by José Alcina Franch. *Erasmus* 15: 757–758.

1964

"La Flora y la Fauna." In *Buying the Wind: Regional Folklore in the United States,* edited by Richard M. Dorson, 454. Chicago: University of Chicago Press.
"Folklore Bibliography for 1963." *Southern Folklore Quarterly* 28: 1–94.
"Moochers." In *Buying the Wind: Regional Folklore in the United States,* edited by Richard M. Dorson, 453–454. Chicago: University of Chicago Press.
"No Estiendo." In *Buying the Wind: Regional Folklore in the United States,* edited by Richard M. Dorson, 452–453. Chicago: University of Chicago Press.
"Some Aspects of Folk Poetry." *Texas Studies in Literature and Language* 6: 213–225.
•Reprinted as no. R659 in Warner Modular Publications, Series on Anthropology, 1973.
•Chapter 5 in this volume.
Review of *Cuentos folklóricos de la Argentina,* by Susana Chertudi. *Journal of American Folklore* 77: 355.
Review of *Treasure of the Sangre de Cristos: Tales and Traditions of the Spanish Southwest,* by Arthur L. Campa. *Journal of American Folklore* 77: 269–270.
[Translator] Cosío Villegas, Daniel. *American Extremes.* Austin: University of Texas Press. Originally published as *Extremos de América* (Mexico City: Tezontle, 1949).
[Translator] "Corrido de Jacinto Treviño." In *Buying the Wind: Regional Folklore in the United States,* edited by Richard M. Dorson, 483–485. Chicago: University of Chicago Press.
•Reprinted in *Mexican-American Authors,* edited by Américo Paredes and Raymund Paredes, 5–7. Boston: Houghton Mifflin, 1972.
[Translator] "Pastorela to Celebrate the Birth of Our Lord Jesus Christ." In *Buying the Wind: Regional Folklore in the United States,* edited by Richard M. Dorson, 466–479. Chicago: University of Chicago Press.

1965

"Vicente T. Mendoza, 1894–1964." *Journal of American Folklore* 78: 154–155.

Review of *Cuentos folklóricos de Chile,* Vols. 1–3, by Yolando Pino Saavedra. *Journal of American Folklore* 78: 171.

Review of *Legends of Texas* and *Happy Hunting Ground,* edited by J. Frank Dobie. *Journal of American Folklore* 78: 163–164.

Review of *Picardía mexicana,* by Armando Jiménez. *Journal of American Folklore* 78: 75–77.

1966

"The Anglo-American in Mexican Folklore." In *New Voices in American Studies,* edited by Ray B. Browne, Donald M. Winkelman, and Allen Hayman, 113–127. Lafayette, Ind.: Purdue University Studies.
   •Reprinted as no. 30 in the Institute of Latin American Studies Offprint Series. Austin: Institute of Latin American Studies, University of Texas, n.d.
   •Reprinted in *Literatura chicana: Texto y contexto,* edited by Antonia Castañeda Shular, Tomás Ybarra-Frausto, and Joseph Sommers, 141–150. Englewood Cliffs, N.J.: Prentice-Hall, 1972.

With George Foss. "The *Décima Cantada* on the Texas-Mexican Border: Four Examples." *Journal of the Folklore Institute* 3: 91–115.
   •Reprinted in "The *Décima* on the Texas-Mexican Border," no. 54 in the Institute of Latin American Studies Offprint Series. Austin: Institute of Latin American Studies, University of Texas, n.d.

"The *Décima* on the Texas-Mexican Border: Folksong as an Adjunct to Legend." *Journal of the Folklore Institute* 3: 154–167.
   •Reprinted in "The *Décima* on the Texas-Mexican Border," no. 54 in the Institute of Latin American Studies Offprint Series. Austin: Institute of Latin American Studies, University of Texas, n.d.
   •Chapter 10 in this volume, with additions.

"El folklore de los grupos de origen mexicano en Estados Unidos." *Folklore Americano* 14: 146–163.

"El folklore en el XXXVII Congreso Internacional de Americanistas." *Folklore Américas* 26.2: 31–33.

1967

"Divergencias en el concepto del folklore y el contexto cultural." *Folklore Américas* 27: 29–38.

"Estados Unidos, México y el machismo." *Journal of Inter-American Studies* 9: 65–84.

•Reprinted as no. 42 in the Institute of Latin American Studies Offprint Series. Austin: Institute of Latin American Studies, University of Texas, n.d.

1968

"Folk Medicine and the Intercultural Jest." In *Spanish-Speaking People in the United States,* edited by June Helm, 104–119. Proceedings of the 1968 Annual Spring Meeting of the American Ethnological Society. Seattle: University of Washington Press.
  •Reprinted as no. 83 in the Institute of Latin American Studies Offprint Series. Austin: Institute of Latin American Studies, University of Texas, n.d.
  •Reprinted as no. R616 in Warner Modular Publications, Series on Anthropology, 1973.
  •Reprinted in *Introduction to Chicano Studies,* edited by Livie Isauro Durán and H. Russell Bernard, 261–275. New York: Macmillan, 1973.
  •Reprinted in *Folk Groups and Folklore Genres: A Reader,* edited by Elliott Oring, 63–77. Logan: Utah State University Press, 1989.
  •Chapter 3 in this volume, with additions.
"A Selective Annotated Bibliography of Recent Works in Latin American Folklore, 1960–1967." *Handbook of Latin American Studies* 30: 385–410.
"Tributaries to the Mainstream: The Ethnic Groups." In *Our Living Traditions: An Introduction to American Folklore,* edited by Tristram P. Coffin, 70–80. New York: Basic Books.
Review of *Proverbial Comparisons in Ricardo Palma's* Tradiciones peruanas, by Shirley L. Arora. *Romance Philology* 21: 358–359.

1969

"Concepts about Folklore in Latin America and the United States." *Journal of the Folklore Institute* 6: 20–38.

1970

"Proverbs and Ethnic Stereotypes." *Proverbium* 15: 95–97.
"The Where and Why of Folklore." *Illinois History* 23.4: 75–76.
Preface. In *Bibliografía del folklore chileno (1952–1965),* by Manuel Dannemann Rothstein, vii–viii. Latin American Folklore Series, edited by Américo Paredes, no. 2. Austin: Center for Intercultural Studies in Folklore and Oral History, University of Texas.
Preface. In *Las miniaturas en el arte popular mexicano,* by Mauricio Charpenel, vii. Latin American Folklore Series, edited by Américo Paredes, no. 1. Austin: Center for Intercultural Studies in Folklore and Oral History, University of Texas.

[Editor and translator] *Folktales of Mexico*. Chicago: University of Chicago Press.

1971

"Folklore e historia: Dos cantares de la frontera del norte." In *25 estudios de folklore,* edited by Fernando Anaya Monroy, 209–222. Estudios de Folklore, no. 4. Mexico City: Instituto de Investigaciones Estéticas, Universidad Nacional Autónoma de México.

"Mexican Legendry and the Rise of the Mestizo." In *American Folk Legend: A Symposium,* edited by Wayland D. Hand, 97–107. Berkeley: University of California Press.

"The United States, Mexico, and *Machismo.*" Translated by Marcy Steen. *Journal of the Folklore Institute* 8: 17–37. Originally published as "Estados Unidos, México y el machismo" (*Journal of Inter-American Studies* 9 [1967]: 65–84).
•Chapter 9 in this volume.

Foreword. In *The Concept of Folklore,* by Paulo de Carvalho Neto, 9–12. Coral Gables, Fla.: University of Miami Press.

Review of *Folk-Lore from the Dominican Republic,* by Manuel J. Andrade, and *Spanish Folk-Tales from New Mexico,* by José Manuel Espinosa. *Hispanic American Historical Review* 51: 556.

Review of *Mexican Tales and Legends from Los Altos,* by Stanley L. Robe. *Hispanic American Historical Review* 51: 544–545.

[Editor] With Ellen J. Stekert. *The Urban Experience and Folk Tradition.* Austin: University of Texas Press.

1972

"El concepto de la 'médula emotiva' aplicado al corrido mexicano 'Benjamín Argumedo.'" *Folklore Americano* 17 (1971–72): 139–176.
•Chapter 7 in this volume, in translation, with additions.

"Dichos." In *Mexican-American Authors,* edited by Américo Paredes and Raymund Paredes, 27–34. Boston: Houghton Mifflin.

[Editor] With Raymund Paredes. *Mexican-American Authors.* Boston: Houghton Mifflin.

[Editor] With Richard Bauman. *Toward New Perspectives in Folklore.* Austin: University of Texas Press.

1973

"José Mosqueda and the Folklorization of Actual Events." *Aztlán* 4: 1–30.
•Reprinted in *Folklore Americano* 20 (1975): 55–82, with addition of the Spanish text of the José Mosqueda legend.

•Chapter 8 in this volume, with additions.

Preface. In *El Nacimiento del Niño Dios: A Pastorela from Tarimoro, Guanajuato*, by Lily Litvak, vii. Latin American Folklore Series, edited by Américo Paredes, no. 3. Austin: Center for Intercultural Studies in Folklore and Oral History, University of Texas.

1976

A Texas-Mexican Cancionero: Folksongs of the Lower Border. Urbana: University of Illinois Press.

"The Role of Folklore in Border Relations." In *San Diego/Tijuana—The International Border in Community Relations: Gateway or Barrier?*, edited by Kiki Skagen, 17–22. Fronteras 1976, no. 3. San Diego: Fronteras 1976.

1977

"Jorge Isidoro Sánchez y Sánchez (1906–1972)." In *Humanidad: Essays in Honor of George I. Sánchez*, edited by Américo Paredes, 120–126. Los Angeles: Chicano Studies Research Center Publications, University of California.

"On Ethnographic Work among Minority Groups: A Folklorist's Perspective." *New Scholar* 6: 1–32.

•Reprinted in *New Directions in Chicano Scholarship*, edited by Ricardo Romo and Raymund Paredes, 1–32. La Jolla: Chicano Studies Program, University of California, San Diego, 1978.

•Chapter 4 in this volume.

"Yamashita, Zapata, and the Arthurian Legend." *Western Folklore* 36: 160–163.

[Editor] *Humanidad: Essays in Honor of George I. Sánchez*. Los Angeles: Chicano Studies Research Center Publications, University of California.

1978

"The Problem of Identity in a Changing Culture: Popular Expressions of Culture Conflict along the Lower Rio Grande Border." In *Views across the Border: The United States and Mexico*, edited by Stanley Ross, 68–94. Albuquerque: University of New Mexico Press.

•Chapter 2 in this volume.

"'El romance de la Isla de Jauja' en el suroeste de Estados Unidos." *Logos: Revista de la Facultad de Filosofía y Letras de la Universidad de Buenos Aires* 13–14 (1977–78): 399–406.

1979

"The Folk Base of Chicano Literature." Translated by Kathleen Lamb. In *Modern Chicano Writers: A Collection of Critical Essays*, edited by Joseph Sommers

and Tomás Ybarra-Frausto, 4–17. Englewood Cliffs, N.J.: Prentice-Hall. Originally published as "El folklore de los grupos de origen mexicano en Estados Unidos" (*Folklore Americano* 14 [1966]: 146–163).
•Chapter 1 in this volume.

1982

"Folklore, Lo Mexicano, and Proverbs." *Aztlán* 13: 1–11.

1983

"The *Corrido:* Yesterday and Today." In *Ecology and Development of the Border Region,* edited by Stanley R. Ross, 293–297. Mexico City: Asociación Nacional de Universidades e Institutos de Enseñanza Superior.
"Nearby Places and Strange-Sounding Names." In *The Texas Literary Tradition: Fiction, Folklore, History,* edited by Don Graham, James W. Lee, and William T. Pilkington, 130–138. Austin: University of Texas and Texas State Historical Association.

1987

"The Undying Love of 'El Indio' Córdova: *Décimas* and Oral History in a Border Family." *Ernesto Galarza Commemorative Lecture: Inaugural Lecture 1986.* Stanford: Stanford Center for Chicano Research, Stanford University.
•Chapter 11 in this volume, with additions.

1993

Uncle Remus con chile. Houston: Arte Público Press.

AMÉRICO PAREDES is Dickson, Allen, and Anderson Centennial Professor Emeritus of Anthropology and English at the University of Texas at Austin. He received his Ph.D., in English and Spanish, from the University of Texas at Austin, and has taught folklore there since 1957. He has served as editor of the *Journal of American Folklore* and vice-president of the American Folklore Society. His book *"With His Pistol in His Hand": A Border Ballad and Its Hero,* which was published in 1958, has become a classic of the literature. In 1989, the National Endowment for the Humanities honored Paredes with the illustrious Charles Frankel Prize. In 1990, the government of Mexico bestowed on him its highest award to citizens of other countries: La Orden Mexicana del Águila Azteca.

RICHARD BAUMAN is Distinguished Professor of Folklore and Anthropology and director of the Research Center for Language and Semiotic Studies at Indiana University. He holds a Ph.D. in American civilization from the University of Pennsylvania. He is president of the Society for Linguistic Anthropology, past president of the Semiotic Society of America, and former editor of the *Journal of American Folklore.* From 1967 to 1986 he taught folklore at the University of Texas at Austin. Bauman's two most recent books are *Story, Performance, and Event: Contextual Studies of Oral Narrative* (1986) and *Folklore, Cultural Performances, and Popular Entertainments: A Communications-Centered Handbook* (1992).

CMAS BOOKS

Folklore and Culture on the Texas-Mexican Border was designed
by Leda Black, of Berkeley, California. The text was composed by
CMAS Books, primarily in Minion, with Post Antiqua used for the
title page. Camera-ready copy was produced by RJL Graphics, of
Austin, Texas. The book was printed and bound by Bookcrafters,
of Chelsea, Michigan. The text paper is Glatfelter Natural.